HISTORY
OF RUSSIA

Sergei Mikhailovich Soloviev

The

Academic International Press

Edition

of

Sergei M. Soloviev

History of Russia From Earliest Times

G. EDWARD ORCHARD
General Editor

Contributing Editors

HUGH F. GRAHAM	PATRICK J. O'MEARA
JOHN D. WINDHAUSEN	PETER C. STUPPLES
ALEXANDER V. MULLER	T. ALLAN SMITH
K.A. PAPMEHL	MARTHA L. LAHANA
RICHARD HANTULA	ANTHONY V. KNOWLES
WALTER J. GLEASON, JR.	HELEN Y. PROCHAZKA
WILLIAM H. HILL	ALEXANDRA S. KORROS
G. EDWARD ORCHARD	GARY J. MARKER
LINDSEY A.J. HUGHES	MARIAN J. RUBCHAK
NICKOLAS LUPININ	RALPH M. CLEMINSON
GEORGE E. MUNRO	CATHY J. POTTER
DANIEL L. SCHLAFLY, JR.	BRIGIT A. FARLEY
ANTHONY L.H. RHINELANDER	

SERGEI M. SOLOVIEV

History of Russia

Volume 18

Religious Struggle in Poland-Lithuania
Tsar Alexis' Reign Begins,
1654-1676

Edited and Translated and With an
Introduction By

Marian J. Rubchak

2002
Academic International Press

The Academic International Press Edition of S.M. Soloviev's
History of Russia From Earliest Times in fifty volumes.

Volume 18. *Religious Struggle in Poland-Lithuania. Tsar
Alexis' Reign Begins, 1654–1676.*
Unabridged translation of the text of Volume 10, Chapters 1-2 as
contained in Volume V of S.M. Soloviev's *Istoria Rossii s
drevneishikh vremen* published in Moscow between 1959-1966, with
added annotation by Marian J. Rubchak.

ISBN: 0-87569-237-0

Composition by Llano F. McCowen

Printed in the United States of America

A list of Academic International Press publications is found at
the end of this volume.

ACADEMIC INTERNATIONAL PRESS
Box 1111 • Gulf Breeze FL 32562-1111 • USA
www.ai-press.com

CONTENTS

WEIGHTS AND MEASURES

Linear and Surface Measure

Arshin: 16 vershoks, 28 in. (diuims) 72.12 cm
Chetvert (quarter): 1/4 arshin, 1/2 desiatina, 1.35 acres (sometimes 1.5 desiatinas or c. 4.1 acres)
Desiatina: 2,400 square sazhens, 2.7 acres, 1.025 hectares
Diuim: 1 inch, 2.54 cm
Fut: 12 diuims, 1 foot, 30.48 cm

Obza (areal): c. 10 chetverts, 13–15 acres
Osmina: 1/4 desiatina, 600 sq. sazhens, .256 hectare
Sazhen: 3 arshins, 7 feet, 2.133 m
Vershok: 1.75 in., 4.445 cm, 1/16 arshin
Verst: 500 sazhens, 1,166 yards and 2 feet, .663 miles, 1.0668 km
Voloka (plowland): 19 desiatinas, 20 hectares, 49 acres

Liquid Measure

Bochka (barrel): 40 vedros, 121 gallons, 492 liters
Chetvert (quarter): 1.4 bochkas, 32.5 gallons
Korchago (wine): Rus, unknown

Kufa: 30 stofy
Stof: Kruzhka (cup), 1/10 vedro, c. 1.3 quarts, 1.23 liters
Vedro (pail): 3.25 gallons, 12.3 liters, 10 stofy

Weights

Berkovets: 361 lbs., 10 puds
Bezmen: c. 1 kg, 2.2 lbs.
Chetverik (grain measure dating from 16th century): 1/8 chetvert, 15.8 lbs.
Chetvert (grain measure): 1/4 rad, 3.5 puds, 126.39 lbs., c. 8 bushels
Funt: 96 zolotniks, .903 lbs., 14.4 oz., 408.24 kg
Grivenka: 205 grams
Kad: 4 chetverts, 14 puds, 505.56 lbs.
Kadka malenkaia: 12th-century, small measure

Kamen (stone): 32 funt
Korob (basket): 7 puds, 252 lbs.
Osmina (eighth): 2 osmina to a chetvert (dry measure)
Polbezmen: c. 500 g, 1 lb.
Polosmina (sixteenth): 1/2 osmina
Pud: 40 funts, 36.113 lbs. (US), 40 lbs. (Russian), 16.38 kg
Rad: 14 puds, 505.58 lbs.
Zolotnik: 1/96 lbs., 4.26 grams

Money

Altyn: 6 Muscovite dengas, 3 copecks
Bel: Rus, pure silver coin
Chervonets (chervonnyi): gold coin of first half of 18th century worth c. 3 rubles
Chetvertak: silver coin equal to 25 copecks or 1/4 ruble (18–19th centuries)
Copeck: two Muscovite dengas
Denga: 1/2 copeck
Grivna: 20 Muscovite dengas, 100 grivnas equals 1 ruble, 10 copecks
Grosh: 10 peniaz
Grosh litovsky (Lithuanian grosh): 5 silver copecks
Kopa grosh: 60 groshas, one Muscovite poltina, 1/2 ruble
Kuna: 12th-century Rus coin comparable to Westerns denarii or Eastern dirhems. Varied in value by region. Replaced late 14th century by the denga or serebro (silver). Also a marten skin.
Moskovka: 1/2 copeck
Muscovite denga: 200 equals 1 ruble
Novgorod denga: 100 equals 1 ruble
Novgorodka: 1 copeck

Peniaz: 10 equals one grosh (Lithuania)
Poltina (poltinnik): 50 copecks, 100 dengas, 1 ruble
Poltora: 1 1/2 rubles
Polupoltina (-nik): 25 copecks, 50 dengas
Rezan: 12th century Rus coin. 50 rezan equals one grivna kuna
Ruble: 100 copecks, 200 dengas
Shiroky grosh (large silver coin): 20 Muscovite copecks
Veksa: 12th-century Rus small coin equal to one squirrel pelt (belka)

Foreign Denominations
Chervonnyi: c. 3 rubles
Ducat: c. 3 rubles
Dutch efimok: "lion dollar" or levok, 1 thaler, 2.5 guilders
Efimok: foreign currency, 1 thaler, .75-1 ruble, 1 chervonets or chervonnyi
Levok: Dutch silver lion dollar
Thaler (Joachimsthaler): c. 1 ruble, 1/3 chervonets or chervonnyi

Note: Weights and measures often changed values over time and sometimes held more than one value at the same time. For details consult Sergei G. Pushkarev, *Dictionary of Russian Historical Terms from the Eleventh Century to 1917* (Yale, 1970).

PREFACE

In 1851 the first volume of Sergei Mikhailovich Soloviev's *Istoriia Rossii s drevneishikh vremen* (History of Russia from Earliest Times) was published. Writing at the rate of one volume per year, he took his study to the year 1774 when the twenty-ninth volume was published, where it ended with his death in 1879. The present book consists of an unabridged translation of the first two chapters of the original tenth volume, published three times in Soloviev's lifetime in 1860, 1869 and 1877, followed by three more publications in the Obshchestvennaia Pol'za (Popular Use) edition, in 1895, 1896 and 1911. The present text comprises pages 373-523 of Chapters I and II of Volume 10 of the work published in Moscow, 1959-1966, a reissue in 1961 of the volume of 1877, with added annotation and modernized spelling.

Every effort has been made to render the complex text of the original as precisely as possible. Those matters which the translator considered to be historically inaccurate or questionable have been so noted, either in brackets within the body of the text, or in notes at the end of the work. For easier reading, and in accord with the practice in this series, this translator modernized some of the more recondite language, and simplified the numerous interminable, often turgid, sentences into more manageable units without, it is hoped, doing violence to the original material, style or flavor of the language. Many, although far from all, of Soloviev's subtitles at the beginning of each chapter were retained. All were transferred, and new ones added, to the body of the text to provide suitable breaks, and ease the transition from one topic to the next. Unless otherwise specified the notes which appear at the back of this volume are those of the present editor-translator. Most of the author's original annotations, together with those of the editor of the edition of 1959-1966, were omitted because they are too recondite for English-speaking students of Russian history, and therefore of little value to any but specialists, who in any case would consult the original text. They were replaced by the

editor-translator's notes. Occasional brief clarifications in brackets were
inserted into the text. Explanations in parentheses are always Soloviev's.

One of the most vexing problems in this volume is the spelling of non-
Russian personal names, toponyms, ranks and various terms. The stated
policy in this series is to render them in accordance with the language
native to the particular person, city, region or culture, wherever this can
be determined. Turkish, Tatar, Latin, Greek and Danish names are either
transliterated from or spelled as in Soloviev's text, although at times the text
itself is not clear about nationalities. When these are not ascertainable, as a
last resort they are transliterated from Soloviev's Russian.

There is one notable exception to this overall policy. Previous translators in this series were in the habit of rendering Ukrainian and Belarusian names, terms and toponyms in their Russian variants. This
translator's preference was to correct such a deviation from declared
policy by making these spellings conform to their original languages, as
is the case with all others. In the interest of continuity, the editors of this
series have elected to preserve the established practice of using the Russian spelling.

The term Rus is used to indentify what Soloviev calls Western Russia. Rus corresponds to what Ukrainians and Belarusians called themselves during the early modern period. As we move into the cossack era
the use of Rus gradually gives way to Ukrainian, indicating that Ukrainian, not the blend of Ukrainian-Belarusian that earlier constituted Rus,
cossacks are meant.

Russian personal names are rendered in their original form, except for
Alexander, Alexis, Nicholas, Michael, Catherine and Peter, which widespread English usage with respect to these historical figures has made
familiar. Some terms also were anglicized for the sake of clarity and
consistence—rubles, versts, zlotys—while others were given English
equivalents, thus The Holy Wisdom for Sophia cathedral and the Stone
quarter for Kamennyi gorod.

In keeping with the general practice of this series a modified Library
of Congress system was followed for all transliterations of Russian, the
omission of diacritical marks and ligatures, rendering the initial "ia" and
"iu" as "ya" and "yu", while the suffix "ii" (as in "skii") becomes "y" (as
in "sky"). In some instances "i" was inserted to denote soft signs, or apos-
trophes indicating these signs in the Library of Congress system, hence
"Soloviev" and not "Solov'ev. In other cases, such as in the word Rus,
soft signs are disregarded altogether.

Unless otherwise indicated, all dates are given according to the Julian ("Old Style") calendar. A table of weights and measures is provided at the front of this volume for the convenience of the reader.

Finally, I am indebted to the general editor of this series, G. Edward Orchard, whose command of Russian history and the nuances of the Russian language enabled him to provide invaluable advice, thus immeasurably lightening the arduous task of this translation.

Marian J. Rubchak

INTRODUCTION

There is much to be said for Soloviev's magisterial work, its breadth and erudition, copious references to Russian and non-Russian works alike, abundant quotations from classical texts and the Bible, doubtless reflecting his upbringing as the son of a priest and teacher of religion, as well as extensive use of primary evidence. Soloviev is credited with moving beyond conventional interpretations of Russian history and making a pivotal contribution to Russian historiography by setting new standards for scholarship. His interpretation of raw data, emulated by more than one generation of notable scholars studying the Russian past both in that country and in the West, established him as the principal Russian historian of the age. Soloviev's heavy reliance on archival evidence bespeaks his avowed conviction that primary sources, not the historian's consciousness, should frame historical discourse. Although there are some who view as a weakness his failure to analyze or comment upon primary sources sufficiently, Soloviev's insistence that they must speak for themselves is judged by many to be the single most important feature of his methodology. It is seen as marking a decisive turning point in the way subsequent histories of Russia were written.

Somewhat earlier than Soloviev's pioneering work made its appearance this approach to scholarship was introduced in France. It could be found in the oeuvres of such radically different Restoration thinkers as Augustin Thierry, whose writings epitomized romantic historiography, and the "father" of Positivism, Auguste Comte, who insisted that all knowledge must be empirically verifiable. What is more, he affirmed, insofar as we can apprehend phenomena only within the context of their sequential relationships to other phenomena, we must arrange all data in such a way as to unify it within a system of natural laws. The essentials of Comte's Positivism created a dominant mode of thought in France, as a result of which the focus of historical inquiry shifted from viewing the past merely in terms of a series of political events, driven by wars and diplomacy and dominated by great men, to one that elicited an awareness of social issues as well as elite concerns. No longer was the emphasis, as Thierry so aptly characterized it, simply "on pompous narratives in which a few privileged personages monopolize the historical stage while the mass of the whole nation is hidden behind the mantles of courtiers."[1] Like Comte, Soloviev believed that the raw data, systematized to project a coherent whole, presents the most authentic picture of past civilizations. Accordingly he assembled the particulars of Russia's past from chronicles and archival evidence, then organized them into an exciting, if unevenly arranged, panorama of binary oppositions, of virtues and vices, grandeur and meanness, heroic deeds and petty actions. Soloviev's historical narrative does delineate the achievements of grand princes, kings, khans and other outstanding personages of the time. At the same time it leaves no doubt that he has scrutinized documentary evidence about less remarkable, and altogether unremarkable, human beings, those who were pushed beyond the limits of endurance, and sought means to oppose their oppressors either by flight or rebellion.

Emulating the Positivists although he never purported to be a disciple, by his own attestation Soloviev stopped short of analyzing his material in the mistaken belief that such "readings" somehow diminished the objectivity of his work. Soloviev was firmly persuaded that the historian has an obligation to apprehend and evaluate any period under study in the ways that it understood itself. Accordingly, rather than invoke parallel studies to support his assertions, Soloviev adamantly insisted that raw data must be the defining element in any objective historical synthesis. Yet when all is said and done neither Soloviev's commitment to the primacy of minutely sifted archival evidence and his penchant for quoting long passages from the documents, nor his sequential grouping of sources yielded a detached, impartial account. It is axiomatic that the selection and ordering of documents is a subjective process, that individual judgment is indispensable for breathing life into primary data. By one means or another it is the historian who ultimately assigns meaning to the documents. Without his own imaginative insights Soloviev's accumulated archival evidence tended toward only a mechanistic chronicle of Russia's past.

For all of Soloviev's commitment to objectivity in historical scholarship, it eluded him in his own work, resulting in some perplexing historical misrepresentations. Most notable was his view of the organic evolution of the Russian people, beginning with the Kievan Rus era. This rendition bears the unmistakable stamp of Soloviev's ideological environment in which Russian identity was fused with that of the non-Russian

Slavs. Accordingly, when his documents "spoke for themselves," in this author's text they might be heard to say things at variance with their original intent. At one with his age and place and their governing tenets in which the national-imperial Russian myth, the "Russian Idea" was elevated to the status of official policy, the author proved all too susceptible to evaluating the past in the light of such contemporary assertions.

Taking his cue from the Romantic Russian myth which, the reader is reminded, makes no ethnic distinction among the Eastern Slavic peoples, Soloviev compromises objectivity most palpably when he offers as impartial history primary material which he has selected and arranged, then interpreted in accordance with his own convictions. Nowhere is this better illustrated than in his portrayal of Ukraine, Belarus and Lithuania as western appendages of ethnic Russia. Indeed, on occasion the author refers to all three simply as "Western Russia."

The highest official expression of attempts to squeeze all Eastern Slavic people into this Procrustean bed of Russian Imperial ideology was embodied in a number of decrees promulgated in the nineteenth century. First came the Valuev Circular of 1863, issued by the minister of the interior, prohibiting the publication of most books in the Ukrainian language. The second was an even more disabling document known as the Ems Ukaz, signed in 1876 by the reforming tsar Alexander II at the German spa of Ems, aiming at the suppression of Ukrainian culture and language.

Similarly, imperial policy was directed at Belorussia and what constituted Lithuania at the time. An 1836 edict prohibited the teaching of the Belarusian languages. In 1840 it was followed by an ukaz issued by Nicholas I which mandated that henceforth Belarus and Litva (Lithuania) would be referred to as the Severo-zapadnyi krai, or Northwestern Land, of Russia. On the heels of this, a law enacted in 1863 made book smuggling into Belorussia a capital crime.[2]

Soloviev's penchant for utilizing his documents in a less than objective manner is never more evident than when, without warning or acknowledgment, he integrates lengthy excerpts from non-Russian archival sources into his own narrative. Thus the unsuspecting reader receives them in free and truncated Russian translations which produce stylistic discontinuities and, worse still, historical distortions. A case in point are the passages from the epistles of the monk Ivan Vishensky (Vyshensky), writing from Mount Athos in the late sixteenth century in the Ukrainian language, which Soloviev renders into nineteenth-century Russian. No

xiv INTRODUCTION

indication is given of the language in which the original was written. Moreover, his omission of ellipses to indicate internal cuts in Vishensky's magnificent prose, and its presentation as components of Soloviev's own sentences, is tantamount to "editing" the monk's work to make it conform to some ideological design. This can be observed in Vishensky's tirade against the "godless" Ukrainians, Lithuanians and Poles who embraced Catholicism and other non-Orthodox "heresies." To his unsuspecting readers Soloviev presents the monk's diatribe as the sentiments of a "Russian monk" pleading an ostensibly common Russian religious cause, directed at apostates from an all-embracing Russian Orthodox church. Wherever we encounter such an argument it is useful to remember that the two Orthodox churches, Ukrainian and Russian, were separate ecclesiastical institutions answerable to different patriarchates, one in Moscow and the other in Constantinople. The Ukrainian church was annexed to the Muscovite patriarchate only in 1685-1686, nearly a century after Vishensky's impassioned plea to the Uniates to return to their mother Ukrainian Orthodox church.

Eastern Orthodoxy was a critical determinant in the formation of the Russian view of the world, especially its anti-Western orientation. Notwithstanding Soloviev's purported Westernizing sympathies, he too advanced Eastern Orthodoxy as the only true faith, and crucial key to the Russian identity. His unequivocal equation of the Orthodox religion with moral perfection enabled the author to contrast it, in Orthodoxy's favor, with the ostensibly inferior infidel faith of "Russia's" Asian (Mongol) enemies during the Kievan era. Soloviev contends that insofar as belief systems differentiate young nations the Orthodox faith of Kievan Rus set it apart from its Islamic neighbors, and reinforced the Old Rus (read Russian) nationality. He appropriates for Russia alone the entire history of Kievan Rus, and in so doing projects Russian national concerns belonging uniquely to a much later age onto the history of the earlier Eastern Slavic polity. Having thus defined what it means to be "Russian" he proceeds to advance the notion of Russia's messianic mission as one of restoring its people to their essential totality, in other words reintegrating the allegedly indivisible Russian family of peoples. By thus essentializing the continuity between Kievan Rus and Muscovite Russia Soloviev confirms his own romantic fascination with the persistence of a Rus past, embodying the unique spirit of "Russia," in the Russian present. Accordingly, he misses the critical fact that in the seventeenth-century Ukrainians and Belarusians (collectively called Rus or Ruthenians) and Muscovites still looked upon each other as foreigners.

Among the contributing factors to Muscovy's rising distrust of alien peoples Soloviev lists Poland's political ambitions, leading to its sponsorship of some bizarre pretenders to the Muscovite throne. Beginning with their initial occupation of Muscovy in 1605 the Poles grew intimately involved in Muscovy's internal affairs. Not surprisingly, such foreign encroachment on Muscovy's domestic affairs affected the psyche of its people, and contributed to their paranoia about all things Western. In Soloviev's estimation this strengthened the people's resolve to defend their sovereignty, and compelled them a year after their liberation in 1613 "to elect a tsar from amongst themselves to ensure the independence of the Russian state."[3]

A true measure of the depth of Soloviev's imprint on the work of subsequent students of Russia's past is found not only in the publications of the succeeding generation of Russian historians, but in those of more recent Western scholars as well. Many of the latter especially continue to expostulate as the foremost achievement of the second Romanov tsar Alexis the reincorporation of the eastern part of Ukraine after four hundred years of alleged separation from Russia. This is pure Soloviev, an advocate of the monolineal and exclusivist school of Russian history, resting on political and juridical theories.[4] It comprises apologists for a powerful state dedicated to bonding the dispersed masses of "Russia" into an indivisible unity.

Such an ingenuous formulation suggests that the original "Russian" inhabitants of Rus somehow, how is never made clear, metamorphosed into Ukrainians, or Belarus, or even the non-Slav Lithuanians. Meanwhile, in his estimation, a branch of the Russian ethnos evolved on territory to the northeast of its Kievan homeland, from which position it moved teleologically forward toward reunification with the reinvented "Russians" left behind in the Kievan state.

In point of fact there is no valid, let alone irrefutable, historical case to be made for any such claim for a direct ethnic connection between the people of Kievan Rus and the original inhabitants of Muscovy. Except for a branch of the Kievan ruling house, the origin of which has no bearing on the ethnic composition of the Muscovites, inasmuch as no mass population transfer occurred, the only ethnic connection consists of their roots in an ancient East Slavic family of peoples. Muscovites-Russians themselves were products of new, post-Kievan, forces which emerged on separate territory. They developed into a separate ethnos from admixtures of peoples other than those who comprised the inhabitants of Kievan Rus.

Admittedly a measure of religious and cultural indebtedness to ancient Rus did exist, and the two peoples shared a minor dynastic tie, but these factors establish neither an uninterrupted dynastic nor ethnic development.

All such questions of interpretation aside, this volume of Soloviev's history of Russia is a finely wrought recreation of memorable events and a colorful collage of baroque characters whose stories enliven its pages. With his flair for the dramatic, the author describes the abuses and disarray in the Orthodox church during the early modern period of history in which distribution by Polish kings of high ecclesiastical office among unqualified candidates played such a disastrous role. To draw the reader into this era, the author employs details that most felicitously display the human weaknesses of such appointees to episcopal sees, their depredations, cupidity and rapacity. His accounts of a pious laity determined to promote church reforms offer a dramatic contrast to the scurrilous conduct of the clergy in high office.

The spectacle of events leading up to the Union of Brest, which created the Vatican-oriented Uniate church in 1596, unfolds before the reader in Soloviev's descriptions of behind-the-scenes machinations, intrigues, and unsavory, not to mention uncanonical, deals struck by the church of Rome with the defecting bishops of Rus. Illuminated also is the striking contrast between the conduct of the negotiating ecclesiastics and their subsequent insistence upon strict adherence to established protocol and procedural rituals as the fateful assembly in Brest commenced its work. In depicting the exciting events that occurred on the eve of church union Soloviev creates a colorful canvas portraying the excesses of defecting Orthodox churchmen and Catholic persecutors alike. By way of an interesting and suggestive counterpoint, his representations of Muscovite prelates are drawn with a softer brush, blurring somewhat their all too human weaknesses.

As one antidote to clerical abuses a significant phenomenon known as the Rus (Ukrainian) brotherhood movement emerged in the late sixteenth century. Ecclesiastical disarray in the Orthodox church, caused in large measure by the projected union between the Orthodox Rus and the church of Rome, provided the catalyst. Notwithstanding the author's detailed accounts of the inner workings of such organizations in Ukraine and Belarus, he fails to differentiate between them and the Muscovite brotherhoods. Instead he equates the entire Rus brotherhood movement in the

Polish-Lithuanian Commonwealth with the different guild-like fraternal associations in Muscovy. In contrast to the Rus brotherhoods, whose cultural and educational activities helped to spread literacy and inspire the emergence of a Ukrainian national consciousness, the purposes of the Muscovite fraternities were confined to the economic and social concerns of their individual members. Soloviev's seamless linkage of the two, which functioned in such divergent ways, deprives the reader of a true appreciation of their disparate natures and agendas.

The first, most prestigious of the Ukrainian brotherhoods was organized in the heart of Lviv (Lvov, Lwów), home to Western Ukrainians whose Orthodox faith long exposed them to discrimination in the Polish-Lithuanian Commonwealth. They paid dearly for their religious convictions by exclusion from the political, social and cultural mainstream. As a consequence, such marginalization in the beleaguered community created an inner space which enabled its members to retreat into their own culture and spiritual world. Here they could preserve their culture and Ukrainian Orthodox faith with little intrusion from the dominant Catholic center. When in the late sixteenth century ecclesiastical controversy erupted in the Polish-Lithuanian Commonwealth, Lviv's Ukrainians became the first such group to emerge from isolation, and organize into a powerful, reform-minded lay brotherhood.

A patriarchal mandate solicited by the organization endowed it with unprecedented jurisdiction over the life of its secular and spiritual community. The brethren became effective leaders in the fight to preserve Ukrainian Orthodoxy, encouraged much-needed ecclesiastical reforms which the hierarchy avoided, and provided a model of Ukrainian community organization which was reproduced in cities and towns throughout the country. Although Soloviev's portrayal of this brotherhood, and others founded subsequently, is enriched by archival details that offer insights into the life of one of the most important and influential associations in the history of early modern Ukraine, certain lapses in his use of primary documents are troubling. Instead of referring to the readily available "School Regulation," a virtual copy of the Lviv prototype that governed the administration of the school attached to the Lutsk Brotherhood, for his treatment of this educational institution Soloviev relies on a questionable document. It appears to be a hastily compiled set of school regulations drawing heavily on the Lutsk Brotherhood Charter. Its interdictions against commercial transactions and possession of firearms or tools of any kind, in addition to a mandate of strict secrecy in the matter of internal affairs, reflect the concerns of the parent brotherhood organization, not a school for young people.

Notwithstanding that the hierarchs of Rus reached an accord with Rome by 1596, religious strife in the Commonwealth continued to escalate. Until the death of the most Catholic of all Polish kings, Sigismund III, in 1632, the Jesuits persecuted with special zeal all Orthodox who had rejected union with the church of Rome. Soloviev's eye for particulars ensures that his readers will have a historical narrative based upon an impressive accumulation of factual evidence conveying the intensity of that ecclesiastical confrontation.

In the seventeenth century the fortunes of Ukrainian Orthodoxy became intertwined with the activities of the Zaporozhian Cossacks,[5] and the newly-created Uniate church joined the Jesuits in their relentless persecution of the Orthodox faithful. Soloviev incorporates the documents which most vividly recreate the atmosphere of that distant age, and help vitalize the struggles of its colorful historical figures. They form part of a kaleidoscope that teems with Catholic leaders, Orthodox magnates, cossack hetmans, ranking churchmen and the numerous lesser "Baroque" figures entangled in the turbulent events of the early seventeenth century. The polemical acrimony proliferated on both sides of the ecclesiastical confrontation, mutual accusations hurled with mounting fury as the religious drama unfolded. All was complicated from within by a projected, if ultimately unsuccessful, Orthodox-Protestant confederation.

Instances of acute religious strife are juxtaposed as exploits of the Zaporozhian Cossacks, whom Soloviev was disposed to cast in the role of cruel and vicious predators. Apart from a brief reference to the cossack-Polish imbroglio as one that exhibited certain characteristics of a national-religious war, the author interprets their central interest in attacking neighboring territories to be looting and pillaging, not uncommon in most wars of that period. Soloviev makes no attempt to reconcile their warring with the early stirrings of a Ukrainian national consciousness, although he allows that a quest for justice from "their Polish masters" might have been a motive. He describes cossack activity as that of barbarians who tortured their victims with a relish that betrayed a fine disregard for their international ramifications, and a total absence of human sensibility. Whatever motives might have driven them to fighting, we cannot gainsay the strong sense of communality that the Zaporozhian Host had developed by this time, enabling its members to coalesce into a homogeneous Orthodox polity within what now was a cossack political entity.[6] Indeed the cossack feats themselves represent the stuff of which national legends were made, and subsequent generations of Ukrainians, especially those in Soloviev's day, drew upon them in their own quest for a modern national identity.

By the early seventeenth century the Union of Brest, which required extreme machinations and exertion to bring to fruition, was proving to be a devil's bargain by sowing dissension within the Uniate-Catholic coalition itself. Accusations of broken promises multiplied when Uniates recognized the bitter reality of a political union with Rome. The eagerly awaited benefits and much anticipated equality in the Commonwealth promised by the Catholic center failed to materialize. Soloviev conveys the depth of Uniate disillusionment and the related brutality of Orthodox persecutions by Jesuit fanatics undeterred in their resolve to proselytize. The author renders the key events by quoting the entire speech of an Orthodox deputy from Volhynia, a Ukrainian province, to the Sejm in Poland, in which he excoriates the Catholics for their aggression.

In 1620 the beleaguered position of Orthodox Ukrainians in the Commonwealth prompted them to chart a daring course of action. A visit to Kiev by Patriarch Theophanes of Jerusalem provided the pretext. In a suspense-filled secret ceremony he illegally reconstituted the Orthodox hierarchy which was decimated in 1596, although its legitimation in the Commonwealth had to await the coronation of the succeeding Polish king, Władysław IV, in 1632. The role of the new ruler was that of healer, destined to end the controversies that marred his predecessor's reign. Entering into negotiations with dignitaries from both ecclesiastical institutions, Orthodox and Uniate, Władysław presided over a religious compromise which brought official recognition to the Rus Orthodox church in the Polish-Lithuanian Commonwealth.

The consequences of this compromise were not lost on the Jesuits, still passionately committed to their proselytizing mission. Accordingly they trained their arrows on a new target, notably the growing network of Orthodox brotherhood schools established largely, although not exclusively, by laity. The Jesuit "schoolmen of Europe" appreciated the significance of capturing youthful minds while still in a state of formation, and hastened to establish their schools throughout the Polish-Lithuanian Commonwealth. Rival Orthodox educational institutions also began to proliferate in Ukraine and Belarus, in conjunction with their parent brotherhood organizations. To deepen our understanding and appreciation of this important Orthodox institution Soloviev fills his account with intriguing details about the structure and administration of their schools.

The prospect of an educated Ukrainian Orthodox laity represented an intolerable threat to the Jesuit crusade for religious unity in Poland. The Society of Jesus determined to curb such expansion. Although the Jesuits targeted brotherhood schools in general, they reserved their most vigorous exertions for the one in Kiev. Its new learning reflected an Orthodox culture thoroughly attuned to the intellectual climate of the Latin West, and it boasted a school curriculum modeled on Latin lines. This development was an alarming challenge to the Jesuits' cherished designs for religious unity in the Commonwealth, an ambition that never was realized. Indeed, Kiev was destined to become an important conduit for the transmission of Western-style learning to Russia, where it remained for long a bitterly resented alien innovation, and fed the continuing hostility to all things foreign.

The Russian penchant for equating form with substance is exemplified in the second half of the seventeenth century when an ecclesiastical controversy over outward symbols and corrections to religious texts raged with astounding intensity. It produced a breach in the Russian church known as the Schism, which was never repaired. This seventeenth-century example of insistence upon the sanctity of established form echoed a number of incidents of the sixteenth century. Polish-Muscovite wrangles at that time over protocol, the tsar's titles and proper forms of address presented unmistakable evidence of the latter's obsession with ritualized formalities. An account of the spectacle of diplomatic meetings between Muscovy and Poland, during which Muscovite representatives made much of real or imagined slights caused by improper Polish renderings of the tsar's title, produces some absorbing reading. Polish diplomats attempted to justify their allegedly willful diminutions of the tsar's titles by pleading ignorance, or simple lack of attention to things in which they did not put much stock. In the minds of the Muscovites, however, the issue of deliberately, or even carelessly, inscribed titles assumed ludicrous proportions. They demanded punishment without mercy, extending even to the death penalty, for the guilty Polish scribes. Soloviev relates details of endless quibbles over such petty concerns as whether the tsar's title is rendered in the plural or the singular. These controversies might be viewed as masking a profoundly experienced, perhaps unconscious, sense of Muscovite inferiority vis-à-vis the West or, possibly more to the point, a Muscovite craving for the respect of the outside world.

During the Polish-Muscovite negotiations the return of fugitive peasants became another highly charged issue. Each side suffered substantial
losses of peasant labor, although runaways from Polish lands appear to
have outnumbered those who fled Muscovy. Accordingly the Muscovites
refused to entertain any possibility of assisting Polish landlords in the
recovery of their Orthodox peasants. They reasoned that returning Orthodox fugitives to a Catholic country would be to thrust them into the jaws of
heretics and schismatics who, they prophesied ominously, would be sure to
abuse them. Such rationalization confirmed not merely the significance for
Muscovite leaders of Orthodoxy as a symbol of Russian religiosity and
identity, but the importance of economic considerations as well. The country
suffered from a severe shortage of labor, and Muscovite benefits from re-
ciprocal peasant flight far outweighed those of the Poles. Hence it was in
the interest of the former to reject any scheme for peasant repatriation.

Some picturesque "Baroque" vignettes, portraying the bizarre claims
of a motley array of spurious pretenders to the Russian throne, take us
into other recesses of seventeenth-century Russian life. From the details
of their adventures, which sometimes read like picaresque tales, we gain
fresh insights into the world view of a people disposed to entertain outrageous claims of impostors, together with the social and political factors
that motivated them. True to their Russian character and molded by centuries of acculturation that rendered them meekly submissive to the
authority of patriarchal leadership, the people exhibited an almost patho-
logical craving for a father figure. This made them vulnerable to the
claims of various charlatans. The only concern of the narod (people) was
that *a* tsar, any batiushka (little father) occupy the throne. The actual
human being behind that figure was of little consequence so long as the
people had their symbol of a strong patriarchal ruler.

Returning to the issue of the people's antipathy to foreigners, readers
also are introduced to the commercial class in Muscovy. In 1634 and
again in 1636 the Holstein and diplomat Adam Olearius journeyed to
Muscovy. He noted the paradox of a realm's economic reliance on the
same foreigners who profited from special trading privileges while simultaneously inspiring xenophobic reactions on the part of the local populace. Caricatures seemingly straight out of Gogol vitalize this work with
stories of unscrupulous trading practices by scheming foreign merchants
conspiring to impoverish their Muscovite competitors. Even as Muscovites complained bitterly about the prejudicial trading charters facilitating the foreigner's cynical exercise of privileged trades, their time-honored

habit of submission to authority did not permit them to push their demands for justice too far. Such unequal opportunities naturally exacerbated the antagonism that Muscovites harbored toward the foreigners. Expanding Olearius, Soloviev portrays a convoluted Muscovite-Russian economy, an enfeebled merchantry, and the country's neurotic relationship with the world that lay beyond its borders.

The government's task of regulating such an economy was complicated by the fact that the people themselves, at all levels of society, were not above evading their fiscal responsibilities. Indeed, so pervasive was this practice that the seventeenth century witnessed cities like Novgorod facing the prospect of virtual depopulation. Nearly every inhabitant sought a way out of the city to avoid or lessen the tax burden, with the disastrous result that it fell increasingly on individuals incapable of paying anything. This impelled tax-exempt officials to squeeze even further a shrinking tax base. What emerges is a portrait of a country where scoundrels, local and foreign alike, discovered ways to dodge their fiscal obligations. Even the poor and middling peasants, the most exploited class in all the realm, learned from their betters, and found ever new and more creative ways to circumvent their fiscal obligations. In Soloviev's apparent desire to portray the Russians as ethical, honest and selfless victims of unscrupulous foreigners who cunningly exploited their privileges he also paints a picture of a nation of tax dodgers with no sense of civic responsibility, hedged in by a bungled Muscovite economy and inept government.

Soloviev's story of the country's mounting xenophobia continues with Tsar Alexis Mikhailovich's marriage to a woman from the Miloslavsky clan, well known for its pro-Western sentiments. Her sister married the boyar Boris Ivanovich Morozov, who contrived to become the tsar's brother-in-law by shrewdly manipulating the sovereign's choice of bride. From his new position of power Morozov introduced a number of Western-style reforms which aroused popular suspicions. In due course, driven by mistrust and desperation, the population vented its rage on corrupt Muscovite officials and hapless foreigners alike. The public fury thus unleashed had its roots in the preceding years. An unsuccessful war with Sweden during Tsar Michael's unremarkable reign resulted in the loss of Muscovite territories to the enemy, producing the spectacle of hordes of Muscovite peasants fleeing the conquered lands, and the Swedes demanding their recovery. Rather than relinquish the Orthodox peasants who fell to an alien and Lutheran master, Alexis elected to purchase their freedom.

Unlike the earlier instance of runaway peasants to Polish-Lithuanian lands, now the tsar was prepared to make substantial sacrifices rather than surrender his peasants to the mercy of "heretics."

Scenes of carts filled with meat and grain rolling out of Muscovy and rumors of the tsar's treasury emptied for the benefit of foreigners inflamed an already restive populace. Popular sentiment exploded into destructive violence, and riots spread throughout the land. Disregarding altogether the fact that the fate of their co-religionists was at issue, aroused by feelings of xenophobia, dismayed by the prospect of famine in Muscovy as more and more provisions left the country, and infuriated by the arrogance of corrupt and greedy Muscovite officials, mutinous mobs ran amok. Soloviev describes in dramatic detail their gruesome deeds, as foreigners and unscrupulous officials alike were swept into a murderous maelstrom of witch hunts and escalating violence, until the rebellion had run its course.

These events amply demonstrate the potential for popular resentment exploding into violent action when an exploited people is driven to exasperation by the seeming hopelessness of their situation, and their perception of a callous officialdom unresponsive to their fundamental human needs. By depicting the protagonists as human beings with human weaknesses—villainous and disdainful officials and a superstitious and suspicious populace easily swayed by rumors, and embittered by the immense gulf that separated their lot from that of the privileged classes—Soloviev's study draws the reader deeply into the life of the ordinary people and their uppermost concerns.

After the disturbances subsided and harsh punishments were inflicted, the people's attention fastened on their patriarch-designate, Metropolitan Nikon. Soloviev provides his readers with some rare glimpses of Nikon's life, from his humble beginnings as the son of a poor peasant, through his rise to prominent church office while losing touch with his origins along the way. In many ways Nikon's story is the story of church-state relations in early modern Russia. It also illustrates the unpredictability, indeed the volatility, of a people's sentiments towards the clergy, especially when they perceived a high churchman making common cause with Russia's ruling classes. In his person Nikon exemplified all of the worldliness of the Russian church and the corruption of its clergy. Although Soloviev tends to spare his readers many of the grisly details of crimes committed against the people by other men of the cloth, this did not extend to

Nikon. The author illuminates the prelate's cruelty, his hubris and pride, his arrogance and boundless ambition, a lamentable combination in Nikon's character, especially when added to what is described as his innately obstreperous personality. Such qualities revealed at once a talented son of the church and a thoroughly despicable human being.[7]

Instead of detecting in this peasant's son some sympathy for their suffering, the people found themselves dealing with a haughty prelate who would not hesitate to advance his own cause at the expense of their misery. When lay-clerical relations degenerated to the level of uncontrollable mob violence a rebellious rabble fell on Nikon, beating him so severely as to cause life-threatening injuries. The implication of their actions is not difficult to imagine. Not even the tsar would so have affronted a man upon whose soul God had impressed his spiritual seal. Nikon assiduously encouraged this submission in his patron the tsar by his uncompromising insistence on the complete surrender of crown authority to the higher power of the church. The relationship between the two opposite characters of dominance and subservience offers a fascinating psychological study.

Tsar Alexis did indeed acknowledge Nikon's spiritual authority. He humbled himself before the very prelate whose candidacy for the patriarchal throne he so sedulously promoted, even to the point of subterfuge. The indispensable secrecy that enshrouded Nikon's impending elevation exposed the limitations that boyars still imposed upon an autocrat's maneuverability in seventeenth-century Russia. Soloviev's portrayal of the respective behavior of sovereign and subject towards a high-ranking churchman creates an interesting study in contrasts. In the common eye Nikon was the embodiment of corrupt authority. When popular hostility turned into open rebellion this son of the church found himself as much at risk as any secular official in a similar situation. Ordinary people went where tsars and angels feared to tread. The sensational events surrounding Nikon's career illustrate the characters of rulers and ruled alike. Soloviev exposes their depredations as well as their sacrifices, their superstitions and phobias, all of which helped to mold the early modern Russian mind and shape the people's historical evolution.

In sum, Soloviev's finely crafted work brings Russia's past to life in new ways. Except for the lapses already noted the author's fascination with detail and scrupulous examination of the evidence serve him well. Melding an active imagination and primary sources to produce a vivid pageant, laced with memorable vistas of life in early modern Russia and its neighboring countries, this historian offers his readers intimate glimpses into that Russian society of a kind that few scholars before him thought to reveal. In doing so he transforms and deepens our knowledge of the country's past and our appreciation of Russians as flesh and blood beings confronting a changing world, in ways heretofore not charted. Even so, the shortcomings of the work must be pointed out. Let me reiterate and comment on the most obvious. The author is often misled by his ideological commitment to the "Russian Idea," as even a cursory examination of the contents of this volume will testify. Regardless of the validity of any claim to a shared Kievan legacy, it cannot be utilized to validate some essential "Russianness" of the Kievan state. Neither can it sustain an argument for an essential, inseparable ethnic connection between the peoples of Muscovy and Kievan Rus. Such interpretation of the data places Soloviev in the ranks of imperialist myth makers. In many respects this work is a *tour de force*, and its author must be given his due. At the same time a historian of Soloviev's stature might have done more to advance the cause of objective history, to the extent that this is a realistic goal. By applying a less subjective interpretation to his rendering of archival data Soloviev could have generated a significant corrective to the prevailing and frequently distorted renditions of Russian history. Choosing, perhaps in spite of himself, to do otherwise, the author contributed to the proliferation of ahistorical fictions and untenable claims in Russian historiography.

On a final note, at issue here is not the primacy of archival evidence, or even Soloviev's selection and ordering of the data, although the reader is reminded that such an exercise is itself an act of interpretation. It is the author's penchant, all disclaimers to the contrary, for allowing the dominating idea of the era in which he lived—the national romantic myth as justification of empire—so completely to animate his historical narrative.

HISTORY OF RUSSIA

Volume 18

Religious Struggle in Poland-Lithuania

Tsar Alexis' Reign Begins, 1654-1676

I

PREPARATIONS FOR CHURCH UNION

RELIGIOUS CONFLICT

In the beginning of this work I noted that Russia does not have clear-cut natural borders, neither to the West nor to the East. Nature provided little support for establishing the country's national sovereignty and uniqueness. Yet history soon granted it a powerful weapon when Christianity, more significantly Eastern-rite Christianity, was introduced into ancient Rus.[1] Christianity provided a sharp line of demarcation between the people of Rus, upon whom it left a strong European imprint, and their Asian neighbors to the East, the Muslim infidels. At the same time a moral boundary was drawn between them based on the Eastern confession which the Rus [Ukrainians] embraced, and the Roman faith of Western nations.

Religious differences figure very strongly in the belief system of a young nation, generally constituting the basis of divisions into "ours" and "theirs." It was precisely these differences which reinforced the fledgling and undeveloped Rus nationality, promoting its national uniqueness and sovereignty. Exhibiting great religious fervor, struggling always under the banner of Christianity, the Rus people waged an unrelenting fight with their heterodox barbarian Asian neighbors to the East. While the Muscovite realm was threatened with the loss of independence during the seventeenth-century Time of Troubles,[2] driven by religious inspiration and aware of their spiritual distinctiveness, Western Rus resisted Poland and Lithuania. This is what compelled the Muscovites [Russians] to elect a tsar from amongst themselves to ensure the sovereignty of their state.[3]

Having briefly reviewed the events known as the Time of Troubles in Muscovy, and the restoration of self-determination and tranquility in Russia in the reign of Tsar Michael,[4] we now turn our attention to Rus, where another religious battle raged. Michael's successor was instrumental in its resolution. Already we are aware that certain deficiencies in its political evolution stood in the way of Ukraine's preservation of independence, resulting in its subordination by a stronger political entity, the grand principality of Lithuania. Later, with Lithuanian mediation, the Rus and Poles were united but, as noted earlier, the confessional differences in their respective territories became a source of considerable embarrassment from the moment of unification.[5] Under Jogaila and some of his successors Polish Catholics felt free to display their religious zeal by persecuting worshipers in the Eastern Orthodox faith. We have observed how similar attempts at religious uniformity created national antagonisms in the past, causing the Rus people to seek separation from the Polish-Lithuanian union in order to join Orthodox Muscovy.[6] Until the mid-sixteenth century there was no strong, sustained commitment to forcing the Rus into the Catholic confession, or at least into accepting Catholic dogma while retaining the Orthodox rites, liturgy and liturgical language. With the passage of time even the existing meager attempts grew progressively more feeble, primarily because the Jagiellonians were more concerned to maintain a solid, unbreakable political union of Lithuania and Rus with Poland, and so respected the civil rights of all their inhabitants.

The Jagiellonian rulers understood well that persecuting Orthodox Rus, and attempting to force a union with the Catholics, would jeopardize their primary objective of political union. Accordingly, as they expended ever more time and energy on their political aims these rulers tended to minimize efforts to encourage religious uniformity which in any case could be accomplished only through coercion. Moreover the Jagiellonians found themselves increasingly helpless in reviving the earlier Catholic enthusiasm for a union, which already was waning during the years preceding the Reformation. This caused them to abandon their hopes of joining the two churches.

What happened to the flow of events which were once so advantageous to Poland? What subsequently rekindled the dormant Catholic fanaticism and induced Poland's Catholic leaders to begin anew the religious persecution of their Rus subjects? Clearly such actions could only end as they had earlier, under similar circumstances. Rus regions[7] would simply break their ties to Poland and join Muscovy.

Earlier periods of our history have far more in common with the history of Western Europe than is evident at first glance. The great religious question, namely the ecclesiastical conflict in Western Europe which followed Luther's Reformation, also had important consequences for the fate of Eastern Europe, indeed of our own fatherland. Momentous seventeenth-century events in Western and Eastern Europe alike were fuelled by religious issues and the confrontation they engendered. In the West the Protestant and Catholic struggle resulted in the decisive liberation and self-determination of nationalities hitherto pulled and chained together by Roman Catholic aspirations for political and economic unity. In the East, Orthodox clashed with Catholics to defend the process of self-determination and national awareness of the Rus, as well as other Eastern Slavic peoples. All of this testified to the fact that struggles in both East and West were closely related.

THE JESUITS[8]

We know that Luther's teachings and their offshoots were disseminated with alacrity throughout the Polish domains, whereas elsewhere the Catholics pitted their celebrated Jesuit warriors against the enemy. Employing skillful methods the Jesuits defeated Polish Protestantism, itself sickened and weakened by internal dissension. They then turned their attention to a more dangerous foe, the ancient Eastern or Rus confession, which had put down such deep roots among the people. The Jesuits excited fanaticism among the Catholic people, helping to inflame their hatred of Orthodoxy. They also influenced local leaders, blinded by their zeal and incapable of recognizing their best interests. The leaders believed, or at least tried to convince others, that church union would cement the unity of the realm. What they failed to comprehend was the fact that only peaceful measures, not coercion, could achieve this aim. So these Jesuits sent their restless scholars to wage war on the Rus faith. They delivered sermons and wrote learned treatises against it, they agitated in the homes and in the schools, all in their attempt to alienate Rus youths from the faith of their fathers.

In 1577 the celebrated Jesuit Piotr Skarga published a book entitled *The Unity of God's Church and the Greek Departure from this Unity.*[9] The first two parts were dedicated to a dogmatic and historical survey of the initial split in the Roman church. In the third segment, especially interesting to us, the author posited three reasons why order was impossible to achieve in the Rus church. First, that church condoned a married secular clergy which, concerned only with worldly affairs, neglected to tend its flock. Because of this, all learning in Rus deteriorated, and priests were transformed into peasants. Second is the Slavonic tongue. The Greeks cheated the people of Rus by depriving them of the Greek language, leaving them with Slavonic instead. As a result, they might never aspire to true learning and understanding inasmuch as Latin and Greek are the only languages in which learning and religion can be acquired. Nowhere in the world was there ever, nor could there ever be, a single college or academy where theology, philosophy and other subjects were taught and learned in any other language. No one can be educated in Slavonic. Indeed no one even understands it in its authentic form. There is not a people in the world that speaks it the way it is written in the books. It never had, nor can it have, its own rules or grammar. Never do we hear that among the Rus there are scholars who know both ancient and modern Greek, whereas we Catholics all share the same faith and language the world over. A Christian from India converses about God with a Pole without difficulty. Third is lay interference in ecclesiastical affairs and the denigration of the clergy.

Skarga speaks directly of union, pointing to its advantages for laity and clergy alike. According to him church unity requires only three things. (1) That the metropolitan of Kiev accept the blessing of the Pope rather than that of the patriarch. (2) That every Rus agree with the Roman church on all articles of faith. (3) That the Rus also acknowledge the jurisdiction of the Holy See. Everything that related to church rituals was to remain unaltered.

In 1590 Skarga reissued his book, dedicated to Sigismund III. In it the author claimed that his writings had benefited many, had opened the eyes of many, and proposed that more new editions be issued. Skarga charged that the current edition was unavailable because wealthy Rus had bought all the copies and had them burned. "God grant that all heretics be brought together," he continued, "there are not too many of them left now, and were secular authorities allowed freely to exercise their authority and privileges each day, the number of heretics would dwindle even more. Most problematic of all are the Rus, who respond to attempts at conversion by invoking their ancestors and their ancient history." He went on to complain that the present government no longer invoked the same measures that earlier kings used to attract Rus to the Catholic faith, measures such as barring them from the Senate.

Yet another Jesuit, Antonio Possevino, whom we mentioned earlier,[10] failed to persuade Ivan the Terrible to become a Catholic. To accomplish this he attempted initially to introduce church union into Rus, and established schools for them [Uniates] in Rome and Wilno.[11] Possevino was convinced that the sole way to convert Eastern or Muscovite Russia was to begin with the Rus in the Polish-Lithuanian Commonwealth.

As for church union, the Jesuits referred to it as a transitional phase, indispensable for bringing the stubborn Rus, still secure in their ancient faith, into the Catholic fold. They openly advocated compulsion, such as withholding certain benefits, as an effective measure to induce the reluctant Rus to change their minds. Skarga's works amply demonstrate the Jesuits' view of such a union as a temporary state. He argues for the desirability of a uniform liturgical and scholarly language, as opposed to the use of Slavonic. For those Rus who accepted merely church union instead of total conversion Slavonic naturally must remain the liturgical language. At a time when European nations, growing into maturity, increasingly were inclined to extricate themselves from the medieval diapers of Latin and Catholic unity, and to develop their national character with the aid of their native languages, the Jesuits audaciously defied history with their claim that nowhere in the world was it possible for an academy or college to offer instruction in any language but Latin or Greek. The Rus resisted this kind of retrograde thinking, which threatened Europeans with permanent stagnation. They waged a struggle for their faith and identity, but where were they to find the resources for a successful solution of their dilemma?

We have observed the unenviable position of the Rus church during the second half of the sixteenth century. A realm so indifferent to the needs of that church, and with its own religion to assist, would never support Orthodoxy. It preferred instead to nourish its Catholic clergy with the Orthodox bread of the Rus. Accordingly the Polish Catholic administration appropriated Orthodox resources for its own purposes, turning over not only the monasteries but entire eparchies to individuals who felt no calling whatsoever for such offices. They received their appointments not as rewards for service to the church, rather for services rendered exclusively to the Polish Catholic realm.[12] Such shepherds could never lead their Orthodox flocks to their own faith or strengthen their morals. Indeed the elevation of unfit candidates served merely to weaken discipline in the Orthodox church, undermined the moral conduct of the lower clergy and caused learning to stagnate. Naturally the crown's hostility to Orthodoxy and its refusal to lend any support roused the Rus community to action. It turned out that the very thing that Skarga insisted would prove detrimental to the Orthodox church, lay interference in internal affairs, actually was indispensable to its salvation. As we already are aware, the Catholic government ignored the needs of the Orthodox, and because the Orthodox hierarchy was in a state of decline, laymen reacted in their own interest by strongly influencing ecclesiastical affairs.

RUS ELITES

What sort of resources did the Rus community have at its disposal, what strengths could it draw upon, how could it solidify and unite these strengths? At the time it boasted a powerful aristocracy consisting of illustrious magnate families, some of which traced their lineage all the way back to Riurik and Gediminas.[13] This elite strongly supported the Rus church and its people, especially in the earlier epochs. We have discussed the activity of Prince Konstantin Ostrozhsky,[14] as well as the help given to the Rus by the Muscovite émigré Prince Kurbsky[15] and his friends, in their struggle with the Catholic church. Eventually, notwithstanding its earlier determination, the Rus nobility began to falter in its defense of faith and nation. Their focus of activity shifted to Crown Poland,[16] its court and Senate. This culminated in a merger of the Rus elite with the Polish aristocracy, within which the Rus strove for equality. Rus aristocrats equated the interests of their own people with provincialism, and disdained them as something beneath their dignity. Generally speaking, the older generation continued to hold fast to its heritage whereas the youth, alienated from its ancient native environment by upbringing, marriage and service, easily lost ties to its cultural legacy.

If the magnates, once so protective of the Western Rus faith and nationality, subsequently withdrew this support, the same could not be said of the middle class, the local inhabitants, who formed strong associations. In both the Rus and Muscovite regions we saw that brotherhoods or confraternities acquired a special significance within the more independent and highly developed communities.[17] In Muscovy they were most influential in cities like Novgorod and Pskov whereas their prestige, comparatively speaking, was weaker in the less developed towns downstream. In Western or Lithuanian Rus they became a vital part of the urban scene.[18] Owing to the Magdeburg Law,[19] the towns of Rus routinely adopted older communal forms of guild-like structures, which in turn facilitated the founding of brotherhoods. Besides this powerful base for integrated public activity and development of community life and brotherhood organizations, the town dwellers were capable of a more compact social struggle than the aristocracy in the Polish-Lithuanian Commonwealth. Moreover, they had stronger connections to the provinces, and Rus relationships in the Commonwealth were after all largely provincial. Thus it is quite plain why the urban brotherhoods, modeled on medieval guilds, attracted even some of the gentry to the confessional conflicts.[20] The Jesuits increasingly found that brotherhoods, those powerful urban alliances generated by Rus town life, were stumbling blocks which persistently thwarted their plan for church union.

From the outset, first with the aid of the aristocracy, then especially with the assistance of the brotherhoods, the Rus fought for their faith and national identity against mighty adversaries supported by the crown. Cooperation between aristocracy and brotherhoods enabled the Rus community actively to influence ecclesiastical affairs. We have been apprised already that Skarga considered this sort of lay interference disastrous for the church, and certain Rus bishops who suffered from the effects of lay influence more than others also began to incline to this position. Those bishops who promptly embraced church union proclaimed themselves the only lawful, hence indispensable, agents for delivering the church from such unwelcome intrusion. They looked to union as a way to restore tranquility to their ecclesiastical institution, and provide it with at least a semblance of well-being. Accordingly they were not averse to accepting the legality, indeed the indispensability, of such an arrangement.

EPISCOPAL CONDUCT

For a fuller understanding of the state of the Rus church hierarchy at this time we will examine conditions in a number of its most important [Western] hierarchies. Some of the Rus bishops there possessed substantially more landed wealth than their Eastern counterparts. The Vladimir eparchy in Volhynia owned a fortified castle in the town of Vladimir, and several manor houses; the town of Krasnov; sixteen settlements in the districts of Lutsk and Vladimir; the Kupetov region, which contained the small town of Ozerany, eleven settlements and fishing grounds; and Voloslav island on the Lug [Luh] river, site of the St. Onufry monastery. The Lutsk and Ostrog eparchies owned four towns and thirty-four settlements in the districts of Lutsk and Vladimir. Of these the towns of Khorlup and Zhabche were protected by fortifications, cannons, culverins, muskets and a variety of other firearms. It is therefore understandable that such lucrative appointments, with their preeminence and luxurious lifestyle, were much sought after by the prominent laity. Once episcopal sees were acquired through the good offices of secular authorities, the recipients manifested little interest in abandoning their secular way of life. Indeed it would have been a difficult transition even if they were so inclined.

We know already about the condition of Poland at the time, the arbitrary behavior of the mighty, their disdain for laws, and the weakness of crown authority. Force needed to be met with force, so it was small wonder that episcopal castles were fortified and defended with artillery. Frequent armed clashes with avaricious, powerful and unruly neighbors, people of another faith who deemed it no sin to profit at the expense of schismatic bishops, led to repeated appearances in the courts, to complaints and attempts at self-defense. Consequently, instead of praying and writing sermons, the bishops applied themselves to poring over passages in the law books.

Following the death of the current bishop Joseph, in the year 1565 there appeared two candidates for the eparchies of Vladimir and Brest. One was a member of the Polish nobility, Ivan Borzobogaty-Kraseński, the other the bishop of Kholm, Feodosy Lazovsky. Upon receiving a royal charter to the eparchy the first man took control of the episcopal castle, in which he installed his son Vasily. At the same time King Sigismund Augustus issued letters patent for the office of bishop of Vladimir to Lazovsky,[21] who arrived in Vladimir with military retainers and demanded that Vasily Kraseński surrender the castle. When Kraseński refused, Lazovsky stormed and seized it. Kraseński complained to the king, who dispatched one of his noblemen to summon Feodosy Lazovsky to court. The nobleman, together with some of Kraseński's retainers, confronted the bishop in Vladimir cathedral and served him with the royal summons. Lazovsky refused to appear in court, attacked Kraseński's servants with his staff, and ordered his personal retainers to beat and kick the intruders who were in the cathedral. He then scattered Kraseński's servants, declaring "Had Borzobogaty-Kraseński appeared here in person I would have had him hacked to pieces and tossed to the dogs." Lazovsky's actions testify to the sort of man with whom we are dealing. Having ensconced himself in the eparchy, he behaved like any powerful secular lord. Much like other nobles he was the subject of written complaints in which he was accused of gathering armed bands to attack neighboring landowners, of robbing and pillaging on the open road.

In his old age Feodosy Lazovsky placed himself under the care of his son-in-law Dubnitsky, the mayor of Vladimir, who squandered the property of the church, ravaged its estates and stole its letters patent. Still, in judging Lazovsky's conduct it must be considered in the context of its time, not subjected to the standard of our own age and society. Feodosy Lazovsky belonged to a savage breed of people with ruthless characters whom society was forced to tolerate because it was defenseless against such lawless conduct. Once his passion cooled Lazovsky recollected "In my lifetime I caused many to be beaten and robbed, now as my end approaches the time has come to think about the salvation of my soul." Accordingly he determined upon the following amends. A portion of the proceeds from the small town of Ozerany and eleven settlements, both of which belonged to the church, were to be used to beautify Vladimir cathedral. Feodosy designated another portion of the proceeds for the support of two preachers. The school was to have two university graduates, one to teach Greek and the other Slavonic. He also received permission from King Stefan Bathory to turn over the Vladimir eparchy to Melety Khrebtovich-Bogurinsky [Khrebtovych-Bohurinsky], archimandrite of the Caves monastery in Kiev, with the stipulation that Feodosy retain the use of the income from the eparchy until his death (which occurred in 1588). Then it would pass to the exclusive control of Khrebtovich.

A royal decree stipulated that because Feodosy Lazovsky had deprived Ivan Borzobogaty-Kraseński of the eparchy of Vladimir, the latter was to be compensated by the Lutsk and Ostrog eparchies. Marko Zhoravinsky [Zhoravynsky] held the Lutsk office between 1561 and 1567 without benefit of holy orders. After his death it passed to Borzobogaty-Kraseński, who tried to emulate his predecessor by avoiding holy orders, but in 1571 Metropolitan Jonas of Kiev forced his ordination as Bishop Jonas. Together with his children and various relatives the new bishop administered the church property as though it were his own personal estate. He added the little town of Zhabche to his daughter's dowry, while his sons plundered the churches and dispersed the monks. In the end Jonas fell into dispute with King Bathory, who objected to the bishop's overbearing behavior, and he died under a ban of anathema.

After his death in 1585 Ivan Borzobogaty-Kraseński was succeeded by the bishop of Pinsk and Turov, Cyril Terletsky. He too had a gentry background, was intelligent, well educated, energetic and fully qualified to administer the eparchy according to the demands of the time, although by character he was a totally unsuitable candidate for episcopal office.[22] Terletsky found the Lutsk eparchy in a deplorable state. Because it had been so thoroughly ravaged by Kraseński and his relatives the bishop decided to seize Zhabche. He resorted to the courts to secure the inviolability of his church properties and rights and kept his episcopal militia constantly at the ready, prepared to ward off all challengers.

The Dormition Cathedral in Lvov
View of the Apse from the East. First consecrated in 1571, then rebuilt after a
fire, the present structure was consecrated in 1631 by Petro
Mohyla, founder of the Mohyla Academy.

THE FIRST BROTHERHOOD

The third Rus eparchy that deserves mention is that of Lvov [Lviv] in Galich [Halych, Galicia in the West], or Red Rus as it was also called at the end of the sixteenth century. Gedeon Balaban, son of Bishop Arseny of Lvov, was its current bishop. Having received the eparchy in the form of a legacy, he was convinced that he had an even greater right than his colleagues to treat it as personal property.[23] This landowner-bishop met with some formidable opposition from the local Orthodox Dormition brotherhood. During a visit to Lvov in 1586 by Patriarch Joachim of Antioch the town dwellers, as wardens of the Dormition Orthodox church, persuaded the pontiff to bless their brotherhood charters, in effect to approve the founding of the organization.[24]

They drafted the following regulations. (1) On appointed days the brethren shall meet in a designated building, in a spirit of love, peace and mutual respect, to engage in good works as witnessed by God and the people. (2) Every four weeks, or as the need arises, one of the brethren, bearing the brotherhood banner, is to announce an upcoming meeting, after which all members shall assemble, and each contribute half a grosha to the organization's treasury.[25] (3) Anyone desiring to join, be he a burgher, member of the gentry or someone from the provinces, regardless of rank or place of origin, local or foreign, shall pay an initiation fee of four groshas. (4) A member who lives at some distance from the brotherhood's meeting place shall be given the option of making an annual lump-sum payment of six groshas. (5) Each year the brotherhood is to elect four officers from amongst themselves. (6) The senior brother is to take charge of the strongbox and the junior brother will keep the key. (7) Every year, upon completion of their term of office, the four ranking officers shall submit a report to a plenary session of the brethren. (8) Should a proposed candidate for office refuse nomination without a valid reason, he shall be fined three measures of wax. (9) Punishment is the same for all—confinement in the belfry.[26] (10) If one brother insults another verbally he goes to the belfry, and in addition is to be fined fourteen pounds of wax. After that, although not asked to resign from the organization, the offender shall beg forgiveness of the injured party and the entire body. (11) Use of unseemly or vulgar language carries a penalty of one pound of wax. (12) At the conclusion of business on meeting days the brethren are to read religious works and engage in modest conversation with one another. (13) Any brother who learns that a member has committed a misdemeanor must not keep it a secret, rather reveal it so that the guilty one can be punished. The brotherhood shall pass a separate sentence on anyone attempting to conceal such information. (14) A senior brother is to be punished for the same transgression two or three times more severely than his junior counterpart. (15) As soon as a brother is convicted and sentenced to time in the belfry, or assessed a fine, he is to seek forgiveness from the injured party. (16) Any brother who cannot pay the fine shall ask two of his brethren to vouch for him until the subsequent meeting. (17) Each is to be tried by the entire brotherhood, with junior brethren speaking first, then senior members taking their turn. (18) If a member is engaged in an enterprise which he is unable to handle personally, he is permitted to seek advice and assistance from two fellow members. (19) All brotherhood affairs shall be held in the strictest confidence. If two people testify that someone has violated this rule the individual in question is to be sentenced to the belfry and fined a bezmen of wax.[27] (20) Anyone who disdains the ecclesiastical brotherhood court is to be considered in contempt of the church. Should he fail to repent within four weeks' time the offending brother is to face excommunication as a heretic and blatant sinner. It is the duty of the priest to denounce him in church before the whole congregation, and to pronounce the ban of excommunication. (21) Anyone found associating with an excommunicated individual is to incur a like penalty. (22) In the event that an indigent brother finds himself ailing the brotherhood is required to render financial assistance, and tend him during his illness.[28] (23) The recipient of such assistance in time of crisis pays no interest. These loans are only for the sick and needy and may not be made to anyone intending to develop a commercial enterprise at brotherhood expense.[29] (24) The entire organization is to accompany the remains of a deceased brother to the parish cemetery for burial, and a brotherhood candle is to be lit in church. (25) If a member is absent from a meeting or a funeral without good cause, an officer of the brotherhood must be so informed. Any unexcused absence will incur a fine of one pound of wax. (26) Each brother shall enter the names of his mother, father and all other deceased kin in the parish book of the dead. The priest of the Dormition church must read these names at matins and vespers on the Saturdays designated as remembrance days, and also during Lent, in accordance with the provisions of the church charter. (27) Two liturgies for the brotherhood are to be celebrated annually, one for its well-being, and the other a requiem mass. On both occasions distribution of alms for the poor is to increase substantially.

A society which cannot guarantee the security of all, where force prevails, will have individuals or groups who strive to seize as much power as possible in the belief that this alone protects them from other powerful forces. That is why the Dormition Brotherhood took such pains to secure from Patriarch Joachim the important prerogative of exposing those who violated the laws of Christ, to cleanse the church of scandalous excesses, to supervise and censure all violators, not excluding the bishop himself.

Let us continue our perusal of the brotherhood charter. (28) Should the brotherhood decide to seek excommunication of a brother by a parish priest, not even an archpriest or a bishop is empowered to reinstate that individual until he agrees to submit to the authority of the brotherhood. (29) When the brethren see or hear from members of other brotherhoods that individuals—clerical or lay, in a local parish or one in another city—are violating canon law, they shall issue a warning to the offenders, either orally or in writing. If the warning is ignored, a brotherhood officer is to be informed. (30) Should the bishop comports himself in any way contrary to the law, let all oppose him as an enemy of truth. (31) Should a bishop accuse a brother of a transgression the brother must not defend himself personally, but wait for his fellow brethren to come to his defense. The case will come up before the bishop, who is to judge it according to the laws of the holy fathers. (32) As the senior organization, the Dormition Brotherhood shall expose any brotherhood which violates these rules. No one is permitted to challenge its decisions on the basis of seniority by claiming that certain brotherhoods were founded earlier because bishops [often not qualified] created such associations improperly.[30] "We decree," the patriarch stated, "that all brotherhoods everywhere shall submit to the Dormition Brotherhood." (33) All brotherhoods in cities and outlying areas, as well as in the villages, must keep themselves informed on the conduct of both laity and clergy and, concealing nothing, report on unlawful behavior to the bishop. (34) Whosoever violates these ecclesiastical rules, be he bishop, prince or ordinary individual, shall be anathematized by all four patriarchs and the holy fathers of the seven ecumenical councils.[31]

At this time Patriarch Joachim sent out a circular letter informing everyone in Lvov that the Christian church wished to renew itself completely, that is to say by studying the scriptures. To this end the [Rus] inhabitants of Lvov proposed to found a school for Christian children of all classes. They were to learn the scriptures in both Greek and Slavonic,

so that all Christian folk not languish in ignorance for lack of enlighten-
ment.[32] For fifteen hundred gold pieces[33] they purchased a printing press
with Greek and Slavonic type to serve the needs of the school. They also
planned to construct a new church as well as a building to house their
school, printing press and a hospital. The patriarch solicited donations for
those worthy projects from all Orthodox Christians.

Conflict soon erupted between the brotherhood with its sweeping
powers, and Bishop Gedeon Balaban, who jealously guarded his own
authority. Before too long news of their differences reached the patriarch
in Constantinople, Jeremiah II,[34] who sided with the brotherhood. In November 1587 he wrote to Gedeon "We have deliberated, have sought and
found an assassin in our midst, one who despises goodness. You dare not
utter a single word against a brotherhood in which God dwells, and by
which He is glorified. If we hear that you obstruct its blessed work you
shall be excommunicated, and face further church sanctions." This stern
injunction pushed Gedeon Balaban toward Skarga's position. He became
convinced that lay interference in ecclesiastical affairs would have an
adverse effect upon the church. Joining the dominant [Catholic] church
would liberate the bishops from such humiliating lay control. Thereupon
Balaban approached the Catholic bishop of Lvov, proclaiming his willingness to accept church union.

JEREMIAH IN RUS

Such was the state of the Rus church when Patriarch Jeremiah of Constantinople visited it on his way home from Moscow in 1589.[35] The laity lost
no time in presenting him with a list of strenuous objections to the anarchy
reigning in their church, for which they blamed the depraved and negligent
bishops. Among them was Metropolitan Onisifor Devochka [Onysyfor
Divochka] of Kiev.[36] In 1585 the nobles of Galich sent him the following
interesting letter while at the Polish Sejm.[37] "The great misfortune that has
befallen us can be traced to the fact that under your pastoral office we have
been oppressed terribly. We weep and wander about like sheep without a
shepherd. Although we acknowledge your holiness as our superior, your holiness fails to protect his sheep from the rapacious wolves. You give no
thought to piety or virtue. We came to the Sejm in Warsaw to complain of
the injustices against us, hoping that you would keep your promise to be
here, so that together we might petition the king to protect the rights and
liberties guaranteed by our Greek law. Yet your holiness refuses to honor
his obligations, refuses to act in the face of such unparalleled misfortunes.

"During your tenure of office our faith has been subjected to such villainy. Shrines are desecrated, Holy Communion denied, churches closed and sealed, bell ringing prohibited, priests dragged away from altars and out of churches like thieves, and laity denied prayer in the house of God. Not even pagan kings would have tolerated such outrages, yet all these abuses occur under your holiness as our shepherd. Nor is this all. Holy crosses are hacked apart, bells taken to the castles and turned over to the Jews for disposal, and your holiness encourages such actions by distributing circulars in support of aid to the Jews against God's church. Our churches are transformed into Jesuit temples,[38] and the Jesuits appropriate our ecclesiastical property. Decent monasteries once run by abbots and their brethren now have become home to [lay] abbots, their wives and their children. Such are they who govern the churches. Large crosses are cut up into small ones. All that once existed for the glory of God is now blasphemy. Holy church items are turned into sashes, vessels and spoons, and church vestments fashioned into coats and mantles. Even worse is the fact that your grace arbitrarily and unilaterally appoints bishops without witnesses present and without consulting us brethren. This violates the laws of the church and transforms unworthy individuals into bishops. They occupy episcopal sees, shamelessly flaunt wives and sire children. Thus do our misfortunes multiply. Too many bishops have been appointed, sometimes two to a see, leading to a breakdown of order. We are duty bound to warn your holiness, to pray and to plead, for the love of God remember your holy predecessors the metropolitans of Kiev, and find inspiration in their true faith. Do not be angry with us, for we pity your soul and your conscience. You shall have to answer for everything to the Lord God."

A NEW METROPOLITAN

Upon his arrival Jeremiah removed Onisifor from office and replaced him with Mikhail Rogoza [Rohoza], already familiar to us as archimandrite of Minsk.[39] There he became the representative of all Rus Christians, in other words, all Orthodox believers. It is instructive that during Mikhail's elevation Jeremiah turned to all the assembled nobles and made the following pronouncement. "If he is deserving, your words shall confirm it. If he is unworthy and you present him as being deserving, you will find that I am absolved." His remarks plainly point to the lay influence in Rogoza's election, as well as to the fact that the patriarch completely disassociated his own wishes from the process. The laity had proposed installation of this unknown archimandrite, the patriarch acquiesced then acquitted himself of all responsibility for the elevation.

A careful scrutiny of Rogoza's character and conduct shows us why he was the laity's choice. They sought in their pastor one who would in no way resemble other Rus bishops of the time who had nothing in common with genuine prelates. Mikhail was pious, modest, of comparatively irreproachable morals and not given to coercion. Unfortunately he did not combine with his virtues as a private individual and monk certain other traits essential to the Rus church in these turbulent times. Mikhail lacked toughness and force, was timid and unaggressive. Thus he was destined to play a dismal, indeed hypocritical, role in the events surrounding the union of the two churches.

Be that as it may, Rogoza was the laity's choice, and the patriarch sided with the brethren. He took some steps with that in mind. From Wilno in 1589 the patriarch issued a circular letter to the bishops enjoining them to unfrock all priests who had married two or three women in succession, and reprimanding Bishop Leonty for concealing such offenders.[40]

In the same circular the patriarch noted that he heard from many trusted princes, magnates and Christians in general, and saw with his own eyes that twice-or thrice-married clergy continued in office. Jeremiah also blessed the founding of a brotherhood in Wilno, attached to the church of the Holy Spirit, whose members pledged to distribute alms to hospitals, prisons and beggars on the streets twice a year, at Easter and at Christmas. In addition the organization undertook to offer free education to orphans and children of all brotherhood members. They were to be taught Slavonic, Greek, Latin and Polish. The vernacular Rus language was included in the curriculum. The brethren resolved to staff the school with reputable scholars, and to publish books in Greek, Slavonic, Rus and Polish.

Jeremiah confirmed the rights and regulations approved earlier for the Dormition Brotherhood and added some new ones. (1) Only the brotherhood is permitted to operate a school in Lvov. It alone is authorized to teach Orthodox children the scriptures and the Slavonic and Greek languages. (2) The brotherhood is authorized to publish not only church books, such as the Books of Hours, Psalters, Books of the Apostles, Lives of Saints, service books, prayer books, the metaphrases of the scriptures, texts for holy days, chronicles and theological works, but also school texts such as grammars, poetics, rhetoric and philosophy. (3) The bishop is to ordain without objection or reservation any priest whom the Dormition

Brotherhood recommends for its church. The brotherhood may remove any priest guilty of what it deems to be inappropriate conduct.

Soon after agreeing to the recommendation of the laity that Rogoza be elevated to the metropolitan see, as a sign of his kindness and goodwill and because he considered Cyril Terletsky to be a man of skill, shrewdness and erudition, Jeremiah conferred the title of exarch on the bishop of Lutsk.[41] By this act Terletsky became the ultimate ecclesiastical authority in the Ukraine. The rank of exarch, or patriarchal deputy, made him responsible for disciplining the bishops, maintaining order among them and removing the unfit from office. What prompted Jeremiah to make such an appointment, especially in light of the fact that the metropolitan already held that office? Why did he choose to hand over *de facto* authority to the bishop of Lutsk? Had Terletsky somehow influenced the patriarch? Had he revealed some weakness in Rogoza or hinted at the danger of a powerful laity which Rogoza's elevation demonstrated, or did he perhaps express some personal objection to the appointment? Maybe it had something to do with the patriarch's recognition that Rogoza lacked the true qualities of leadership for such a perilous and turbulent time, impelling him to install quickly a more canny and aggressive representative. It is even possible that the laity, the powerful magnates, realized they had offended Terletsky by passing him over for the office of metropolitan. Reluctant to lose the support of such an active and learned man, might they have been responsible for, or at least have offered no objections to his appointment as exarch? The sources are silent on these matters. Setting aside all such speculation we shall only remark that Terletsky's appointment was strange and ultimately detrimental.

PROBLEMATIC APPOINTMENTS

Trouble began even before the patriarch had time to cross the Rus border. Terletsky maligned the other bishops to the patriarch, while the bishop of Vladimir, Melety Khrebtovich, accused Terletsky of violently coercing the patriarchal envoy. Jeremiah then sent a representative with instructions for Metropolitan Rogoza to convene a council so that these matters might be settled. The patriarch also demanded fifteen thousand aspers,[42] or two hundred and fifty thalers, for a certificate of installation. To justify his demand the patriarch argued that had Rogoza come to Constantinople to fetch the document, it would have cost him considerably more. Rogoza, displeased that the patriarch appointed him metropolitan then proceeded to confer real authority upon his subordinate, replied to the envoy "I am not obliged to pay the patriarch anything nor am I in any position to convene a council at this time."

Clearly the metropolitan was disgruntled over Terletsky's appointment as exarch. For his part, Terletsky resented the fact that his new title did nothing to help him win the trust of the patriarch who, after all, ordered a council to deliberate on the accusations brought against the exarch. Then there was Bishop Balaban who also was extremely unhappy over patriarchal confirmation of the rights of a brotherhood he detested. For the same reason all of the bishops must have been very disturbed over having been placed under lay jurisdiction. There were also disagreements between the privileged Dormition Brotherhood and the smaller, less privileged brotherhoods. In 1590 four Lvov citizens, along with their supporters from the St. Nicholas, St. Theodore and Epiphany brotherhoods joined forces with Bishop Gedeon. Together they mounted a campaign against the Dormition Brotherhood and its school, agitating for a boycott of its institutions. Taking the side of the Dormition Brotherhood, Metropolitan Mikhail excommunicated all four organizers.

FIRST COUNCIL OF BREST

Such was the state of affairs when in June 1590 a council was convened in Brest. Metropolitan Mikhail Rogoza, Bishop Melety Khrebtovich of Vladimir, Bishop Cyril Terletsky of Lutsk, Leonty Pelchinsky of Pinsk, Dionisy Zbiruisky of Kholm and Gedeon Balaban of Lvov all attended. Also invited were the castellan from Brest, Adam Potey, and canons from each of the cathedrals. The prelates discussed the terrible oppression of the Orthodox church, the appalling disarray within the ranks of the clergy, the depravity, disagreements, disobedience and excesses of certain Christians. To avert similar disorders and future arbitrary behavior, to establish order, discuss schools, education, hospitals and other virtuous and pious endeavors, the fathers agreed to assemble in Brest-Litovsk annually, on June 24. Absentees would contribute fifty kopa grosh in Lithuanian money for various spiritual needs. If illness was the reason for absence at the succeeding council the prelate would confirm by oath that he had indeed been ill. If he missed yet another year and failed to take the oath he would be removed from episcopal office. The hierarchy pledged to bring to the council archimandrites, abbots and other religious elders who were learned in the scriptures.[43] They also agreed that no laymen might govern monasteries, promised not to visit eparchies other than their own and undertook not to install unqualified elders on pain of fines of one hundred kopa grosh. Anyone refusing to pay the penalty would be damned.

Seven deputies (including two Greeks) from the Dormition Brotherhood appeared at the council with a grievance against Bishop Balaban, who refused to acknowledge the patriarchal mandate regarding it and the Rogatin [Rohatyn] Brotherhood.[44] The bishop persisted in his opposition even after reaching an agreement and making peace with the brethren. Gedeon had only one answer to all of their complaints. "I am angry at the brotherhood because it refuses to show me the respect due to a bishop." Nevertheless the council found for the brotherhood. Gedeon's refusal to ordain brotherhood candidates for the priesthood deprived the church of services for the inspiration of Christians. Hence jurisdiction of the brotherhood was transferred directly to the metropolitan of Kiev, who never failed to ordain its candidates.

TERLETSKY

After the conclusion of the council's business Cyril Terletsky was taken ill and left for Sandomir to convalesce. Soon news of his imminent demise was out. Acting upon this information a certain Borovitsky, an officeholder in Ostrog castle, entered the bishop's home and seized his belongings. Terletsky recovered unexpectedly. When he returned from Sandomir, counting on the great man's affection for him, he complained to Prince Ostrozhsky. Borovitsky also enjoyed the favor of the prince and knew only too well how to protect himself. When Terletsky left Ostrog, Borovitsky proceeded to malign him to the prince. So effectively did he tarnish the bishop that the prince's affection turned into profound loathing for the exarch. We can sympathize with the subsequent position of the bishop of Lutsk, who fell out of favor with this pillar of Orthodoxy and most prominent nobleman in his eparchy. Thus on one hand he faced opposition within his own community in the person of the mightiest of them all, and on the other was obliged to deal with increasingly severe persecutions by foreigners.

With a band of armed men the royal secretary Marcin Broniewski attacked the ecclesiastical estates of the Falimich family, appropriated the church and all of the episcopal holdings. Moreover the city elder of Lutsk, Alexander Semashko, an Orthodox turned Catholic, took it into his head to charge an entrance fee to Lutsk cathedral. In April 1591, on Holy Saturday and Easter Sunday, Semashko decided to admit only the bishop and his servant, but no priests, to the castle church, rendering services impossible.

For two days the bishop was deprived of food and drink, while a drunken Semashko presided over games and dancing in the atrium of the cathedral, ordering his musketeers to shoot at the cathedral cupola and the cross.[45]

According to prior agreement, in June the bishops assembled for a council in Brest. They determined to present their complaint to the king, charging that officeholders and landowners of the principality of Lithuania were interfering in ecclesiastical affairs, passing judgment of priests and dissolving marriages. Terletsky and some of his colleagues decided unceremoniously to rid themselves of the numerous troubles inflicted on them by both their community and certain strangers by accepting the ecclesiastical union proposed by the Jesuits. To King Sigismund they sent the following declaration. "We, the undersigned bishops wish to acknowledge as our pastor and head the apostolic vicar of St. Peter's, his holiness the Pope of Rome. We anticipate that such a move will cause the numbers of those who honor God in His holy church to rise. Yet even as we long to become subjects of the Holy Father we ask that all rites, services and customs of our sacred ancient Eastern church be left intact, that his majesty the king issue a charter ensuring our liberties and confirming the article, we submit entirely. We pledge to place ourselves under the authority and benediction of the Holy Father. This letter, bearing our signatures and seals, we turn over to our senior brother, Father Cyril Terletsky, exarch and bishop of Lutsk and Ostrog. The signatories consist of Cyril of Lutsk, Gedeon of Lvov, Leonty of Pinsk and Dionisy of Kholm."

The king waited until January 1592 to respond to a petition from the metropolitan prohibiting lay interference in spiritual affairs. A royal privilege addressing the bishops' desire for church union was not issued until March 18. It read "On behalf of ourselves and our successors we the sovereign solemnly promise the bishop, the presbyters and the entire clergy of the Eastern church and the Greek religion, and them alone, that should any patriarch or metropolitan anathematize them, no harm shall come to them. We pledge not to use such accusations or anathemata to deprive them of their eparchies, to be turned over to someone else during their lifetime. We promise to multiply our benevolences toward them and all who embrace church union, to endow them with the same liberties and exemptions that the Roman Catholic clergy enjoy. All this we intend to confirm by additional charters."

CORRESPONDENCE

For the time being the Orthodox were unaware of the plans Terletsky and his colleagues were laying. At least the Dormition Brotherhood, still locked in a struggle with its own bishop, did not mention anything to that effect in its letter to the patriarch dated February 6, 1592. "The bishop of Lvov, Gedeon Balaban," the brethren wrote, "torments us with endless aggravations. He has divided the people and instigated them against our brotherhood, demanding that everyone turn way from it or face anathema. He has pillaged St. Onufry monastery although it was placed under the jurisdiction of our church and shares in its stauropigia status, and has dishonored its abbot. We showed the council the charter confirmed by your holiness for the monastery and priests in our brotherhood church, which the archbishop [that is to say, Metropolitan Mikhail] has taken under his blessing even as the bishop himself curses it. We complained about the bishop to the council, yet owing to its already full agenda no decision was taken on this scandal. Hence the matter was put off until the next meeting. Together with the other bishop, the archbishop decided that for the time being the priests of the Lvov and Wilno Brotherhoods enjoy the benediction of the archbishop and the protection of the entire council. Yet in keeping with his former hostility the bishop continues to disseminate lies about us among the people of all ranks, denying us our right to build a church and open a school. That is why we released the teachers. Kiril went to Wilno, Lavrenty to Brest, and the rest scattered to other cities. Only Stefan remains. Episcopal persecution drove the best priests away to other parishes, while the digamists settled everywhere. The bishops of Kholm and Pinsk cohabit with their wives and, following their example, the digamists boldly celebrate the liturgy. The church is in a very confused state and continues to deteriorate. At one time prominent individuals who lapsed into various heresies wished to return to the Orthodox church, but now they have lost all desire to do so. Church scandals are under severe scrutiny, and everybody cries out with a single voice 'If the church is not reformed, we shall place ourselves under the jurisdiction of Rome, so that we may live in peace and tranquility.' Moreover your holiness has been deceived. Some would have you believe that there are those among us who do not revere the holy icons. There are none such among us, neither in the brotherhood nor indeed in the entire city.

"This is what really happened. When our archbishop (Mikhail) came here, to Galich, he found an icon in the city of Rogatin. Instead of Our Savior the icon portrayed God the Father with gray hair. He found a similar icon in Galich. The archbishop demanded that the icon be removed from the church, and replaced with one portraying Jesus. Yet as soon as he left Bishop Gedeon of Lvov ordered that in Galich the icon of God the Father, Who must always remain invisible, be placed above the other icons. He gave it the title 'Ancient Man' and in his sermon accused the archbishop of iconoclasm. At Easter he insisted that some sort of bread called paska be blessed in accordance with the old heretical custom.[46] They celebrate on Good Friday, a holy day, and on the second day of Christmas demean the Virgin by bringing to the church tarts and pies, the so-called 'Virgin's labor,' or 'gifts to the newborn' as we refer to them. The bishop instructs us to observe all such ancient customs, and to pay no attention to what your holiness says.

"We also have some good news for your holiness. In Wilno the brotherhood is flourishing. Fedor Skumin, governor of Novgorod Seversk, and Bogdan Sapieha, governor of Minsk, along with many other high officials, have joined the church brotherhood. They announced their solidarity with the Dormition Brotherhood that together we might work for our mutual good. Besides that, Adam Potey, castellan of Brest and royal senator, founded an order in Brest modeled after that of Lvov."

Imagine the astonishment of the brethren when, shortly after they had filed their complaint, their enemy Gedeon produced a patriarchal charter ordering that the St. Onufry monastery be removed from the jurisdiction of the metropolitan. In September the brotherhood wrote to the patriarch "How did this happen? Was it diabolical jealousy or the slander of treacherous people, or was it because you forgot what was in your previous charter?"

Revealing for the first time its concern over the disarray in the church, the brotherhood apprised the patriarch of its plans for a church union. "To begin with, as your grace knows well, we have among us so-called prelates, although they really deserve to be called villains who live openly with their wives in violation of their monastic vows. Some of the digamists are high-ranking clergymen, others beget children with loose women. When prelates behave thus, what can we expect of ordinary priests? After the metropolitan exposed some of the clergymen at the council, demanding their resignation from the priesthood, they responded 'First let the hierarchy resign their offices and obey the law, then we shall do likewise.' The bishops have stolen the offices of archimandrite and abbot, filled monasteries with their families and various lay officials, robbed the churches of their wealth, corrupted the monks and keep horses and dogs on monastery grounds. Many already have announced their intention to accept the jurisdiction of Rome, with the stipulation that they retain their Greek canon law. To this end the Roman Catholic pope sent one of his own prelates with an order to celebrate mass in every church with his unleavened bread, as a sign of church union.[47] Piotr Skarga, the Jesuit in Wilno, published books on his faith and the Greek heresy, which he then presented to the king. People are beginning to convince themselves that Christ's faith can be practised legitimately under Rome, just as it was at the beginning. Because of the anarchy reigning among our leaders our native laws are trampled, and the lies of teachers who play dissembling games with Orthodoxy have blanketed the church."

The brotherhood could not name, indeed they did not yet know, the names of the bishops who elected church union, so carefully and secretly was it all done. It is understandable that this situation made it necessary for the bishops to proceed slowly. There is no need to seek the reason for their caution in any external circumstance. The brethren wrote to the patriarch about an idea gaining popular approval, urging submission to the papal throne as the only way to rid themselves of the anarchy and disorders reigning in the Rus church. Yet there were difficulties and dangers inherent in such overt action. Terletsky could not make this decision alone, and allies would be extremely difficult to find. We have noted earlier that he no longer could count on the friendship of Prince Konstantin Ostrozhsky.

BISHOP OF VLADIMIR

Soon a new man came to take the place of Terletsky in the prince's good graces. Early in 1593, following the death of Bishop Melety Khrebtovich of Vladimir, Ipaty received the eparchy. His civil name was Adam Potey, that same senator and castellan of Brest whose fervent piety the Lvov Brotherhood mentioned in its letter to the patriarch. Potey turned out to be worthy of his new office, "a great ascetic, abstainer, a pious observer of fast days, a keen defender of church rights and one who disdains worldly pursuit." The former castellan was not very well versed in Orthodox dogma, so he was relatively indifferent to the details which separated the two churches. If follows, therefore, that in all likelihood he was receptive to the idea of church union.

Terletsky began working on the new bishop. "It is dangerous," he pointed out to Potey, "to rely on the goodwill of Prince Ostrozhsky. He used to be well disposed toward me, yet now he despises me. The patriarchs will be travelling frequently to Moscow in search of donations, and they will stop here on the way back. Jeremiah has defrocked one metropolitan already, and has founded brotherhoods which are certain to persecute the bishops, indeed are doing so already. Prelates will be slandered and censured. Should the brethren succeed in having any one of us removed from episcopal office, consider carefully the disgrace. The reigning king grants lifetime appointments, nor does he revoke them for any reason except a criminal offence, whereas the patriarch degrades and unfrocks on the strength of a silly denunciation. Judge for yourself what bondage! When we become subjects of the Roman pope not only will we retain our eparchies for life, we also shall sit in the Senate together with the Roman bishops, and thus will recover with greater ease the estates which have been confiscated from the church."

OSTROZHSKY CORRESPONDENCE

We are in the dark as to who initiated the discussions on church union, Potey or Prince Ostrozhsky, but we are aware that on June 21, 1593 the prince wrote the following in a letter to the bishop of Vladimir. "Everyone ought to try to love and propagate the glory of God. Although many worldly pursuits prevent me from devoting myself fully to spreading His glory, nonetheless my Christian duty long has caused me to cherish a desire that intensifies with time, which is to find a way for the highest of all churches, the church of Christ, to return to its original pure state. Yet I see that worthiness comes only from the worthy, and honesty only from the honest. In my case either bad luck or unworthiness prevented my launching this noble cause. Holy Scripture tells us that 'the power of God is attained through weakness'[48] and 'What is impossible for man is possible for God.'[49] As God is my witness, these words caused me to do what I did, not for worldly fame but because I mourn the decline of the church of Christ, and cannot tolerate the insults of heretics and apostates against that church. Not too long ago I took the liberty of discussing and debating some of the essential points in the Holy Scriptures with the papal legate Possevino,[50] not personally, but through my superiors and the court chaplains. This did not please God, although I know not whether to our benefit or our detriment. Yet He was pleased by what subsequently came to pass.

"Now intending for the sake of my physical health to set out for countries not far from where the Pope of Rome resides, and unable to suppress my anxiety about God's church, I propose to promote a union of the churches there. God willing I shall accomplish this if you, the clergy, can find a way at your next council to stop your bickering in God's church. In my opinion, my lord bishop of Vladimir, after reaching an accord with the archbishop and the bishop, and receiving permission and a royal charter from his majesty the king, you should journey to the grand prince of Muscovy, there to consult with him and the clergy of that land. You should tell them what persecution, victimization, desecration and disparagement the Rus here endure in procedures, canons and church ceremonies, and beseech them, as brothers in faith, to endeavor to eliminate these troubles in Christ's church, this persecution and bitterness among the Rus. I implore you, my lord bishop, you who are a gentle master, friend and ardent champion of the love of faith in Christ, to use all your influence at the council to initiate, if not union, then at least some measure of amelioration in the life of the people. For it is known to all of you lord bishops that the people of our faith are in a state of moral decline, that they are ruled by sloth and neglect their piety. Not only do they ignore their Christian obligation, the defense of their church and their ancestral religion, many of them go so far as to ridicule it and scatter among various sects. Should you fail to address the problem you know well who shall answer for it, because you are the leaders, mentors and shepherds of Christ's flock. Why have the people become so lazy and negligent, why do they abandon their faith? Because there are no teachers, no preachers of God's word, no religious instruction, no sermons. That is why God's glory has dimmed in His church. A veritable craving to hear God's word has set in. At the same time a retreat from the faith and God's law has begun. We have reached the point where we no longer find comfort in our religion. We have reason to ask as did the prophet 'Who shall give our head water and our eyes a source of tears,'[51] so that day and night we might mourn the fall, the deterioration of our faith and the church? Everything has been overturned and has fallen, everywhere there is sorrow, mourning and misfortune. If this continues, God alone knows what will become of us in the end."

In that same letter the prince included certain clauses he considered essential for a successful church union. (1) All rites and rituals of the Eastern church must be retained in full. (2) The Roman Catholic lords shall refrain from confiscating our churches and their possessions for their

own Catholic church. (3) Once union is accomplished they will not accept any of our people who wish to become Catholics, or coerce our
people into embracing the Catholic confession, especially through marriages, as frequently happens. (4) Our clergy will enjoy the same high
esteem as do theirs, and the metropolitans and bishops (even if not all)
shall have a place on the council and in the dietines. (5) The patriarchs
must be convinced of the need for church union so that we might praise
the Lord with one heart and one voice. (6) We need to contact the Muscovites[52] and Moldavians to reach a consensus on the union. In my opinion it would be best to dispatch the bishop of Vladimir to Moscow, and
the bishop of Lvov to Moldavia. (7) Some things in our churches have
to be corrected, especially when it comes to certain popular fantasies. (8)
It is imperative that we have learned presbyters and good preachers, because inadequate learning is responsible for the growing baseness among
our clergy.

TOWARDS CHURCH UNION

Common sense should have prompted Potey and Terletsky to realize that
the prince was making unrealistic demands. The Eastern Greek and Eastern Russian, or Muscovite, churches would never recognize the Pope as
their head, without which a union of the churches was unthinkable. Thus
travel to Moscow or Moldavia would be futile. Ecclesiastical councils
could not decide the matter. The sole solution seemed to lie in the hands
of a few influential activists capable of inspiring by example a people
grown weary of the painful situation in the church.

Less than a year after the council of 1593, on May 21, 1594 Terletsky
and the participating clergy presented themselves to the Lutsk government. They stated that in accordance with the will and intent of God,
glorified in the Trinity, and consistent with the painstaking efforts and
encouragement of his majesty the king and the lords spiritual and temporal, the long desired church union was accomplished and brotherly love
restored between the Eastern and the Western churches. His Holiness the
Pope of Rome was acknowledged as supreme pastor and apostolic vicar.
To confirm this union and demonstrate submission to the Pope he, Terletsky, together with Bishop Potey of Vladimir, would set out for Rome as
commanded by the king. Church property in Vodirada was mortgaged to
cover the costs of this journey.

As June 24, the customary date for the council, drew near, Metropolitan Mikhail Rogoza, Ipaty Potey and Cyril Terletsky came to Brest. On

the day after the metropolitan arrived no service was held. The bishop of Vladimir, Potey, simply delivered a sermon on the calling of the Christian pastorship based on the scriptural words "I am the Good Pastor."[53] After the sermon the bishop asked those present to tell him whether or not he had spoken well. Everyone answered "Very well indeed." Just then a voice was heard from the crowd "The bishop preaches against himself." There was consternation in the church. The accuser was apprehended and brought before the church assembly, where he confronted Potey with "You teach us to do good, yet your personal behavior is despicable. For eight kopa [grosh] you transform foolish youngsters into priests." The commotion accelerated. The crowd beat and tortured Potey's accuser, then chained him in the almshouse.

COUNCIL OF BREST

On the third day after matins orders went out for bells to be rung to summon the council. The clergy assembled in the church, opened the "holy gates" or the central doors in the iconostasis, put the lectern on the pulpit and placed the open *Gospel* upon it. The metropolitan sat down in his special place, and the bishops took their prescribed seats, the archimandrites also occupied theirs, then the archdeacons, archpriests, abbots, priests and brotherhoods all sat in their customary places. There were some members of the gentry present although not many. It was rumored that certain Roman Catholics also would be present.

Following a prayer for the descent from heaven of the Holy Ghost to inspire the proceedings, the council commenced its work. The brotherhoods registered a complaint against Bishop Balaban of Lvov, and Potey added his own grievances against him. The Lvov and Wilno brotherhoods produced charters from the Eastern patriarchs formalizing the establishment of their organizations and according them various privileges. Many of the landowners presented lists of complaints to the metropolitan, and to all of the bishops.

Evening arrived and everyone dispersed for dinner. Suddenly there appeared an official communiqué from the archbishop-primate of Gniezno informing the metropolitan that the council was unlawful inasmuch all conferences, Sejms and councils were prohibited in the absence of the king, who currently was in Sweden. This caused the council to confine itself to judicial matters. It confirmed the rights of the brotherhoods, and ordered that Gedeon Balaban be deprived of his episcopal see for acts of violence against the Lvov Brotherhood. For his part the bishop protested against the assembly, stressing its illegality. Terletsky simply abstained from participating in what had turned out to be an unlawful gathering.

On December 2, 1594 several of the bishops issued an act embodying an episcopal consensus on the projected church union. The prelates blamed the widespread heresy on the fact that the Rus were separated from the Roman Catholic gentry. Children of one mother were divided and unable to help each other. Although they prayed for confessional unity the Rus themselves did nothing to achieve it. Instead they looked to their superiors, waiting for the leaders to take appropriate steps towards unification. But their faith in episcopal guidance was growing fainter, the bishops continued, because the prelates, still in pagan bondage, were incapable of action, irrespective of their good intentions.[54] "In such circumstances," the bishops wrote, "the Holy Ghost has inspired us to understand that the lack of unity in the church is a powerful obstacle to the people's salvation. Our ancestors dwelt in unity because they acknowledged one supreme pastor, namely his holiness the Pope of Rome. As long as this order reigned God's praises ever more reverberated in the church, and heretics found it difficult to disseminate their heresies. It is obvious to us that the proliferation of hierarchs has produced discord in God's church. Because we are unwilling to carry the perdition of human souls on our consciences, we are determined to unite in the sacred cause. We do this so that together with our dear Roman Catholic brethren we might praise God the Father, the Son and the Holy Ghost with one voice and one heart, under the one and only incarnate shepherd of God's church, just as in days gone by. Before God we solemnly pledge that together, and separately, we shall employ sincerely and diligently all just means to bring our remaining spiritual brothers, as well as the rank-and-file, to spiritual unity. To encourage this we are circulating this epistle." The original was signed only by Bishop Ipaty Potey of Vladimir and Bishop Terletsky of Lutsk.

ROGOZA REACTS

The metropolitan still remained to be persuaded. As Terletsky set out to see him Mikhail Rogoza gave him the following articles to present to Crown Hetman Zamoyski.[55] "Owing to disagreements among our highest superiors, the patriarch along with several of the bishops, I wish to acknowledge the primacy of the most holy Pope of Rome, while fully preserving all rites and customs of the Eastern church. I ask the hetman for his assurance that the king will issue a suitable charter enabling me as metropolitan peacefully to occupy my see in all honor and dignity until the day I die, and that he will guarantee me a place in the Senate with rights equal to those of Roman Catholic clergymen. Should the patriarchs write epistles against us they must be ignored. Moreover the monks from Greece no longer can be permitted to remain on the territory of his majesty the king, or gain entrance to the hostile Muscovite lands by way of our territory, because we consider them spies. Pilgrims carrying patriarchal charters must not be admitted into our presence."

They also wrote an instruction to be delivered orally to the king by an authorized messenger. "We have observed in our superiors the patriarchs a dereliction of duty and neglect of God's church and holy law. We see their bondage, we see that instead of four patriarchs there are now eight. We see the way they live in their patriarchates, how one after another they accept bribes, and how they have forfeited cathedrals. When visiting us they make not the slightest attempt to enter into disputations with those who worship in other faiths, concentrating instead upon extorting money from us, taking it wherever they can find it, then moving on in search of bribes in pagan lands. That is what we, the bishops, have observed, and are therefore not willing to remain in this state of disorder to be led by such pastors. We have agreed unanimously (and firmly guarantee it if his majesty wishes to spread the glory of God under one pastor and give us, along with our bishops, our churches, monasteries and the entire clergy the same freedoms accorded the Roman clergy) that we wish to proceed to the unification of the two churches to which we have been entrusted by the Redeemer himself, under one supreme shepherd, the most holy pope of Rome. We are prepared to acknowledge him as our pastor, asking only that the ruler protect us with his charter, and forever confirm the following articles. (1) Our principal churches and eparchies shall remain for all time inviolable in their liturgies and ceremonies. (2) The Rus church hierarchy, monasteries, properties, grants and the entire clergy shall remain forever intact in their ancient customs, under our episcopal authority, benediction and letters patent, with all customary deference. (3) All church affairs, the liturgy, ceremonies and rituals shall remain unchanged, and are to be carried out in accordance with the old calendar.[56] (4) We shall enjoy dignity and respect at the Sejms, and receive seats in the Senate so that we can rejoice and be happy under the benediction of the most holy pope of Rome. (5) No patriarchal curses shall have power to harm us. (6) The monks from Greece who come here to rob us, whom we regard as spies, shall no longer wield any power over us. (7) All privileges which the brotherhoods have received from the patriarchs and others shall be cancelled because they lead to the proliferation of various sects and heresies. (8) Every new bishop shall be elevated by the metropolitan of Kiev, whereas the metropolitan shall be consecrated by all the bishops with the blessing of the pope of Rome, without payment of fees. (9) All foregoing articles shall be confirmed by royal charters from his majesty the king, one in Latin and the other in the Rus language. (10) His holiness the pope also shall approve the articles. The signatories were Ipaty Potey, bishop of Vladimir, Cyril Terletsky of Lutsk, Mikhail Kopistensky of Peremyshl and Gedeon Balaban of Lvov.

DYNAMICS OF CHURCH UNION

Terletsky dissembled and concealed his motives from his rival Potey because he wanted exclusive control over the entire process. Moreover when he met Potey in Torchin, at the residence of Bernard Maciejowski, Roman Catholic bishop of Lutsk, he was silent about his discussion with the metropolitan about this matter, and failed to mention the articles for Zamoyski with which the metropolitan entrusted him. In view of this in January, 1595 Potey wrote to Mikhail Rogoza "Be advised that the bishops all have agreed to a union with the Roman Catholics, and we believe that this is already well known to prominent individuals. When the prince-bishop in Lutsk [the Roman Catholic bishop] and I discussed this, noting its considerable benefits for the church of God, he asked that the bishop of Lutsk [Cyril Terletsky] and I include our superior, your grace, in this endeavor. I reminded the prince of the previous harm inflicted upon us not only by them, meaning the Roman Catholics, but by our own people as well. We cannot agree amongst ourselves, nor do we respect our own hierarch the metropolitan. We revolt against him, ignore both his charters and his curses, and in point of fact desire him to have no authority over us. 'I am aware of this, but why is it so?' he asked. 'Because there is no order among you. Your own patriarchs ignore such things. They only come here to solicit donations and sow discord among you, issuing charter after charter. Once you have joined us, things will be different. Your hierarch will enjoy greater esteem and authority, and everyone shall obey and fear him.'

"There was more talk of how to unite the two churches without violating either our conscience or our faith. We did not forget to discuss the issue of Senate seats and received a positive response, together with pledges of assistance. We also discussed the fact that even though your grace might personally wish to set our church affairs in order, in light of the impoverished senior eparchy in Kiev you lack resources for the task at hand. 'This is outrageous,' the prince-bishop of Kiev[57] responded. 'In order to enhance properly the stature of the metropolitan see we shall provide a decent endowment.' He mentioned the Caves monastery and commented 'It is more fitting that the monastery be administered by the metropolitan of Kiev than the drunken monks who run it now.' He also insisted that we approach your grace to come to an understanding on these matters, and when we reach an accord, the Pope himself will send emissaries with an invitation for church union. The king shall convene a synod. First and foremost we must discuss with you at the synod whatever remains unresolved, and provide guarantees for all you seek for your faith and your ceremonies.

"We parted with the understanding that we would meet with your grace, and now implore you to let us know where we can find you. No one pays any attention to the patriarchs, and we cannot go on beating our heads against a wall, without assistance from them. For the love of God we do not ignore this matter. Let us meet and of these matters. God knows, and of course we ourselves can see, what is happening to us. We are aware that our church leaders help neither us nor themselves, that they send people who wish only to quarrel with us. They issue edict after edict yet are powerless to maintain order. In the office of the bishop of Lutsk [Terletsky] I saw a document from the crown chancellor in which he indicated that the king himself wishes to meet with your grace. He also suggested that he and the bishop of Lutsk seek an audience with the king, at which the bishop of Lutsk promised not to pursue this matter until we communicated with you. Meanwhile I humbly ask you not to show my letter to anyone, because it is confidential."

ROGOZA TO SKUMIN

Rogoza elected cunning. He would navigate between the two dangerous shoals without severing relations with either side. He would temporize and delay his decision until the last possible moment. In addition to the lures outlined in Potey's letter—enhanced authority and increased revenues—church union would be advantageous to Rogoza because he did not see eye to eye with the patriarch. It is rumored that recently the patriarch pronounced some provisional bans upon the metropolitan. Yet is was also extremely hazardous simply to ignore the church union which the king so ardently desired. The officials in power would never forgive his indifference, his refusal to support it. On the other hand the bishops crafted plans for union without consulting the laity, Prince Ostrozhsky, Skumin or the other dignitaries, and proceeded without the knowledge of the brotherhoods, whereas Mikhail Rogoza was after all the choice of the laity.

Upon reading Potey's letter Rogoza wrote to Skumin on January 20, 1595. "Gracious Sir! Striving to keep your grace, a pillar of our church, informed of all news relating to both the church and me, I wish to apprise you of the latest tidings, the like of which neither you nor our ancestors have ever heard. I am forwarding a copy of the letter so that you can assess the situation for yourself, and send me your answer as quickly as possible. I fear that such machinations might conceal treachery and temptation for our church, therefore I have no intention of arriving at an independent decision."

Even as the metropolitan dissembled, Terletsky did likewise, and Potey attempted an air of secrecy, the decisive step was about to be taken in Lvov by the local bishop, Gedeon Balaban. After all, as we have seen earlier, his position was the most precarious of all. He summoned a council of archimandrites, abbots, monks and the secular clergy for January 28, 1595. They declared their intention of following the example of the highest-ranking Rus pastors to recognize the Roman Catholic church as the one true church, with the authority of a universal institution. They swore never to renounce the most holy Roman Catholic leaders, to curse those who renounced them, and earnestly implored the metropolitan and the bishops to conclude without delay this redemptory task.

The entire affair remained so precarious that it was in danger of disintegrating. Like Terletsky, Balaban chose to act alone. The metropolitan went along with Potey and arranged a meeting with him at Nowogródek, then instead of waiting for him there he went on to Słuck. On February 11, 1595 Potey decided to write to him again. "Your grace did not respond to my letter, and I have no idea what will happen next. Never should you have ignored this matter. For the love of God I entreat you to reveal your true intentions. For better or worse, I am prepared to bear anything for you grace. Under no circumstances will I ever desert you, but it is easier for your grace there among your own kind than it is for us here in the jaws of the enemy. If they are determined to devour someone, devour him they will. I do not know whether I mentioned in my first letter to your grace that at the house of the bishop of Lutsk I saw a letter from the crown chancellor indicating the king's desire for a meeting with you.

Should you elect to accommodate him, visit me first. It is very important
that we speak! When I asked the bishop of Lutsk why he was going to
see the king, he swore to me 'I have no idea what they want with me, for
I have no business with them, neither my own nor that of anyone else.'
Yet now, probably in response to the second letter, he met with the chancellor and proceeded to Cracow without me. God alone knows what his
is all about, but I am sure of one thing, that they say in court about me
'The one person whom we trusted turned out to be the worst of all.' That
is why I have received no letters from the king or the chancellor, neither
have any dietine decrees been sent to me, whereas the bishop of Lutsk
has been privy to it all. For God's sake see to it that we are not excluded.
As for the matter in the East, do we hope in vain? You can judge from
the news I send you just exactly what is happening to our people there.
If we cannot get there immediately, for the love of God try to convene a
council on St. John's Day [June 24], for it is imperative that we all meet
soon. For God's sake send me your reply. Do not be afraid to write, everything will remain confidential. It will be as if a rock sank to the bot-
tom of the sea. For my part, I will see to it that you receive all the news
from Poland."

Terletsky anticipated everybody. He visited the king and returned with
a letter dated February 18, 1596. "We have learned," it read, "of your
profound desire and good intention of uniting God's Greek church with
the universal Roman church under one spiritual leader, just as the
churches were united in the past. We not only applaud your decision, we
accept it gratefully, viewing it as the work of the Holy Spirit which takes
its inspiration from God. Just as He is One in the Holy Trinity, so He
desires unity and harmony in His holy church and the Christian faith.
Over it He has placed one pastor to tend not only His young ewes, that
is to say ordinary folk, but also young rams, such as priests, bishops,
presbyters, deacons and all other servants of the church. We desire, indeed urge, you to conclude your good and blessed deed. Almighty God
from Whom all blessings issue will assist you in this endeavor, and reward you a hundredfold in His kingdom of heaven. In taking you under
our royal protection we wish to be your gentle and gracious lord for all
time. We shall make a point of testifying to your efforts before the most
holy pope of Rome. Only do not procrastinate. This matter needs to be
settled as soon as possible. We have instructed the bishop of Lutsk, whom
you should trust in all matters, to discuss it with you in greater detail."

ECCLESIASTICAL INTRIGUES

Terletsky acted alone without any constraints whatsoever because the enmity between him and Prince Ostrozhsky had destroyed links with the most powerful laity. The pillars of the church, Potey and Rogoza, found themselves in a different situation. They were still obliged to correspond with these magnates in order to justify their actions and to conceal their true intentions. Prince Ostrozhsky wrote to Potey that Terletsky had been in Cracow and acted there on behalf of all bishops who agreed to church union. On March 17, 1596 Potey responded "I heard that the bishop from Lutsk was recently in Cracow, but I swear to God that I heard nothing about him acting as anybody's deputy. I do not believe he went bearing messages from anyone to anybody, neither have we ever dreamed of deciding anything amongst us, or of conspiring together for any purpose whatsoever. Is it so difficult to understand that even if every single one of our bishops were to agree to the union, as long as the rest of Christianity opposes it, such a union will remain a vain endeavor which can only dishonor us in the eyes of our flock? It would never do for us to conclude or even to initiate something like this in secret, without convoking a council to notify our younger brethren. They are all equally servants in the church of God, along with the rest of the faithful, especially your graces, you Christian lords."

Ostrozhsky sent yet another letter couched in terms which obviated all further need for secrecy. In it he reproached Potey for failing to maintain order in the church, pointing to the Protestants as models in such things. Potey angrily responded on March 25 "Although I have not replied to your grace's communications," he wrote, "nonetheless I humbly thank you for your warning. I regard the church union not as that which contributes to my benefit and prestige, rather as something that mandates our complete transformation. I see it as an act that permits us to keep our religion intact, correcting only what is false while continuing to steer the customary course. God grant that everyone live in harmony, even those more important than we.

"In the light of all that is transpiring we are beginning to lose hope, for the patriarchs are powerless to do anything even should they prove willing to help. We, however, have the capacity to act, if only we harbor a genuine desire to do so. Yet we merely deceive God when we do nothing more than pray for confessional unity. Do not marvel that the rivers disappeared when the springs dried up. Do not wonder why neither they nor we possess scholarship or order. You remind me that the councils at

Brest have issued a number of decisions on schools, printing shops and other things that God's church requires, yet there has been no action. My response to this is that even though my hierarchs would not have benefited personally from these decisions, I would permit no one to hinder such good and noble deeds. Indeed I would not even begrudge what remains of my meager possessions to promote them, although already I have wronged my children by selling off two estates. I would sacrifice everything for the good and pious people, but nothing at all for witless people who simply chase profits. In Brest it was the teachers themselves in search of fat dumplings [lucrative benefices][58] who brought the school to ruin. They departed for no good reason, inviting sneers from our enemies to the sorrow of the poverty-stricken faithful. You know well enough how difficult it is even for you, the great magnates, to bring all this about. What can be said of us wretched cripples who live among the wolves? They even forbid us to perform church services in a decent manner.

"I could tell your grace much more about what goes on in my Brest bishopric, and what oppression Christians in other places endure. We might take heart if this cross were patiently borne by all. Observing our weakness, many are deserting, not one at a time but in droves. God alone knows who shall remain. As for the news from Cracow, in my opinion it is false. Even if it happens to be true, do not involve me, for I have no desire to become a cardinal or metropolitan. Indeed, I have often regretted my willingness to become a bishop, and I hold you responsible for having persuaded me, especially in light of what is going on in the world. Never having given blank forms to anyone, I know nothing about them, but I know other things very well indeed, probably better than anyone. Were it possible to commit such information safely to paper I would prove to your grace that the news from Cracow is false. There are those who would pass themselves off as saints even as they malign us, and there is nothing secret that does not eventually become public. Although I have not begun anything, if others are willing to support a good cause it will not go against my conscience, for I have no wish to be left behind. Since you are so kind as to instruct me in the orderly formation and customs of other faiths, I say let the formation be of the best kind, for if it does not rest upon a proper foundation everything in it will come to shame, whether the schools, the printing presses or hordes of preachers. They will be known by their fruit. Some may appear beautiful on the outside, but inside they shall be all stench and maggots.[59] I do not look

with favor upon them, and I caution your grace that it is better to unite
with those who truly sing the praises of the Lord, the One in the Trinity,
than with the obvious enemies of the Son of God."

Rogoza denied even more vehemently than Potey his complicity in
any attempt to unify the churches. In March, 1595 he sent Prince
Ostrozhsky an interesting piece of news about Gedeon Balaban's innocence. "A very timely thing occurred," he wrote, "as I was concentrating upon the furtive hypocrisy. Just then I found the bishop of Lvov at
the monastery in Słuck. He, I believe, will not precipitate a conflagration
so destructive to our Eastern church and the entire Orthodox population.
He knows nothing about the machinations of the rest of our bishops, is very
much opposed to their evil intentions, and has sworn to this on the Bible.
He also has promised to follow carefully all developments in this affair in
Poland, and to inform me and your grace of everything that transpires.
Because of this I thought it best to annul the decision against him in the
ecclesiastical court. It is especially important that your grace, as the eye of
the Orthodox church, use every means at your disposal to study the church
union. Beware, even so, of the serpent from the Garden of Eden and the sly
fox [Terletsky], about whom I have cautioned you already."

SKUMIN CORRESPONDENCE

We see that Mikhail wrote differently about Balaban to another pillar of
the church, Skumin, judging by the latter's response of May 10 to
Rogoza. "I was heartened by your letter," he wrote, "in which you informed me about your good health, but what you wrote about ecclesiastical affairs saddens me. Even a blind man can see that every problem
stems from the disagreement between the brotherhood and the bishop of
Lvov [Balaban]. Let the impartial judge of blood and innocent souls summon to account those who are the cause of this. In all fairness, we consider most guilty of all our patriarch of Constantinople, whose charters
have brought so much grief upon us. In my opinion the bishop was so
exhausted that not only was he prepared to embrace the union, he might
happily have accepted help from the Devil himself. If this be the will of
God it shall go forth. If not, things are bound to change. At the moment
I do not intend to philosophize about any of this. Your grace seeks my
advice as to what should be done about it. Yet Almighty God, Who sees
into our hearts, knows that I have none to give. I do fear one thing, which
is that your opposition might be in vain. There are many reasons for this,
but I do not trust the written word. I would be pleased to meet with your
grace to discuss the matter in person."

Skumin refused to give advice while Terletsky and Potey were approaching the king in Cracow. For Mikhail Rogoza they secured everything for which he was prepared to sell his church to the pope. Upon their return to Lithuania they requested a meeting with Metropolitan Rogoza. It was set for May 18 in Kobrin but he deceived them again, causing Potey and Terletsky to write him the following letter. "In accordance with the wish and written instructions of your grace our superior we came to Kobrin on the fifth Sunday after Easter. Failing to find either your grace or any messenger from you, and not knowing the reason for your grace's absence, we were obliged to return to our respective domiciles. Now we are writing to your grace to express our dissatisfaction with the contempt you showed, not only for us, your brothers, but for one who is much greater [the king], who was aware of our projected meeting. Remember what you were charged with, and how favorably it was resolved? You have everything you asked for, privileges, charters and the right to excommunicate Archimandrite Nikifor Tur of the Caves monastery. We are surprised that, having requested all this, you now ignore and scorn the kindness shown to you. Had we known where to find you, we would have come to you, but we had no idea where to look. We implore you to set everything aside and join us in Brest as quickly as possible. Do this, both for the sake of your own affairs, which must not be put off, and for the general good. Should you fail to do so you will destroy us and yourself as well. This is not like trifling with one of your own."

The metropolitan refused to budge. He waited six weeks, then on June 14 wrote to Skumin once more. "I sent my servant Grigory to you with news of everything about which I now have reliable information. Approximately four years ago the bishops of Lutsk, Lvov, Peremyshl, Kholm and Pinsk agreed to a church union, papal jurisdiction and the new calendar. They even have a royal charter to this effect. The bishop of Vladimir concurred. I sent your worship the charter displaying the bishops' consent to church union. In this connection they recently summoned me to Brest, and I too would have received such a charter, but without the counsel and decision of your grace and of my colleagues, as well as a general sanction, I have not reached a final decision and I am taking six weeks to deliberate. I promise that both you and the governor of Kiev [Prince Ostrozhsky] shall have an answer at that time. If I agree to church union the king has authorized substantial benefits. If not, it will mean disgrace and the persecution of Christians.[60] I will probably have to give up my see. A new metropolitan, Terletsky, is waiting in the wings already. My sole wish is to leave mother church with its liberties intact, without the burden of anybody's yoke, under conditions guaranteed by some sort of charters."

Skumin sent a distressing response, distressing not because of any threats or sharp words, but because of the ingenuousness of an honest and humble man without any pretensions to aggrandizement. "You have been so kind as to apprise me of what the bishops who have their sees in Crown Poland have initiated without your consent, as you explained. I, however, received a communiqué from the Polish court indicating that after the Sejm in Cracow deputies representing all of our clergy went to the king with a written statement of consent from your grace, together with the appropriate credentials. Now you seek my advice, yet it is difficult to offer advice on what already has been settled, ratified and sent to the king. Any advice I have to give would be superfluous and laughable. To begin with what we really need is for people of our faith truly to be aware of what is happening. Such new and momentous matters ought not be initiated without their knowledge. That is why I cannot offer your grace any advice at this time, nor would it be appropriate for any individual to give such counsel. I, a lamb of Christ's flock and under the pastoral care of your grace, will have to follow my shepherds, and you my lord should know where to lead us, because it is you who will answer for us."

MORE LETTERS

Prince Ostrozhsky, to whom Potey was obliged to write a conciliatory letter on June 16, expressed his anger against the bishops more forcibly than Skumin. "If it took me so long to write to your grace," Potey wrote, "it was because I possessed no reliable information, even though all this time people have been disseminating various false reports about us. They implied that we have accepted fully the Roman Catholic faith, that we agreed to celebrate the Catholic mass and distribute the communion wafers. To be sure, you as a God-fearing and intelligent gentleman can decide on the veracity of this for yourself. For if an ordinary individual, concerned only for his own soul, needs to think well about how not to bring it to harm, how much more important is it for those to whom God has entrusted the souls of others to avoid anything violating the consciences of themselves and others. Do not believe everything you hear, for I know that people carry to your pious ears all kinds of rumors about us, about our alleged decisions that contravene the interests of our faith and church.

"Although no decision has been made yet, neither bad nor good, we are so unfortunate as to be accused of being renegades and heretics. The effect of this is to prevent us from thinking and worrying about God's church and its tranquillity. Our gatherings and other church-related matters are viewed with suspicion. It is an astonishing thing! Heretics from all sects are free to gather, to make plans at their councils, and issue works not only against the Christian [Orthodox] faith but against God's religion and the everlasting faith of His only-begotten Son. This is enough to turn Christians away from the ancient faith toward their accursed heresies.[61] We hapless bishops, who enjoy an unbreakable succession from Christ and the apostles, cannot even assemble to mediate and hold council on God's church, that we might keep intact our houses of worship and our Orthodox faith, and ensure something good for our heirs. This is especially important in light of the fact that we still have devout leaders and lords, patrons of our faith among whom, with no flattery intended, we consider your princely grace to be the leading light.

"Yet instead of inspiring us to do good as a gentleman and our protector, word has reached us that your grace refers to us only in harsh and unfriendly terms. If you just can set aside your anger and carefully examine this matter, I believe that you will prove willing to help us. I am sending your grace in writing the items to which we are prepared to agree. At the same time I would be happy to meet with you in person, to explain to your grace why we are doing this. I remember the admonition that your grace sent to me in Brest. You urged us to pursue union with the church of Rome while taking care not to violate our own faith and religion. God grant that in the spirit of that advice your grace will now help us in our cause. Tearfully and in all humility I beg you not to act in anger, but calmly and compassionately to read the conditions of the church union. You will find in them nothing new except the calendar, which is no dogma of faith. Rather it is a ritual that God's church can in good conscience change."

OSTROZHSKY'S CIRCULAR

In response to Potey's letter of June 24 Prince Ostrozhsky sent out a circular to all Orthodox faithful, which boded ill for the bishops. "My exemplary pious parents," he wrote, "brought me up in the true faith in which, fortified by God's help, I abide even now. I have received the word and grace of God, and am convinced that there is none other than the one true faith planted in Jerusalem. Now through devious machinations of the Evil

One, tempted by the glory of this world and befogged by affluence, our would-be pastors and the most important leaders of our true faith, the metropolitan and the bishops, have turned into wolves. They reject the Eastern church, renounce our most holy patriarchs, our pastors and our ecumenical teachers, and embrace the Western faith. Only with the outward cover of their hypocrisy worn like a sheepskin do they conceal the wolf within. These accursed ones do not expose themselves. Rather they surreptitiously connive with one another like the betrayer of Christ, Judas, with the Jews. They have chosen to rush headlong into perdition, taking all virtuous souls with them, as their own pernicious and secret writings attest. In the end God the friend of man will not permit them to realize their devious plan, if only you stand firm in your Christian love and duty. This is not a matter of perishable possessions and transitory wealth, rather of the most precious things of all, eternal life and the immortal soul. It is because so many inhabitants of this region, the laity, brothers and sisters of the holy Eastern church, look upon me as the leader of Orthodoxy in the land, contrary to my own perception of myself as equal to all who profess the true faith. It is because I am reluctant to commit a guilty act before God and you that I hereby apprise you of the traitors in God's church. I wish to stand with you as one so that with God's help and your efforts they will fall willingly into the very nets they have set for us.

"What can be more shameless and more lawless than their actions? Six or seven depraved individuals have connived villainously, repudiating their pastors, the same holy patriarchs who installed them. Considering all the Orthodox faithful to be witless they dared to tear them away from the truth, and drag them into ruin along with themselves. What is their worth to us? Instead of a beacon of peace they have turned into an abyss of darkness and sinful temptation for all. If Tatars, Jews, Armenians and others in our realm safeguard their faith as inviolable, do not we true Christians have an even greater right to protect our own? We shall accomplish this as long as we stand united as one. I who up to now have served the Eastern church with my labor and my goods by spreading religious works, by doing other pious deeds, vow to exert every effort and work to the very end for the good of my brethren."

ANTI-UNION ACTIVITY

Prince Ostrozhsky did not confine himself to circulars. Soon one of the bishops, Gedeon Balaban of Lvov, who had commenced church union,

separated himself from the Uniate bishops. As we have seen from
Skumin's letter Balaban's contemporaries viewed him as a man driven
to despair by his struggle with the Lvov Brotherhood, and prepared to
reach some agreement with anyone, even his enemies, to escape his onerous impasse. Even as that struggle was slowly working itself out Balaban
was beginning to find it relatively simple to abandon the entire question
of union, especially as he was much less implicated in it than Terletsky
and Potey, given their journeys to Cracow and their obligations to the
king. As early as the beginning of June (1595) Balaban visited Prince
Ostrozhsky and asked him to promote peace between him and the brotherhood, which the prince promised to do. He in turn elicited from the
bishop a promise to become part of an open struggle against the union,
thereby enlisting the bishop to assume an active role in the cause.

On July 1 Prince Ostrozhsky was in Vladimir. In his presence and that
of other prominent individuals Balaban testified before the town officials
that he and other bishops attended two separate assemblies where he gave
Cyril Terletsky four blank sheets with his seals and signatures. They were
to be used to write complaints to the king and the senators about the
oppression of the Rus church. Since then Balaban learned that Bishop
Terletsky of Lutsk wrote something entirely different on those blank
sheets, a resolution of some kind against the Orthodox religion and the
rights and freedoms of the Rus. Because of this Balaban was registering
his protest against any such resolution. It was presented contrary to the
rules and customs of the Orthodox confession and the prerogatives and
liberties of the Rus, without the knowledge or approval of the patriarchs,
without an ecclesiastical council and without the wishes of the people,
whether prominent old families or ordinary folk of the Orthodox faith. In
their absence bishops were not empowered to make any decisions or take
any action. Prince Ostrozhsky then lost no time in writing to the Lvov
Brotherhood, advising its members to make peace with their bishop. For
his part Cyril Terletsky hastened to accuse Balaban of slandering the
king, who then summoned Balaban to court.

Meanwhile, having moved from Lvov to Wilno, the schoolteacher
Stefan Zizany agitated the Orthodox community of that town with news
about the impending church union, and inflamed its inhabitants against
the traitorous bishop. "Zizany waged a mighty war against the Romans,"
a chronicler writes, " in the town halls and on the streets of the marketplace, and inside the holy church itself." Denying the rumors circulating
about his complicity in the matter of church union, the metropolitan wrote

to the priests in Wilno on July 16 to caution them, and Zizany as well, not to spread such rumors among Christians. The Orthodox inhabitants of Wilno looked for a more promising way out of so dire a predicament. They believed a council was in order. Together with Skumin they turned to Prince Ostrozhsky with a request that he secure royal permission for a public meeting between bishops and laity.

ROYAL REACTION

Under such circumstances the action of the bishops who orchestrated church union amongst themselves was bound to give rise to the question of whether it was possible for the church hierarchy alone, without the laity, to determine such ecclesiastical matters. This issue stood out prominently in the polemics surrounding the union. Suspicious of the bishops' motives, the Orthodox faithful insisted upon lay participation in all decisions concerning the affairs of the church. It was their right, clearly set out in the patriarchal charters of the brotherhoods. They demanded that a council allowing for lay participation be convened. Both the bishops and the Catholic administration used every means at their disposal to oppose the council once they made a clear-cut division between "the rams and the ewes," as King Sigismund described them in the letter referred to above. This did not bode well for the union.

The Orthodox faithful expected the patriarchal exarch from Constantinople, Nicephoros, to attend the council,[62] but King Sigismund instructed the border guards not to admit any patriarchal envoys to Lithuania (July 28). That same day the king wrote to Prince Ostrozhsky admonishing him not to obstruct the business of church union. He also took the opportunity to state his objection to the council. "We do not think this matter warrants a council of the sort for which your bishops have asked our permission. Everything pertaining to the salvation of souls lies within their pastoral authority. It is up to us to honor the decisions of pastors whom the Spirit of God has appointed as our leaders. Besides, rather than resolving anything, these councils merely make things worse."

That same day the king sent a flattering and encouraging letter to the timorous, vacillating metropolitan, whom he attempted to persuade not to be diverted by any distractions or yield to any threats, rather to stand firm in his efforts to resolve the issue successfully. King Sigismund then issued a charter protecting the metropolitan and all Uniate bishops from patriarchal bans of anathema, and confirming them in the rights enjoyed by the Roman Catholic clergy. He also promised to discuss the issue of

Senate seats for them with the gentry and high officials of the Polish-Lithuanian Commonwealth at the next session of the Sejm, and pledged to issue mandates and manifestos against all who would object to church union. Sigismund vowed that no Rus monasteries or churches on royal estates would be converted to Roman Catholic churches, although he stopped short of making the same promise with respect to monasteries and churches on gentry estates. Next he decreed that brotherhoods must obey the metropolitan and other bishops. Finally he gave his permission for the founding of schools using Greek and Slavonic as the languages of instruction, and to establish printing presses, with the one reservation that they not publish anything detrimental to the church of Rome.

OPPOSITION FORCES GATHER

Fierce and open Rus opposition to church union caused the government to persuade Potey and Terletsky to journey to Rome and petition the pope to place the Rus church under his jurisdiction. Meeting personally with Prince Ostrozhsky, Potey pacified him, and gave his assurance that everything began and would end in accordance with the prince's own wishes, and that the entire matter would be decided by the Orthodox community, if not by a formal council. He wrote to Ostrozhsky on August 23 "I see that the time is growing nigh for our journey to Rome yet I have not yet received any instructions from your grace. I have no idea how to extricate myself from this journey. My sole hope is that you will write to the king and restrain him, so that he summons us only after the council has finished its work."

Even more adamant in his objection to this journey was Rogoza who, in spite of the king's letter, remained fearful and distracted. On August 19 he wrote to Skumin once again denying his intention to recognize the authority of Rome. "It would be very difficult for me to do such a thing in my declining years. For this I would need to be reborn, to return to my studies, for knowing no Latin I would not know how to serve at the same altar alongside Roman Catholic chaplains. Whoever aspires to this, let him achieve both a seat in the Senate and the favor of the king. I, a sinful man, would rather have a place with the sons of Zebedee than among the proud and vainglorious.[63] As for the new calendar, there was talk about it earlier among us, especially since the tradesmen find it difficult to follow the old one. We do not, wish to take any action without the advice of all your lordships. After all, as one swallow does not make a spring, so I cannot undertake anything by myself. Word has reached me that, after an audience with the king the bishops of Vladimir and Lutsk [Potey and Terletsky] received permission to travel to Rome. I tried to dissuade them from this plan of theirs, which is certain to produce much unrest and even bloodshed in our Christian nation, but it is difficult for me to restrain anyone so determined."

On September 1 the metropolitan distributed a circular letter to the clergy and the laity in which he explained that he never considered, nor did he now contemplate, trampling on his rights and faith, retreating from his confession, or turning his back on his patriarchal ordination. "Stand firmly by the Eastern church," he wrote, "do not sway like a reed in a violent wind, and I will pledge you my support until the day I die."

ORTHODOX BISHOPS IN ROME

Meanwhile, on September 24, King Sigismund made a public announcement to the effect that the Eastern and Western churches were united, and that Rus pastors as well as a multitude of the laity were now in communion with the Roman Catholic church. He expressed the wish that everyone who earlier rejected the union would follow the example of these pastors. Finally he notified the people that the Rus bishops were on their way to Rome.

These bishops, Terletsky and Potey, left Cracow at the end of September and arrived at Rome in November. On the third day after their arrival they had a private audience with Pope Clement VIII,[64] during which they presented letters from the king and some of the senators. "The pope," they wrote, "received us with ineffable love and grace as an affectionate father would welcome his own little children. We live close to the castle of his holiness in a palace tastefully decorated with wallpaper and furnished with everything we require. Provisions have been allotted to us in abundance by the Pope's generosity, although we were in Rome for six weeks and his holiness had yet to grant us a formal audience. Instead he advised us to 'rest well after our journey.' Finally, after persistent entreaties, our audience was scheduled for December 23 in the great chamber called the Hall of Constantine, where the Pope receives only the most important spiritual personages. Here his holiness was pleased to be arrayed in all of his ecclesiastical vestments and attended by the entire senate, cardinals, archbishops and bishops. Ambassadors from the French king and from other places sat apart. Both sides of the hall were occupied by higher dignitaries, senators and numerous spiritual notables, princes of Rome and members of the gentry. When we were escorted to this gathering we kissed the feet of his holiness, and presented our epis-copal credentials. The Catholic priest Evstafy Volovich read the docu-ment aloud quite well, but insofar as virtually no one (save our Polish and Lithuanian lords who reside here in relatively large numbers) understood Rus, we had a Latin translation prepared, which was read immediately afterward.

"Then, speaking through his chamberlains, his holiness delivered a beautiful oration conveying his gratitude for our unification and our jour-ney. He vowed to protect the inviolability of our ecclesiastical rituals, and to confirm them in perpetuity. In the name of our spiritual father the metropolitan, all of the bishops, in our own name and on our own behalf, we read our pledge. I, the bishop of Vladimir, read mine in Latin, while the bishop of Lutsk rendered his in the Rus language. Next we swore an oath on the Holy Bible in the name of all the bishops and ourselves, then we signed the pledge. His holiness beckoned us to come closer, although we were already quite near, and bowing to us in a truly paternal manner he uttered a few words which included the following. 'I have no wish to exercise dominion over you, but rather would like to take your suffering upon myself,' and so on. The next day, that is December 24, on Christ-mas Eve, his holiness himself officiated in the new church of St. Peter's, where he was attended by large numbers of his clergy.[65] Attired in full regalia, we too attended with the blessing of his holiness."

Even as Potey and Terletsky were kissing the pope's feet, and Rome was celebrating the union of the Rus church by striking a medal with the inscription *Ruthenis receptis*,[66] the parish clergy of Wilno wrote the fol-lowing to Skumin. "The people of the Greek Orthodox faith understand that the metropolitan and bishops are undermining their faith, that they are sending it into captivity without the knowledge of their superiors or us, their subordinates, or indeed the entire clergy, you the gentry and the Christian Orthodox people. Four or five bishops are acting on their own whereas we the clergy of the Greek Orthodox confession swear before God and the Christian people that we never considered such defection from our superiors the patriarchs, that we neither knew about nor agreed to it."

SEJM OF 1596

An important Sejm was scheduled for the beginning of 1596, in Warsaw. The Orthodox gentry, assembling at provincial dietines for preliminary conferences, instructed their deputies to request the following from the king. (1) Any bishop who abandons his Orthodox faith shall be deprived of his office. (2) Men of the Orthodox faith shall be installed as bishops in accordance with the resolution of 1573, and charters issued by previous kings, to which the present king himself has sworn.[67]

We have observed already that the king undertook to protect Potey and Terletsky, so naturally he could not accept the deputies' petition. Accordingly, together with Prince Ostrozhsky, they ceremoniously informed the king, the Senate and the entire Sejm that they and the Rus people would not acknowledge either Terletsky or Potey as their bishops, nor would they accept their control over their estates or submit to their ecclesiastical courts. In addition the deputies wrote a protest listing the abuses against them, and the various persecutions the Rus endured.

On the final day of the Sejm a secretary in the office of the governor of Poznań,[68] Marcin Buchowiecki, was delegated to read it aloud in the presence of the king, but the Sejm denied him a hearing. Drowned out by shouts and compelled to retire, Buchowiecki protested this outrage, whereupon Prince Ostrozhsky registered his protest in the official records of the Warsaw Sejm. He enumerated the criminal acts of Terletsky and Potey, and stated his firm resolve to oppose their declared intentions. In the same spirit deputies from the Orthodox nobility added two more protests, appending them to the registers of the town council. Subsequently signed copies of these protests were distributed to the various provincial governors.

For his part, in fulfillment of earlier commitments, the king granted Terletsky a charter confirming him in his Lutsk eparchy, and pledging on behalf of himself and his successors that Terletsky would be bishop of Lutsk and Ostrog for the remainder of his life. He further guaranteed that Terletsky retained all episcopal holdings in Lutsk, and promised to defend the bishop against ill-wishers who dare attempt to drive him from the episcopal see or seize his church property (May 21, 1596).

Following this, on May 29, 1596 the king issued a manifesto to his Orthodox subjects on the consummation of church union. At the same time he assumed full responsibility for the act, affirming that neither Terletsky nor Potey brought any innovations from Rome. "Ruling happily in our dominions, and reflecting upon how to improve them, we have, among other things, conceived a desire for our subjects of the Greek faith to be brought into the original and ancient unity with the ecumenical Roman Catholic church and obedience to one spiritual pastor. The bishops have brought no innovations from Rome, nothing that would jeopardize your salvation, no changes in your ancient church rituals. All dogmas and rites of your Orthodox church shall remain inviolable in accordance with the resolutions of the holy apostolic councils and the ancient teachings of the holy Greek fathers whose names you glorify and celebrate on appropriate holidays."

With the business thus concluded, the will of the king openly stated, and the union proclaimed to be a matter of state, it followed that the union would be confirmed at the council's conclusion. There the position of the Rus church was to be delineated and the names of friends and enemies of the government entered into its records. In the manifesto mentioned above the king commanded Metropolitan Mikhail Rogoza to convoke a council in the customary place, at Brest, during which Terletsky and Potey would present the details of their mission to Rome. Everyone who worshipped in the Orthodox confession received permission to attend the council, and enjoined to travel as modestly as possible, without unnecessary hordes of servants and retainers. Only Catholics and Orthodox were permitted to participate in the council. Protestants were excluded.

At the beginning of October, 1596 there arrived in Brest the Greek patriarchal exarch Nicephoros representing the patriarch of Constantinople; Metropolitan Mikhail Rogoza with seven Rus bishops, numerous archimandrites, abbots and priests; from the laity Prince Ostrozhsky with his son, and many others. The Catholics were represented by three bishops, Piotr Skarga, three lay nobles and the king's deputies Mikołaj Krzystof Radziwiłł, governor of Troki, Lev Sapieha, chancellor of Lithuania, and Dymitr Chalecki, treasurer of Lithuania.

The council was scheduled to begin its work on October 6 and before long two hostile camps formed. They refused to merge in a plenary session in one church location as was their custom. There was no trace of the metropolitan, who was to have acted as host. The Orthodox were scheduled to meet in a large private house. When they were assembled the clergy sat in a circle with the Gospel book in their midst, while the laity formed a separate circle around their marshal of the nobility. Following the customary prayers Bishop Gedeon Balaban began his speech in the Rus language. An archdeacon did a simultaneous translation into Greek. Gedeon declared that he and the entire assembly clung to their own faith, and were prepared to die for it. In their opinion the metropolitan and his bishops acted uncanonically by their refusal to obey the patriarch. A decision was reached to send for the metropolitan and the Uniate bishops, who failed to appear. Rogoza replied that first he would sit with the Catholic bishops for reflection, after which he would come to the council. The council waited for him until nightfall, to no avail. The next day the metropolitan and his friends again were summoned, which evoked the following response. "You wait for us in vain, we shall not come." On the third day, after yet another summons, they sent this message. "What is done is done. Whether we acted well or badly when we submitted to the Roman Catholic church, it is too late to undo it."

In answer to the exarch's question as to how and when Rogoza and his friends began to work towards church union, Archimandrite Nikifor Tur of the Kiev Caves monastery noted that 'Patriarch Jeremiah, having learned about Rogoza's illegal actions, pronounced a temporary ban upon him. He threatened permanent anathema and deprivation of office if Rogoza refused to mend his ways, whereupon the metropolitan decided to abjure."

Next they turned to the laity to compare the instructions of deputies from various provinces. In all of them they found a common demand, no renunciation of the Eastern church. At the same time the council was notified that in a small room of that very house [in which the Orthodox were assembled], Skarga was exerting all his powers to convince Prince Ostrozhsky and his son of the desirability of church union. "Let Skarga come to the council and argue with learned people," declared Exarch Nicephoros. "Why is he in corners trying to persuade people who are ignorant of theology?" Skarga did not attend.

On the fourth day, October 9, the council decreed that "The metropolitan and the bishops of Vladimir, Lutsk, Polotsk, Kholm and Pinsk are hereby stripped of their office because without the knowledge of their superior they agreed to a church union." The decree stated that such union could not be established by five or ten bishops, that a decision of this magnitude required an ecumenical council. Although the council called upon the bishops to defend themselves they refused to appear, offering no defense. That same day the metropolitan and the Uniate bishops issued their own decree on the deprivation of their office, together with a ban of anathema against the bishops and the communicants who rejected church union.

A CHURCH DIVIDED

Thus was the union accomplished, or rather the Western Rus church was divided into Orthodox and Uniate. Insofar as they declined ecclesiastical unification, the Orthodox went directly against the will of the government, which protected the Uniate faith, thereby weakening the position

of their own church. This grave situation continued even after the administration began to listen to Orthodox complaints, and issued decisions in
their favor. With renewed fanaticism, amidst chaos and arbitrary deeds,
private individuals, especially the strong, ignored official decisions. Finding themselves under the dominion of Catholic magnates or worse, Orthodox apostates, Orthodox peasants increasingly suffered for their faith.

This untenable situation, a struggle with the dominant church and an
enemy with substantial material resources, awakened a moral strength in
the Rus. Opponents fought with their pens and wrote against Orthodoxy.
The Orthodox had to defend themselves in order to support their adherents' decision not to abandon the Eastern church. To protect themselves,
to develop centers for the edification of their people and to refute hostile
accusations of inadequate learning they needed to multiply and improve
both the schools and public morals.

VISHENSKY'S EPISTLES

The East was not as feeble as its enemies would have us believe. A powerful denunciatory voice was heard from Mount Athos, from the Rus
monk Ivan Vishensky who lived there.[69] "To you, Rus, Lithuanians and
Poles of all ranks and ages living in the Polish land, worshipping in various sects and faiths, may this voice reach your ears. I say to you that the
land upon which you tread clamors and cries out against you before God.
It entreats the Creator to send His grim reaper as He did once against the
people of Sodom, preferring an empty and pure land to one inhabited by
your godlessness, and defiled by lawless acts such as yours. For where
today in the Polish land is there faith, where hope, where charity? Where
is truth, where legal justice? Where is humility, where the evangelical
commandments? Where are the apostolic sermons and secular laws?[70]
Where is loyalty to God's commandments? Where is the chaste clergy,
where the cross-bearing monastic life? Where is pious and devout
Christendom? How can you shamelessly presume to style yourselves
Christians when you cannot even respect the power of that name? O
accursed womb which bore such sons for eternal perdition!

"Today in the lands of the Polish Commonwealth churchmen like
Beelzebub's priests of old serve God with their belly rather than their
soul. The lords have become gods to their subjects. Indeed they hold
themselves above God, what with their lawless judgments rendered in
illegal courts where they elevate themselves above a Creator Who has
bestowed equal honor upon all by creating them in His own image. With

their laws the lords have raised mute beasts themselves over God's people. Instead of evangelical sermons, apostolic guidance and canon law, today pagan teachers like Aristotle, Plato and other such mummers and comedians rule in Christ's court. Instead of faith, hope and charity, disbelief, despair, loathing enmity and abomination rule. Repent, all of you! Repent and you shall not perish in mortal and eternal perdition! The Turkish infidels are more worthy before God in justice and righteousness than the baptized Liakhs [Poles]. But do not despair, Orthodox Christians, for God is with you, and I am with you. Have faith in the living God. Do not place your hopes in the sons of men, your Rus lords, for they have abandoned the living God and His faith, and are rendered thereby incapable of offering salvation.

"Cursed be the bishops, the archimandrites and abbots who have laid waste the monasteries, who have turned hallowed ground into landholdings for themselves, in which they lead brutish and lecherous lives with their flunkeys and consorts. Lolling about these estates in beastly sensuality, they appropriate the proceeds donated by the faithful for the worshippers of Christ [the monks] to establish dowries for their daughters, to outfit their sons, adorn their wives, multiply the numbers of their servants and build carriages to which they harness well-fed and well-matched horses. Meanwhile monasteries have no practising monks. Instead of vigils, psalm-singing and prayer, only the howling of stray dogs is heard. Rather than living by the rules, reading religious works and preaching God's law, the godless bishops pore over statute books day and night, and spend their lives in duplicity."

Here is what Vishensky wrote to Rogoza, Potey and Terletsky on the issue of church union. "I ask you, what is meant by the work of self-purification? This question has not even occurred to you. Not only do you yourselves have no notion of it, your Jesus-cursing papal priests, the so-called Jesuits, do not trouble themselves with it and offer no solutions. Show me, you weavers of church union, which of you has attained even the first level of self-denial and sanctity? Was it not your worships who by your evil deeds destroyed the faith even before union? Was it not your worships who cultivated in yourselves an appetite for corruption and worldly avarice? You can never get enough. You are getting sicker and sicker with cupidity and craving for worldly possessions. Show me, you architects of church union, which of you in this worldly life has personally followed the six commandments of Christ?[71] Was it not your worships who not only thwarted and stultified these six commandments among the laity, but are now tirelessly pursuing the same course among the clergy? You sit in one place like idols, and when you need to move that idolized corpse of yours to another location you transport it by chariot at your ease, while your poor subjects labor and suffer for you day and night. When have you ever ministered to the sick? Indeed is it not your worships who make healthy people sick, who beat, torture and kill? Tap your bald pate and ask yourself, you bishop of Lutsk, during your priesthood how many human souls did you dispatch to God? While he was yet a mere castellan, his grace Potey hauled only four servants around with him. Now that he is bishop it seems no fewer than ten will suffice. I doubt that his grace the metropolitan could afford two servants when he was just a little no-body.[72] Now he too keeps more than ten."

In an epistle to Prince Ostrozhsky and to all Orthodox faithful Ivan Vishensky wrote "The reason the Devil wages such a mighty struggle to gain Christians of the Slavonic tongue is that it is the most fruitful of all languages, as well as being God's favorite. Without pagan tricks and artifices such as grammar, rhetoric, dialectic and other perfidies of dev-ilish vanity, it brings us to God without sophistry, through straightforward and diligent reading. It inspires simplicity and humility, it evokes the Holy Ghost, refusing to convey divine wisdom to a perfidious and faith-less soul. The treacherous Latin soul is so blinded and saturated with proud and vainglorious pagan dogma that it leaves no room for divine wisdom, spiritual sagacity, humility, simplicity or goodness. Safeguard your children from this venom, ye Orthodox faithful! It is obvious that you have suffered since you began to covet Latin and secular wisdom. Would it not behoove you to study the Book of Hours, the Psalter, the Oktœchos,[73] the Works and Epistles of the Apostles and the Gospels, re-maining simple worshippers beloved of God and being rewarded with eternal life, rather than to apprehend Aristotle and Plato, and be consid-ered a learned philosopher in this life, only to be consigned to hell in the next?

"The high office of priesthood must be attained according to the rules of the Holy Fathers, not to satisfy personal ambition. Elevation to the higher clerical ranks must not be sought for the sake of estates and noble titles. Do not accept him who forces himself upon you, he who is ap-pointed by the king without your approval. Banish and curse such a man. You were not baptized a papist or a subject of the king that he should send wolves and brigands into your flock.[74] You are better off going to church and defending Orthodoxy without the priests and bishops sent by the Devil than attending a church with such godless priests and bishops, cursing the church and trampling upon Orthodoxy.

"Select your pastors in the following way. First nominate several who have wisdom and life experience. Then designate a day of fasting, hold a vigil in the church and pray to God that He choose and reveal to you your pastor. You will know him by having the nominees cast lots. The merciful God will not ignore your prayers. He will disclose this to you and grant you a suitable pastor. Only then will you turn to the secular authority, to the king, that he might confirm your bishop. If he refuses to approve your choice you will see him grown deaf and dumb because he has been crowned to judge righteously, not to indulge the vanities of his own faith. Only turn to God truly, and He will miraculously set everything right.

"Cleanse these vanity fairs you call councils, both in Zhidichin and in the hills near the village of Spas.[75] Abolish the ancient carols and the Christmas carnival. Christ has no desire to see pagan carols or devilish entertainments commemorating His birth. Drive Epiphany Eve from the towns and the villages into the marshlands. Let it sit there with the Devil.[76] After Easter drag the volochelnoe[77] out of the towns and villages and drown it. Cancel the demonic celebrations on St. George's holiday when people go out to the fields to dance, leap and offer sacrifices to the Devil. Do away with the ritual of eating eggs, pies and dumplings at grave sites,[78] drown the effigy of Kupalo[79] and abolish the practice of leaping over fire on the holiday of St. John [the Baptist]. Peter and Paul implore you. After you have celebrated their holiday [June 29] in Volhynia and Podolia, be sure to smash the swings that were put up at the time of its observance."[80]

In response to the complaint of the Uniate bishops that Patriarch Jeremiah favored the brotherhoods and placed ordinary laity in positions of authority above the clergy, Vishensky writes "How can you call yourselves clergy, or even ordinary worshippers for that matter, when you hold in contempt the brother who was baptized with you in the font of the same faith, who is a son of the same mother, that is God's grace? Whether he be serf, tanner, saddlemaker or cobbler, remember that he too is your brother, equal in all, for he was baptized in the name of the same God in the Trinity."

ZIZANY'S CRITICS

We have learned how profoundly Stefan Zizany aroused Wilno with his sermons when he inveighed against Catholicism and the union of the churches. Rogoza excommunicated him for heresy. Meanwhile on October 8, at the same Council of Brest, the Orthodox bishops proved his innocence, along with that of two of the brotherhood's priests who were excommunicated together with Zizany. "Because the metropolitan sought to abandon the Eastern church he pronounced anathema on those priests for nothing more than a book criticizing the Roman Catholic church." For their part the Catholics wrote a refutation of Zizany's work, entitled *The Tares that Zizany is Sowing*, which appeared in 1595.[81]

In 1596 Zizany published a sermon on the Antichrist given by St. Cyril, patriarch of Jerusalem,[82] in which he argued for the congruence of the era of Antichrist and church union. That same year the Catholics attacked Zizany's book once more in a work called *The Chaff of Stefanko Zizany*. Both its polemical tone and the wit of the age can be illustrated by a short passage. "Not too long ago Zizany brought the noxious tares of spurious learning from Wilno to trade with its inhabitants for genuine wheat, but they were on guard against treason, and prohibited all such commerce with Zizany. Whereupon he wrote a new book, this time trying his luck with chaff instead of tares. Just as chaff scatters with the first gust of wind, so everything he wrote in these books could be dispersed with a single puff of air by each reader. Facilitating this was the fact that Zizany wrote his book in two languages, Rus and Polish, adding even more witnesses to his foolishness."

POLEMICS

The Council of Brest was bound to generate the most heated polemics. Two accounts of it, written from opposite perspectives, appeared in 1597, the Orthodox *Exegesis, or a Brief Description of Events and the Local Synod in Lithuanian Brest*, and the Catholic version, *The Council of Brest and its Defence*, published in Wilno in 1597 by the celebrated Skarga. Consistent with his fundamental point of view, Skarga confirmed the illegality of the assembly, maintaining that only the one convoked by the metropolitan and the bishops, that is the union, had any validity. Laymen had no right to involve themselves in ecclesiastical matters, and owed unquestioning obedience to their pastors.

The Orthodox published a refutation of Skarga's book in the form of the well-known *Apokrisis*.[83] Naturally the author used all of the arguments he could muster to denounce Skarga's pronouncement on lay interference in ecclesiastical affairs. Adducing charters already familiar to us, in which Rogoza and Potey swore that they would not engage in any action without informing the laity, the author of the *Apokrisis* demonstrated that the clerics did not subscribe truly to Skarga's views, that they simply compromised themselves by betraying their own pledges. "Let us assume," the author of the *Apokrisis* wrote, "that the bishops actually do possess the authority to explain an article of the faith in the Creed which reads 'I believe in the one and only synodal apostolic church' in a way that indicates that the Roman Catholic church is meant. In such a case they too would be duty bound to explain this interpretation to their flock as soon as possible, all the more so because, in Skarga's words, belief in the Roman Catholic church is an indispensable condition of salvation. The bishops are blameworthy because they procrastinated in announcing this new salvationist article of faith in the Creed, and many left unaware of it died unredeemed."

Skarga offered the Old Testament as evidence that decisions in spiritual affairs belong exclusively to the clergy. The author of *Apokrisis*, to the contrary, pointed out that Moses was a secular man, yet he formulated the entire procedure of public worship. How can it be that, instead of the priest Aaron, God gave the layman Moses the right to supervise matters of worship? Even if the Old Testament had left the fact of the determination of matters of faith to the clergy alone, still this would constitute a feeble argument insofar as there is a vast difference between Judaism and Christianity. In Judaism only one branch of the Levites was selected to serve as priests, whereas in Christianity all people are cleansed of their sins with the blood of Christ, and become princes and priests of God the Father. There one part of the people served the glory of God in the one temple of Jerusalem. Here all Christians in every place and at all times are dedicated to glorifying Christ. No matter what they eat or drink or in whatever other activity they engage, they do it for the glory of God, to glorify the Lord not only in spirit but by their physical deeds as well.

Skarga wrote that neither the higher nor the lower clergy whom God commands us to obey can be in error. Hence the laity must defer to them in all matters in the hope that even if some fall into error those who followed their spiritual leaders would be acquitted before God, Who has ordered them to obey such errant leaders. "I ask you," argues the author

of the *Apokrisis*, "why did Moses kill three thousand men for worshipping the calf that was cast by the high priest Aaron?[84] I ask you what does
Skarga think of the high priest Uriah who, together with King Ahaz,
sacrificed to idols?[85] I ask you what does he know of priests living at the
time of Christ? Why did no apostles obey them? Why did they not follow them in faith or in its absence? Leaving aside the examples from the
Old Testament, I ask you when Bishop Auxentius of Milan[86] was an ad-
herent of Arianism, when Dioscorus of Alexandria and Eutyches[87] became heretics, when the bishops of Constantinople, Nestor and Macedon,
fell into heresy, was everybody in their eparchies obligated to follow their
teachings? Had they done so, would they have been justified before God?
If so, then as the Holy Scriptures say, everyone must carry his own burden, for 'if the blind lead the blind, both shall fall into the ditch.'[88] Because the laity must obey their pastors in all things, does it follow that
the Germans of Cologne committed no sin when, looking to the example
of their archbishop, they converted to Lutheranism?[89] This would indicate that we too are not guilty when we take our cue from the bishops of
Lvov and Peremyshl, both of whom contend that the Pope is not the
supreme ruler of the church. Moreover, what if the bishop of Lutsk were
to 'go Turkish,''[90] which is quite conceivable in view of his morals,
would his sheep be justified before God were they to become Muslims?
Of course the chronicler of the Synod of Brest will shake his head at this.
He should also know that it is not clerical title but devotion to higher
values that save us from error. It is not necessarily desirable that we take
our cue in all things from the clergy"

   We have offered these examples in order to reveal the position and
rhetorical devices used by the author of the *Apokrisis* but leave the detailed critique and evaluation of his book to ecclesiastical scholars. After the publication of the *Apokrisis* an Orthodox priest from Lvov wrote
an account of the progress of the union entitled *A Forewarning to Orthodox Christians Essential for the Future*.[91] The work contains some interesting details, but its lack of chronology tends to confuse events, making
it difficult for scholars to follow.

   The *Apokrisis* created a furor among Roman Catholics. Their anger was
evidenced by a response entitled the *Antirresis*.[92] In his struggle against this
strong adversary its author resorted to desperate means, to lies and calumny. The author of the *Apokrisis*," he stated, "filled his book with a
multitude of indecencies and improprieties that the Devil himself issuing
forth out of hell could not have fabricated more lies than Christopher

Filalet has written in his books. In truth everyone should call him the
bearer of the Devil and lover of lies, not the bearer of Christ and lover
of truth."

KING SIGISMUND

In his circular to the Rus the king perceived a need to arm himself against
the actions of the Orthodox at the Council of Brest. "The metropolitan,"
wrote the king, "who along with the bishops, other clergy and numerous
people of the Rus Greek faith assembled at the customary place, namely
St. Nicholas cathedral, began the proceedings appropriately enough with
a prayer. For three days the metropolitan deliberated as he considered the
Holy Writ and studied the rules of the Holy Fathers. In a fraternal fashion he summoned Bishop Mikhail Kopistensky of Peremyshl,[93] Gedeon
Balaban of Lvov and their colleagues to a meeting. It was they who initiated a church union and apprised our majesty of it. Now these same
bishops have followed the lead of certain recalcitrant individuals choosing to abandon their senior bishop the metropolitan as well as the majority
of the episcopal fraternity. They have deserted God's church, the holy
place where they were to meet and come to an agreement with their superior. Not once throughout the entire council did they stand in God's
church, electing instead to make common cause with Anabaptists, Arians,
blasphemers and other old heretics, enemies and profaners of the Orthodox faith, that is to say the faith of the Rus. In addition after accepting
spies and traitors into their midst as friends, one Nicephoros and other
Greeks, all foreigners, they assembled in a heretical temple. Here they
acted in the spirit of anger and opposition, with the petrified heart of a
pharaoh, daring to engage in affairs that did not concern them, opposing
their authorities, opposing our majesty their sovereign and the Polish
Commonwealth. They separated themselves from God's church and secretly drew up plots and protests. They affixed their seals and their signatures to blank sheets of paper, brought in all kinds of people who were
not even members of the church and forced them to sign the sheets. After writing something on them they had the audacity to distribute these
sheets throughout our dominions."

Admonishing the Rus to follow the metropolitan's exemplary acceptance of church union, and informing them of the anathema against
Kopystensky and Balaban, the king forbade the people to acknowledge
them as bishops, or even to associate with them. Sigismund also ordered
the officials and others in authority not to oppose the resolutions of the

council at Brest which recognized the church union, and decreed that its opponents be punished. Orders went out to treat the Orthodox like criminals, and their persecution was legalized.

Yet the king's decree could not be implemented fully. Too many people, indeed virtually all, would have had to be punished for rejecting ecclesiastical unification. They included some exceedingly powerful individuals, whereas the government itself was very weak. At the same time as Sigismund institutionalized Orthodox persecution he proceeded to reward the Uniate bishops. Prince Ostrozhsky meanwhile persuaded Balaban and the Lvov Brotherhood to suspend their rivalry for a year.[94] Both sides promised that during the interim they would cooperate in their defense of Orthodoxy.[95]

II

THE AFTERMATH

THE COSSACKS

Even as Western Rus was agonizing over church union there emerged among them a phenomenon of decisive impact upon the future development of the conflict. We noted earlier that both the Muscovite and the Polish governments in Eastern Europe simultaneously became embroiled in a struggle with the cossacks, who were growing in strength on their borders and becoming aggressive in both East and West. Proclaiming themselves defenders of realms, they did not limit themselves to guarding frontiers. In keeping with their savage nature, which they never troubled to conceal, the cossacks made it clear that if they failed to attack their neighbors they would forfeit their livelihood. Then behaving like the predators they were, the cossacks did exactly that. Just when such conduct was adjudged most harmful to the Polish state they raided Turkish territory, drawing both powers [Muscovy and Poland] but especially Poland into a dangerous animus against Turkey. Naturally Poland had to resort to every stratagem at its disposal to forestall any damage to the realm the cossacks might inflict.

When peace was concluded with Turkey, and Poland was assured that there would be no further attacks on Polish possessions, the Sejm of 1590 passed a resolution requiring the crown hetman to survey and make public information about lands inhabited by the cossacks. The hetman was instructed to assign them a commander-in-chief, squadron commanders and captains, all from the Polish gentry, while the cossacks were required to swear an oath of loyalty to the Commonwealth. They were barred from entering foreign territory by sea or land without permission from the crown hetman. They were not permitted to receive any Polish fugitives into their ranks. Their numbers were to be strictly regulated and recorded in the crown hetman's register. The Sejm dispatched two commissioners to take up permanent residence among them, and to monitor implementation of the resolution.

COSSACK MILITARY EXPLOITS

Clearly the cossacks would not accept such restraints without a fight. In 1592, five thousand strong, with someone called Kosiński at their head,[1] they attacked Podolia and laid waste the lands belonging to Konstantin Ostrozhsky and other landowners. Prince Ostrozhsky then sent an army which routed Kosiński near the town of Piatka, not far from Ternopol. Kosiński was surrounded and killed as he attempted to make his way into Cherkasy.[2] Around 1595 the hetman of the Zaporozhian Host, Grigory Loboda, devastated Rus.[3] In Volhynia Prince Ostrozhsky evened the score with him. Loboda then proceeded to the Danubian principalities to fight the Turks, while Ostrozhsky attacked Polesie. Just then Nalivaiko[4] and a band of one thousand men broke away from Loboda and took Ostropol, a landed possession of Ostrozhsky. We have no idea how Ostrozhsky settled things with his guest, but we do know that afterwards Nalivaiko invaded Rus and occupied Słuck. On November 30, 1595 Nalivaiko's troops, now two thousand men strong, entered Mogilev on the Dnieper. They burned houses, shops and the stockade. In all, ninety houses were reduced to ashes while the cossacks robbed and murdered their inhabitants, regardless of sex or age. Then the Lithuanian hetman Radziwiłł moved against them with fourteen thousand Lithuanians and four thousand Tatars. Learning of Radziwiłł's imminent approach, Nalivaiko rode out of Mogilev and arranged his wagon train according to the customary cossack-style encampment.[5] From this temporary fortification he successfully defended himself against Radziwiłł in a day-long battle, after which he left for Bykhov [Bykhiv]. The Lithuanians pursued the cossacks but, unable to inflict any harm, they turned to robbing the local populace instead.

The crown hetman Stanisław Żółkiewski[6] wrote to the king in 1596 "It is terrifying to contemplate the magnitude of such belligerence, such disregard for royal greatness, such a deliberate intent to destroy Cracow and ruin the gentry estate." Finally Żółkiewski defeated and captured Nalivaiko near Lubny, on the border of Solonitsa, and he was executed in Warsaw in 1597. Ostrozhsky was suspected of dealings with Nalivaiko, while a rumor circulated that Loboda had ravaged Rus with the prince's knowledge.[7] In reference to this Ostrozhsky wrote to his son-in-law Radziwiłł, governor of Wilno. "I rely upon God to save me not only from these suspicions, but from death itself."

The Polish crown triumphed over the cossacks but continued to nurse deep festering wounds. The weakness of the government is attributed to the fact that it had no way to deter its powerful men from committing acts of violence upon the populace, or to prevent soldiers whose wages went unpaid from resorting to appalling robberies. During the wars with Nalivaiko, whatever the cossacks left the soldiers seized. It was a religious war, a by-product of church union, but it was also Orthodox persecution. The gentry in particular found themselves in a difficult situation. Village assemblies, not very strong even in the second half of the sixteenth century, as noted earlier, increasingly lost their significance in the seventeenth century, as they yielded their authority to the gentry. Both male and female members of the gentry, together with their friends and even an occasional clergyman, presided over the courts and handed down judgments. Peasant delegates sent by their villages had no voice. They simply concurred with the decisions of the landlord and his supporters. Some of the gentry forbade their peasants to participate either in the village assemblies or the village popular courts. As early as 1557 the gentry and their estate managers received the right to punish their servants and peasants by death. Moreover in leasing their property to the Jews the gentry empowered them to appropriate profits, hand down legal judgments on peasants without the possibility of appeal, and even pass death sentences upon guilty or disobedient peasants, according to the seriousness of their transgressions. So the peasants, or serfs as they were called in the Southwest, fled to join the cossacks even as Żółkiewski was complaining about cossack intentions to destroy the gentry estate.

In the Muscovite realm the cossacks took advantage of the Time of Troubles. To wage a more effective struggle against the government they displayed banners, or took up the cause of imaginary sons and grandsons of Ivan IV. As the Time of Troubles came to an end in Muscovy, so too

MID-SEVENTEENTH-CENTURY ZAPOROZHIAN COSSACK CAMP
Samiilo a, *Litopys*. Vol. 1, Kiev, 1991

did the cossack reign. It was quite different in the Polish state. There, fighting against the crown to protect their interests, the cossacks effectively used church union to present their conflict as a holy war, and to march under religious banners.

THE NICEPHOROS AFFAIR

The year 1595 began with the scandalous case of the patriarchal exarch Nicephoros. As we found earlier, in his circular the king called the exarch a spy. On his way to Wallachia to purchase horses for Prince Ostrozhsky one of his servants was seized on Hetman Zamoyski's property, and letters containing some harsh comments against the Poles were found on his person. They were given to him by the Greek monk Pafnuty, who was about to undertake a journey to Moscow. Because Nicephoros's conduct at the Council of Brest angered the Poles, they charged that it was he and not Pafnuty who authored these epistles. Ignoring the fact that Nicephoros and his lawyer brilliantly proved the absurdity of such charges, the Poles refused to exempt him from trial.

Offended by the proceedings which were meant to discredit him as much as Nicephoros, the old Prince Ostrozhsky delivered a lengthy speech to the king. He reminded Sigismund of his merits and those of his ancestors, recalling that the enmity between him and Zamoyski never prevented Ostrozhsky from taking the side of the king during a royal assembly, for which the king showed him special favors. He placed one of the prince's sons to his right in the Senate and another to his left, thereby filling Ostrozhsky's old age with joy, yet now his enemy Zamoyski was persecuting Ostrozhsky's servants. He kidnapped good innocent people on public thoroughfares, took their money and tortured them because he wanted to dishonor Ostrozhsky in any manner possible. What is more, he attacked Ostrozhsky's clergy and called them traitors. "Although you can see the violence done to us, and are aware of the infringements on our rights, your majesty chooses to ignore the oath by which you pledged not to violate but rather to extend and multiply these rights. Indeed you refuse to keep us in our Orthodox faith enjoying our rights. You will not appoint replacements for the deserting bishops. You permit these renegades to use force against us, shed the blood of those who refuse to follow them in their defection to rob the faithful and deprive them of their holdings. Because of our Orthodox faith you trample on our rights, abrogate our liberties and oppress our consciences. By such acts you break your oath. If earlier you did good things for me, your recent malevolence has nullified them. Not only do I, as a senator, suffer these indignities, I perceive that the destruction of Crown Poland may be at stake, for now nobody is secure in his rights and liberties. Soon terrible devastation is bound to follow. Our forefathers, pledging citizenship, loyalty and obedience to our sovereign, enjoyed in turn his favor, justice and protection. In my declining years my most precious of treasures, the Orthodox faith and conscience, have been assaulted. As I face my own demise I charge your majesty to take care. I hold you responsible for the fate of Father Nicephoros, and on the day of judgment I shall seek retribution for any harm that may come to him. I pray to God that I will never again have to witness such violations of people's rights."

When he finished his speech to the king, Ostrozhsky rose, and leaning on the arm of a friend left the royal chamber. His friend suggested that it would be courteous to wait for the king's reply. "I prefer not to do so," replied the old man, and continued walking. Then the king sent Ostrozhsky's son-in-law, Governor Radziwiłł of Wilno, after him with a plea to return. "I assure you," said Radziwiłł, "that the king shares your grief and will release Nicephoros." The enraged old man replied "Let him devour himself and Nicephoros too!" So saying, he stormed out of the palace. The obstinacy of the proud magnate was the undoing of Nicephoros. He died in Marienburg, which soon held other even more illustrious prisoners.[8] Rumor had it that a lack of food hastened Nicephoros's demise.

OSTROZHSKY-PAPAL CORRESPONDENCE

Eventually Ostrozhsky made peace with his sworn enemy Zamoyski, but he refused to reconcile himself to the project promoted by Potey and Terletsky. In vain did the Pope resort to flattering words to influence his acceptance of church union. Using the most respectful of expressions, Ostrozhsky thanked the Holy Father for his affectionate letter, and let it be known that he too was working for the same cause. Yet at the very moment when he needed all the resources he could muster to bring about the desired results as quickly as possible, suddenly, without benefit of a general council, some of the clergy hurriedly presented his holiness with an unfinished product, indeed one which was scarcely begun. This caused such distress that more people chose heresy over unification with the apostolic see. "We are prepared for an agreement," Ostrozhsky wrote, "but this business of union involved many interested parties. Doubtless your holiness can postpone the affair to a later date when the Greek fathers whom I shall try very hard to persuade shall enthusiastically agree to a union. We know that your holiness has made reconciliation and peace among all concerned a high priority. We believe that by giving everyone what is rightly theirs, to the Roman as well as the Greek church, and by joining the two ecclesiastical institutions like two daughters of one great sovereign, you shall deprive neither of its original traits. I believe it will please the Creator Himself to see peace reign in the world, with the final decision coming simultaneously from the highest Roman bishop and the Eastern patriarchs."

CALL FOR TRIAL

Because the Orthodox believed that by violating a righteous cause Potey and Terletsky were the cause of all their troubles, they insisted that the bishops be tried for their misdeeds. Finally the king was forced, formally at least, to accede to their demands. In January, 1598 Sigismund summoned Potey and Terletsky to appear before the Sejm to respond to the accusations of the Volhynian emissaries. They charged the bishops with going to Rome, where they misrepresented themselves as the deputies of all communicants in the Greek Orthodox Christian confession, and placed themselves under the Pope's jurisdiction in the name of the people. This they did without popular sanction or agreement with the prelates. The bishops were unauthorized deputies. Moreover they dared to pursue the matter against the wishes of their patriarchal superiors. Then at the Synod of Brest, aligning themselves with the Roman Catholic priests (with whom all contact was prohibited by the laws of the holy fathers), they had the effrontery to excommunicate good people who refused to approve their desertion.

Potey responded to the king in a manner which Sigismund found pleasing and familiar. "This is a new and unprecedented business! The sheep complaining about the shepherd when it is the pastor who should complain about them to you, the sovereign, who is duty bound to punish the disobedient and return them to submissiveness. The apostle says that the fool is saved by fear. Now, on the contrary, my sheep make accusations against me and refuse to acknowledge me as their shepherd. Was it not your royal majesty who confirmed me in my eparchy at Vladimir to which, abandoning my position as senator, I only agreed because the tearful entreaties of Prince Ostrozhsky so moved me? Was not your majesty pleased to grant me the metropolitan see after the death of the current prelate? Who in your majesty's domain has the power to

rescind such an appointment without good reason? Who shall be deprived
of it? Is it not withdrawn only from those who forfeit honor and life because they have committed a grievous crime? It is plain that we are guilty
of nothing that merits the death penalty. Why then deprive us of our clerical office? Merely because we revived something that was confirmed
long ago, that we offered our submission to the supreme shepherd of the
church of Christ, that we turned away from the patriarchs because they
offered us no comfort, no spiritual guidance, no order? They only came
or sent to us for wool and milk. Instead of peace they sowed unrest, casting the sword of discord among their children. They gave unprecedented
authority to the common people, to some new unheard-of brotherhoods
not sanctioned by canon law, by exempting them from control and grant-
ing them jurisdictions rightfully belonging to the bishops. In their boor-
ishness these peasants are so imperious that they refuse to submit to the
authority of either the clergy or their secular lords.[9] Are we not right to
flee from such a shepherd who is himself imprisoned, and incapable of
assisting us in any way?"

Naturally the king was expected to be swayed by Potey's speech, but
the Orthodox remained unconvinced. They responded to Potey's charges
with "Shameless talk! Your own evil has rendered you incapable of ut-
tering anything good about anyone. What are you saying about the devout patriarchs and your teachers? You sound like faithless pagans. 'For
you are wise to do evil, but to do good you have no knowledge,' in the
words of the prophet.[10] Have not prophets been sent to you at all times?
Have not the patriarchs sent teachers to instruct you? Have they not constantly written you letters on various subjects and visited you personally?
You say 'When the patriarch arrived he created some sort of brotherhood
and appointed priests and preachers.' Yet Christ did the same thing by
unmasking hierarchs, gathering people and apostles around him and ap-
pointing teachers from amongst them. The patriarch acted in a similar
fashion when he revealed Onisifor the metropolitan of Kiev for the
digamist he was,[11] when he condemned Archimandrite Timofey Zloba of
Suprasl monastery for murder, and elevated Mikhail to the metropolitan
see. Then he enumerated all their evils in letters, and made the necessary
preparations for a trial. What more could he have done? Who if not the
Greeks and the patriarch founded the Greek school? Did not Metropolitan Arsenios of Elasson, sent by the patriarch, teach Greek grammar and
the written Slavonic language in Lvov for two years? When his students
published his grammar, printed works in Greek and Slavonic began to

proliferate, something which never before occurred in Rus. Indeed, after the people of Kievan Rus accepted Christianity, instead of studying they proceeded to build churches which evil neighbors immediately destroyed. They forced their own people to pay tribute. Using their teachings and various other methods they pushed the magnates away from the church and reduced the entire populace to a state of penury. Now there are schools being founded in every town, and hospitals and churches also are being erected.

"In accordance with a decree issued by the ecumenical patriarch all digamists have been expelled, heresy condemned, confessors designated, church councils convoked, the courts have been restricted, the wicked punished and unfit bishops removed from office. Compared to all this, what have you done? Fearing that he might punish you as criminals and demand your removal from office, you caused one of the patriarchs, him from Antioch, to be beaten and ordered the ecumenical patriarch Jeremiah to return home. In all honesty you should have issued a verdict against yourselves as the Jews did, saying 'He will out those wretches to a miserable death, and let out the vineyard to other tenants who will give him the fruits in their seasons.'[12] 'Even now the axe is laid to the root of the trees.'[13] The vine arborist will not persuade his master to spare a barren tree until he has dug around it and dunged it for the coming year. Now is the time to set things right.[14] Yet these days every bishop tolerates bigamous and digamous priests, lechers and murderers in his own bishopric. The bishops themselves murder people, as the court records attest. They destroy churches and monasteries, distribute monastic property and the monasteries themselves among their friends. They marry off the monks and nuns. Then, having conspired together in secret, they flee to the Pope."

ANTI-CATHOLIC UNION

When Catholic authorities denied them appointments some Orthodox determined to ally with Protestants who also were suffering persecution, that together they might force the authorities to hear the following complaints and satisfy the following demands. "The ancient authority of the patriarch of Constantinople is being violated. Neither he nor we have the right to communicate through envoys and charters. Let all patriarchal decrees, particularly that issued in Brest against apostates, remain in force. Our deserting metropolitan and his bishops enjoy the protection of royal favor, thereby avoiding patriarchal control. His majesty enjoins us to go against our own conscience and obey them. If the king refuses to subject them to the decision of our council, let him install a new metropolitan.

"In every town and guild papists deprive individuals of the Greek faith of equal freedoms and honor. Papist artisans mercilessly oppress them.[15] At the expense of the communicants in the Greek faith the papists secure now privileges from papal legates which the king confirms. Everywhere the king's representatives hold the church brotherhoods accountable for violations of civic peace, therefore undeserving of civic honor and freedoms. The brotherhoods, especially in Wilno, suffer intolerable hardship. Would that our brotherhoods and our confessions were simply left in peace. The apostate metropolitan curses and the king condemns all brotherhood priests and preachers, together with all who obey them and attend brotherhood churches.

"In the year 1598, precisely on Easter Sunday, the Jesuits perpetrated a great act of violence against the Wilno brotherhood church. Various mandates were issued and circulars sent out against the brotherhood. Some brethren out of favor with the chancellor (Sapieha) would have suffered the death penalty had not God himself and Governor Radziwiłł (a Protestant) not saved them. Let the mandates be nullified and the chancellor make peace with the brotherhood.

"In the Holy Trinity monastery the brotherhood altar was confiscated by the apostate metropolitan, while the chancellor seized the house in which the brotherhood assembled. Bailiffs registered a protest in the town hall against several members of the brotherhood, an action harmful not only to us but to our descendants, against our having attended the church synod in Brest. They wished great misfortune upon us and our descendants. We are subjected to this abuse from the papists because they want to reverse the patriarchal blessing which we enjoy, deny his jurisdiction over us and coerce us into accepting the papal faith. Such injustice inspires us to enter into a strong union for the defense of our mutual freedoms. Their lordships the Protestant lords must forge a strong bond with us to fight the injustices to which we are subjected as we, by the same token, defend them in their struggle. As a sign of their good will toward us we ask them to stop deferring to the Pope, to reject his new calendar and observe our ancient Julian one in the old way (as the Prussian lords and other Germans observe it along with us) so that together we might protect ourselves against coercion on God's holy days."[16]

Such were the instructions for deputies preparing to leave for a conference with the Protestants scheduled for May 1599 in Wilno. Prince

Konstantin Ostrozhsky, Yury Sangushko and two relatively undistinguished clergymen were there on behalf of the Orthodox. The hierarchs from Lvov and Peremyshl refused to attend. Representing the Protestants were Prince Mikołaj Krzystof Radziwiłł, governor of Wilno, Andrzej Leszczyński, governor of Brest-Kujawy, and other prominent personages. The Protestants broached the subject of consensus on dogma, which the Orthodox refused to consider. Instead they chose to limit themselves to a political union and drew up an agreement which not even many of the Orthodox were willing to sign, causing the conference to produce no palpable results.

That same year (1599) Ipaty Potey succeeded the deceased Mikhail Rogoza as metropolitan of Kiev. His first act was to militate against Stefan Zizany, who continued to preach in Wilno against church union. To retaliate against the Holy Trinity monastery for having granted sanctuary to Zizany, Potey ordered that the monastery church be sealed. An old friend of Zizany, Yury Rogatinets, sent a conciliatory letter from Lvov.[17] "You write that your church was sealed at Ipaty's command. Ignore this order but speak no ill of him, for his despair might move him to even worse deeds, inspired by rage rather than God's work. Such things are nothing new in God's church. Together with the Romans the high priests sealed off Christ's tomb, yet they were unable to restrain His power. Herod murdered infants in order to kill Christ, yet in the end accepted his own demise like other enemies of God who opposed the church from their perches of power as landowners.

"You claim that Ipaty composed certain dialogues between a Rus and a Liakh in which he charged that during our stay at Wilno we separated from the Uniates and joined the Lutherans. He is quite mistaken, for we maintain no friendships with any heretics. As far as the rumors that I correspond with Ipaty are concerned, I can say freely and openly that I am in touch with all kinds of people from the opposition without necessarily sharing their views. I act with the meekness of a lamb, the wisdom of a serpent, the integrity and purity of a dove, as Christ taught. My conversations and correspondence with Potey's son Yan make this perfectly clear. I am sending you copies of the letters."

It is plain from the letters of Yury Rogatinets that the enmity between the Lvov Brotherhood and Bishop Balaban had not abated. "I enclose a copy of another of my works which I have just written on the occasion of the funeral of my niece Anastasia, who died as the result of Balaban's torture. You can see for yourself the nature of our agreement with Balaban." When Prince Ostrozhsky came to Lvov, Balaban avoided him.

POLEMICS PROLIFERATE

Prince Ostrozhsky continued in his former pursuits. A manuscript denouncing the schismatics and heretics was discovered after the death of the Alexandrian patriarch Meletios. The prince quickly took steps to publish it in Greek and Rus languages. He sent to the Lvov Brotherhood for typesetters. Nor was Potey idle. In June 1605 he arrived at the city hall in Wilno to announce that in the church of Krewo he had found an old manuscript, dated 1476. It contained an account of the Council of Florence and a charter to Pope Sixtus IV from the Kievan metropolitan Mikhail, the archimandrites of the Caves monasteries and those in Wilno, as well as from the grand princes and Rus magnates.[18] He published the charter in 1605 as proof that a church union took place in Rus a long time ago. The Orthodox greeted Potey's book with derision. They won a decision from the Sejm which mandated the distribution of clerical offices and possessions exclusively among Rus magnates—of the one true Orthodox faith—a freely conducted Orthodox liturgy and a prohibition against combining in a single individual two clerical offices together with their incomes. In 1609 they won a resolution stating that neither Orthodox nor Uniates would oppress or provoke each other. Anyone found guilty of violating this order would be fined ten thousand zlotys.

There seemed to be no way to stop the disorders. In 1610 a work appeared by Melety Smotritsky under the pseudonym Theophilus Ortologos entitled *Lament of the Eastern Church*.[19] As the title itself suggests, the author wished above all to elicit sympathy for the untenable position of an Eastern church subjected to constant persecution. That same year Skarga produced a work criticizing the book. It was entitled *Warning to the Rus Concerning Complaints and Laments of Theophilus Ortologos*.[20] In 1612 yet another refutation of Smotritsky's book was published, the so-called *Paregoria, or Alleviation of the Lament* (a work by Morochowski).[21] And in 1617 a work titled *In Defence of Church Union*, by the Uniate archimandrite Lev Kreus of Wilno, was published.[22] In it the author sought to prove that Uniate actions were rendered perfectly legal by the unification approved in the fifteenth century.

Neither agitation nor oppression abated. The crown pretended to disapprove of such persecutions, but no one paid much attention. At the Sejm of 1620 the deputy from Volhynia, Lavrenty Drevinsky,[23] spoke this way. "In your war against Turkey your majesty conscripts the largest number of his soldiers from among Orthodox Rus. How can you expect these men to offer their bare chests as a bulwark for your realm when their own needs and requests are ignored? How can these people fight for the lasting peace of their realm when they enjoy no peace at home? The oppression that the Rus of ancient lineage suffer for the sake of their faith is plain for everyone to see. In the larger cities their churches are sealed, church property is plundered and instead of monks populating the monasteries cattle are penned there. Children die without being baptized. The remains of the deceased are carted beyond the city limits like carrion, lacking a proper church service. Men and women live together without the sacrament of marriage. People die having been denied confession and communion. Can it be that God himself is not offended? Can it be that He will not avenge this?

"Setting aside any comments about other cities, I will tell you what is happening in Lvov. Non-Uniates cannot live, trade or join craft guilds in that city. Nor can they bury their dead or openly visit the sick to administer the sacraments. In Wilno when the remains of a pious Rus are to be buried they must be taken out through the gate through which city garbage is removed. Orthodox monks are captured on the open road, beaten and thrown into prison. Deserving and qualified individuals are denied civic and governmental appointments for no other reason than they are not Uniates. To the humiliation of the Rus, louts and simpletons without any conception of justice fill prominent positions. They extort money from innocent Orthodox for no reason whatsoever. The main cause of this evil lies in the fact that your royal majesty chooses to appoint to higher clerical office men about whose origins you know nothing. Who does not know that the present bishop of Polotsk is the son of a cobbler who invented for himself the gentry name of Kuntsevich? We are all aware that Shishka, the bishop of Peremyshl, is the son of a shepherd and his uncle remains to this day one of the peasants belonging to Kiev's governor. It is common knowledge that the bishop of Vladimir is the son of the Lvov townswoman Stetskova, and Pokost, the bishop of Kholm, is the son of a merchant from Wilno accused of stealing cloth. Had his cowl not protected him, he long since would have found himself at the end of a rope.

"Such was the benefit of church union that for twenty years the Uniates have been unable to produce anyone from the ranks of the hereditary gentry for the episcopacy! Why even now they have given us Pochapovsky as bishop of Lutsk, a member of the gentry to be sure, but because of his age totally unfitted not only for the office of bishop, but even for that of deacon. How can we call him "father" when he has not yet turned twenty? All such chaos stems from the fact that they accept ordination from an illegitimate pastor. They have turned away from the patriarch of Constantinople who has been the spiritual authority in the country since time immemorial. For twenty years now at every Sejm and dietine we have been begging through bitter tears to be allowed to retain our rights and liberties. If our wishes continue to be ignored we shall be forced to cry out with the prophet 'Give sentence with me O God, and defend my cause.'"[24]

ORTHODOX RESOLUTION

The Sejm resolved to ratify the Constitution of 1607 to ensure that henceforth spiritual offices and incomes be distributed to people of the Greek Orthodox faith. The Orthodox nevertheless refused to wait until all Uniate bishops were dead (what with twenty-year-olds amongst them) for implementation of the resolution. When Patriarch Theophanes of Jerusalem, whom we already have mentioned, came to Rus [in 1620] he was asked to appoint Orthodox bishops to all the eparchies.[25] In 1621, the moment their bishops were installed, the Orthodox issued a set of rules called *The Exhortation to Piety* for ameliorating the disastrous situation in their church. According to this document "all virtue must emanate from the top, that is to say from the metropolitan, the bishops and the clergy. It is they who must begin by first repudiating all evil and sin in themselves. The bishops are to preach the one true [Orthodox] faith, repentance, pious deeds and avoidance of noble homes. The bishops must also send out their own students capable of teaching in the churches, not wait for the people to come to them, bowing and bearing gifts. Together with those bishops whom they appoint and send, they must openly and decisively teach in the churches, from their own official positions, the confession of the Eastern church which we profess today as the one true faith. They must make it clear that its power of salvation is not open to question. In the Latin-Roman church, as well as in other assemblages which it has spawned, salvation is impossible, because there is no true faith.

"In every way the bishops must approve and praise the faith, dogmas and rituals of the Eastern church, rejecting and denouncing others. They must do this spiritually and thoughtfully, without slander or imprecations, citing common passages from the Bible and using persuasive examples as proof. They must promulgate these truths through their writings. Only

worthy and intelligent individuals whose virtue and piety are above reproach must be ordained. This is always to be accomplished without
charging fees, which neither the bishops themselves nor their representatives may extort by resorting to pretexts or hinting at straitened circumstances. It is up to them to inspire and prepare for holy martyrdom
themselves and the hearts of the people. They shall write and publish
books in defense of virtue and piety and refute our opponents in writing,
after seeking the counsel of others, for there is diversity of opinion among
us. For their part our opponents are firm in their faith, and in their hearts
they bear malice towards us. There is to be no communication with de-
parting Uniates. At confession the people must be instructed to avoid such
contacts. Orthodox converts shall be admitted only at the level of peni-
tents. Councils shall be convened and sermons delivered in church every
Sunday and Holy Day. Schools and brotherhoods are needed in every city.

"We must remember that Ipaty Potey, Rogoza and those sharing their
views were no mean intellects. Yet our ancestors, many of them quite
simple people, dared fearlessly to unmask them, so it is only right that
all Orthodox act in the same way. Inasmuch as the holy apostle Andrew[26]
was the first archbishop of Constantinople, the ecumenical patriarch and
apostle of Rus whose feet stood on the hills of Kiev, whose eyes beheld
Rus,[27] whose lips blessed it, who sowed the seeds of faith among us, it
will be just and righteous solemnly and firmly to restore his holiday.
Indeed Rus is in no way inferior to any other Eastern people, for it too
had an apostle as its enlightener.

"We ought to send to the patriarch of Constantinople for his blessing,
assistance and advice. We should also send to the holy Mount Athos to
summon and bring back the venerable Rus, including the blessed Cyprian
and Ivan named Vishensky, and others who live there flourishing in life
and God's word. There is also a spiritual need to send any Rus sincerely
inclined to a virtuous life to Mount Athos, which is a school for religious
studies. If it is impossible to convert the papists, their cohorts and their
followers, that is to say the Arians, evangelicals and Lutherans, we must
at least attempt to seek out those Rus who abandoned us and the Eastern
church. The hierarchs are committed to this to save their souls, because
the gentry defectors tempt the innocent and grievously injure us." As the
Orthodox and their recently-restored bishops were developing this program it is not surprising that Uniates, especially the hierarchs, were disturbed by the proximity of such dangerous rivals. To undermine the
newly-forged bonds between Orthodoxy and the Greek Orthodox church

they spread rumors that the Orthodox meant to betray Poland and submit to the Turks.

THE STRUGGLE INTENSIFIES

Melety Smotritsky, ordained by Theophanes as bishop of Polotsk, wrote
a defense of his co-religionists. An abbreviated title of his work is *Verification of Innocence* [Wilno, 1621]. The Uniates responded with *A Great
Guilt* [Wilno, 1621] and an epistle to the monks at the monastery of the
church of the Holy Ghost in Wilno. Incidentally it should be noted that
the eminent Wilno Brotherhood split over the issue of church union. The
Trinity Brotherhood supported the Uniates and thereby was severely
weakened when, rejecting union, the majority of the brethren founded a
new brotherhood attached to the monastery of the Holy Ghost. An intense
conflict between the two brotherhoods ensued. The Holy Ghost Brotherhood issued a *Defense of the Verification* [Wilno, 1621]. It advanced the
position that the bishops must not accept their appointments from secular
authorities. This resolution was confirmed by the law of the Rus church,
according to which Rus joined Poles as equals. The law was ratified by the
Polish kings. The document also supported the right of the patriarch of
Constantinople to appoint Rus metropolitans and bishops because the canons of the ecumenical councils gave him jurisdiction over the Rus. The
Defense concludes as follows. "Our side entertains no thought of coercion. It entrusts its affairs to the Lord God and the just royal decree. In
God's church we learned to endure oppression, not to inflict it. The law
will not permit our people to be driven from city councils and the guilds,
or deprived of their liberties. Do not imagine that the laws of our homeland and world justice will deteriorate if your union falls. Terence's fool
Thraso also thought that when he fell the sky would fall with him.[28]
Should they begin to behave as you imply, the Rus would not be pacified. On the contrary they would be transformed into exiles in their native land. Then Lithuania would repay the Rus, and Poland the Greeks
(who enlightened Rus with the light of Christianity) in the same way that
the bad son repaid his good mother for her fine upbringing by thrusting
a knife into her heart." It also noted that Sviatopolk of Moravia,[29] after
accepting the Greek faith from Methodius, converted the Czech Mieszko
I and his wife Ludmila. Through the Czech queen Dubrovka the Polish
Mieszko accepted the Orthodox faith. In Lithuania Algirdas was married
to two Rus princesses. He accepted the Rus faith and baptized his two
sons into it.[30] Thus did religious polemics lead to historical inquiry.

BEYOND POLEMICS

The struggle was by no means confined to scholarship. When Patriarch Theophanes installed Melety Smotritsky as bishop of Polotsk nearly all inhabitants went over to his side. Then the Uniate bishop Josaphat Kuntsevich, a passionate, fanatical man, resorted to desperate measures to strengthen his position and that of the Uniate faith. His decision won him a stern reproach from the Lithuanian chancellor Leo Sapieha. Although Sapieha could not be accused of Orthodox bias, he recognized how politically damaging were Kuntsevich's actions against the brotherhood. Sapieha wrote to Kuntsevich on March 12, 1622 "There is no doubt that I sought church union, and to abandon it would be ill-advised, but it never occurred to me that you would employ such violent measures to effect it. Accusations against you in Poland and Lithuania expose your guilt. Are you oblivious to the grumbling of the foolish people who claim they would rather become Turkish subjects than endure this kind of religious persecution?

"According to you only some monks in the eparchies of Boretsky (the new Orthodox metropolitan in Kiev) and Smotritsky, together with a few of the Kievan gentry, oppose the union,[31] yet the entire Zaporozhian Host[32] has requested that the king confirm both Boretsky and Smotritsky in their eparchies, while you and your supporters are to be overthrown. For its part the Sejm has received complaints from nearly all of the Rus, not just the monks. Your actions spring more from vanity and personal loathing than love for 'your neighbor.' They can be seen as opposing the will of the clergy or even certain laws of the Commonwealth, and have produced the dangerous sparks which threaten us all either with a very dangerous flame or even an all-consuming conflagration.

"Obedient cossacks are far more useful to the government than your church union. That is why you must defer to the will of the king and the wishes of the crown in the knowledge that your own authority is limited, that your attempts to bring about something which goes against the public good and disturbs its peace might, in all fairness, be regarded as an insult to his majesty. If you dared attempt something like this in Rome or Venice you would soon be taught respect for government. You propose to return the fleeing sheep to the fold. They must be converted so that there might be one flock and one shepherd, wherein we must act judiciously, informing ourselves well about the circumstances of a time when everything depends upon free choice, especially in our homeland where the saying *enter by force* simply does not apply. As for the threats upon

your life, each of us is the cause of his own misfortune. Use the situation
to your advantage instead of blindly surrendering to your desires. You
claim that the bishops must be your exemplars. Indeed it is your duty to
emulate the holy bishops in suffering, piety and setting good example.
Read about the lives of the pious bishops where you will find no testimonies, no proclamations, lawsuits or legal witnesses. You on the other
hand have courts, town councils, tribunals, city halls and public offices
filled to overflowing with summons, litigations and denunciations. Not
only will this fail to strengthen church union, it will undo every last public
union of love in society.

"It is the duty of every sensible person to examine all avenues of
popular wisdom before taking up arms. You should not write barbed
comments to the administration, not respond with threats the way you do.
The apostles and saints never conducted themselves in this manner. You
say you have the right to cut up or drown non-Uniates. No! God's commandments unequivocally forbid vengeance, and this applies to you. You
write that not only the church union but the entire pious Roman clergy
are reproached at the Sejm. Who is to blame? When you violate the consciences of the people, when you seal their churches so that the people
die like infidels, without prayer, without Christian rites and without
church services, when you willfully abuse your power of grace and the
privileges granted you by the king, you do not seem to need us. Yet
whenever your abuses spark popular unrest which needs to be put down,
we are called upon to stop up the holes!

"Our opponents believe that we have entered into a conspiracy with
you to suppress the popular conscience and disturb the peace. This never
happened. It is enough that we are joined with you in a church union. You
would do well to tend and to cherish it in a calling to which you have
been summoned and which you should carry out in peace without sub-
jecting us to public loathing and yourself to censure and danger. You
demand that those who refuse to embrace church union be banished from
the realm. May God protect our fatherland from such extreme lawlessness! The holy Roman Catholic faith was well established in these regions before it acquired [in you] an imitator of piety and obedience to the
Holy Father, and up to that time was famous for its majesty and tranquility both within and outside our kingdom. Now, because it has embraced
a quarrelsome and restless friend, it suffers countless reproofs and dis-
sensions at every Sejm and at every public assembly.

"It seems that it would be preferable and more beneficial to our society if we simply cut our ties with this indefatigable ally [the Roman church], for never in our fatherland have we had such ferment as this specious union has generated. Jesus Christ never closed or sealed churches the way you do. 'There are,' you insist, 'decent priests among them [the Uniates]!' May God give us enough of them, but it is not enough for you to praise them because self-praise is always suspect. What is needed is for the infidels to recognize their good deeds and follow in their footsteps. Indeed I have heard about what kind of priests you confirm, those who destroy more than they create in the church.

"Closing and sealing churches and abusing people leads only to the pernicious destruction of fraternal harmony and mutual agreement. Show us whom you have won over, whom you have attracted with your severity, your harsh measures, your closing and sealing of churches? On the contrary, it is readily apparent that you have lost even those who followed you in Polotsk. You have transformed them from sheep into ugly goats,[33] you have brought danger to the crown and perhaps even ruin to us Catholics. Such are the fruits of your much-vaunted church union. If our homeland trembles I know not what will happen to it. You refer to the instructions of our supreme pastor yet if the Holy Father only could see the chaos your union has brought to our homeland doubtless he would support what you so forcefully resist.

"The king has ordered that the [Orthodox] churches in Mogilev be unsealed and opened. In accordance with his instructions I am writing to you in his matter. Should you fail to comply I myself will issue orders that they be opened and returned to the Orthodox. Jews and Muslims have their synagogues and mosques in the king's domains, yet you go around closing Christian churches. You say 'Is it fair to show such indulgence for the sake of some uncertain future peace?' I reply 'Not only is it fair, it is essential , because the more we oppress them in their faith the more inevitable will be social disorder.' Already there are rumors everywhere that they wish to break all ties with us forever. As far as the people of Polotsk and other plotters against you are concerned, this can happen. If the situation is as you describe, it is you who have brought them to this state of rebellion. The church union has alienated us from Novgorod Seversk, Starodub, Kozelets and many other cities and towns. It is primarily responsible for the Muscovite people drawing away from the king's son, as is shown by the letters that the Muscovites have sent to various nobles. We have no desire to see this pernicious union ruin us in the end."[34]

PAPAL DISPLEASURE

Kuntsevich's fears for his life soon came to pass. In November of 1623 the people of Vitebsk murdered him. It is easy to understand how this sorrowful event discredited the Orthodox, who until then could say "Our side never contemplates coercion." We can also understand how the opposition lost no time in exploiting the setback which the people of Vitebsk dealt their own cause by such a deed. The Uniates hastened to circulate the news of Kuntsevich's martyrdom throughout the Catholic land. It needed no special incentives, no exhortations from the Pope, who went against the opinion of Leo Sapieha and encouraged retaliation in the spirit of Kuntsevich.

Here is what Urban VIII[35] wrote to the king on February 10, 1624. "Our enemies do not sleep. Day and night the father of adversity sows noxious tares, so that instead of wheat, thorns might sprout in the garden of our church.[36] For our part, being no less diligent, we must pull out the poisonous roots and prune the useless branches, otherwise all countries will turn into wastelands, and those among them that should be gardens of paradise instead will turn into breeding grounds for venomous weeds and pastures for dragons.[37] Our present disasters show how easily this can happen in Rus. A schismatic heresy, uncompromising enemy of the Catholic religion and monster of profane dogmas, encroaches upon the neighboring provinces. It cunningly insinuates itself into cossack councils. Armed with the prowess of those most courageous warriors it pretends to defend the crown's interests and threatens the destruction of the one true faith. Rise up, O tsar [the Polish king is meant], you who are celebrated for defeating the Turks and despising the impious! Take up your arms and your shield, If the well-being of society requires it, use fire and sword to stamp out that pestilence.[38]

"News has reached us of some schismatic brotherhoods forming there, and new anti-Uniate laws enacted. Let the royal might, whose duty it is to defend the faith, curb these sacrilegious disturbances. Inasmuch as the impious tend to ignore threats not backed by punishment, it is up to your majesty to see to it that those wicked Rus pseudo-bishops, who strive to create discord and lord it over cossack camps, bear punishment befitting such impudent behavior. The patriarch of Jerusalem, torch of mutiny and leader of thieves, should feel the power of royal wrath. The example of his distress should serve to check the insolence of others. Although this seems to be a difficult business, what can devotion not overcome, guarded as it is by heaven and defended by royal might? The prominent Greek Nicephoros, who became the Devil's instrument and standard bearer of rebellion, churned up so many storms against the Rus Uniates that in the end he found himself interned in an eternal dungeon. Thus he showed by example that crime is not only heinous in and of itself, but inevitably leads to disastrous consequences. If the impertinent schismatics see examples like this frequently enough they will cease to assert themselves so haughtily, and will learn to fear the God of wrath. With this in mind we beseech your majesty to defend this cause with all of your enthusiasm and authority, and above all to give Uniate bishops free access to your court and royal council, that they shall be in no way inferior to other bishops."

At the same time Urban wrote about Kuntsevich's murder. "Who will give our eyes the wellspring of tears, that we might mourn the brutality of the schismatics and the death of the bishop of Polotsk. Where so brutal a crime cries out for revenge, cursed be the man who keeps his sword from spilling blood. This applies to you, O most powerful of kings! You must not shrink from fire and sword. Let the heretics learn that punishment inevitably follows crime. Indeed, in the face of such loathsome crime, it would be cruel to show mercy." The Pope was not satisfied with writing letters to the king, he also wrote to many bishops and laymen, demanding that Orthodox bishops be persecuted, and warning that their cossack connections would bring them misfortune.

VENGEANCE EXACTED

Leo Sapieha, recent accuser of Kuntsevich, now found it necessary to accept the chairmanship of the commission named to try Kuntsevich's murderers. The members of the commission arrived in Vitebsk, surrounded by an army of foot soldiers and cavalry for protection from the cossacks, to whom the inhabitants of Vitebsk turned for help. Within three days the commission wound up its affairs. Two bailiffs and eighteen other citizens ended up on the executioner's block, and their property was confiscated. About one hundred citizens, having saved themselves by flight, received the death sentence *in absentia* and lost their property. The town was stripped of its privileges and its fortifications were levelled. The bells which sounded the tocsin summoning the people to rise up against their bishop were pulled down. Two Orthodox churches were demolished. Yosif Rutsky, Uniate bishop of Kiev, concluded his report to Cardinal Bandino about this operation with an observation. "After this," he wrote "a great fear overtook the schismatics. They began to understand that whenever the senators have the *desire* to implement royal directives, they will not be cowed by show of cossack might.

COSSACK DEFENDERS OF ORTHODOXY

The cossack name was on the lips of both the Pope and the Uniate metropolitan. Whereas earlier it was the Ostrozhskys and the Tyshkeviches, the cossacks now became known as the principal defenders of Orthodoxy. We saw how badly cossack matters ended at the close of the sixteenth century. Somewhat later we find in reports in the Western Rus chronicle about cossack actions of a kind that were bound to discredit them in the eyes of the populace. Under the year 1601, for example, the chronicle records the following. There were four thousand Zaporozhian Cossacks in Sweden. Their hetman was Samuilo [Samiylo] Kishka, and he was killed in that country.[39] The cossacks did no good in Sweden, they were of no use either to the hetman or the king. All they did on behalf of the Rus was to cause unimaginable damage to Polotsk, and devastate the renowned city of Vitebsk. They took huge quantities of silver and gold, butchered prominent citizens and committed sodomy worse than anything the Tatars could have imagined.

This account was entered for the year 1603. There were Zaporozhian Cossacks. Some sort of hetman called Ivan Kutska[40] and four thousand men extracted protection payments from the Borkubalov and Shupensk settlements, fifty kopa [grosh] of cash, five hundred measures of rye and so forth. In Mogilev that same year Ivan Kutska surrendered this hetmanship because there was so much anarchy in the ranks. Everyone did as he pleased. An emissary came from the king to cajole and threaten the cossacks not to engage in violence in towns and villages. One townsman brought a six-year-old girl in his arms to the emissary. She had been raped and beaten half to death. It was grievous and shocking to behold. The people wept and prayed to the Savior to destroy forever such ungovernable men. As the cossacks made their way back to their camp they inflicted huge losses on towns and villages along the way, taking many women, girls, children and horses with them.[41] A single cossack might take as many as eight, ten or twelve horses, three or four children, as well as three or four women and girls.

COSSACK EXPLOITS

About that time Petro Konashevich Sahaidachny, with whom we are already familiar,[42] a highly intelligent and skillful military leader and member of the [Rus] gentry by origin, received the title of hetman. To avoid a quarrel with the government, that is to say with the nobles, he tried to separate the affairs of the cossacks from those of the common people. "Konashevich," remarks one chronicler, "always lived in peace with the landowners. That is why the cossacks had such an easy time of it. Only the common folk suffered greatly." Sahaidachny also served the Polish government well in war. He marched on Moscow in support of Władysław and fought with both Turks and Tatars. In 1621 his cossacks played a key role in the celebrated battle of Khotin in which Poland was saved from an invasion by Sultan Osman who, as we saw earlier, was expected to ally himself with the Muscovites in the war.[43] This was Sahaidachny's final heroic deed. He was seriously wounded, withdrew to Kiev in 1621, and died there the following year.

Although he served the Polish king and maintained peaceful relations with the nobility, Sahaidachny believed that it was in his best interest to offer his services to the Muscovite tsar as well. In 1620 an emissary from Sahaidachny, Ataman Peter Odinets [Otaman Petro Odynets] and his comrades appeared in Moscow to declare "We are here in the name of the entire Zaporozhian Host, Hetman Sahaidachny and his comrades with a petition for the tsar. We request the right to serve the great sovereign as we once served his mighty predecessors, marching against their enemies and destroying their Crimean encampments. Even now the cossacks serve the great sovereign. Some five thousand strong, they attacked the Tatar encampments and fought the Tatars on this side of Perekop, close to its wall. There were about seven thousand Tatars there and eleven thousand more were waiting at the town gate. With God's grace and the tsar's good fortune, they defeated a multitude of Tatars and liberated numerous Christians held captive. Now they come before the great sovereign to offer their services and Tatar informants. God and the tsar's majesty are free to decide their fate, but they are of one mind in wishing to pledge themselves to the service of his majesty, and wish to seek his favor now and forever."

Praising them for their performance, the conciliar secretary[44] Gramotin[45] said "Here in the Muscovite realm a rumor has circulated that the Polish king Sigismund came to an agreement with the Turks for peace

and friendship, yet he wishes to attack their faith. Would they reveal how
he expects to handle the Turk? What about the Pope and the [Holy Ro-
man] emperor? Have the Poles no such design on their faith?" The
Cherkasy[46] responded "The Polish king has no designs on us. He is at
peace with the Turk, and we Zaporozhians are forbidden to move against
them from the Dnieper delta to the Black Sea. There are, however, no
restrictions upon our moving out to sea by way of smaller rivers. We
know nothing of any emperor or Pope, nor have we been forbidden to
conduct raids upon Crimea. In the spring we are all going to Zaporozhie
to pay our homage to his majesty, asking him to receive us into his service." The tsar sent Sahaidachny three hundred rubles as a small reward,
and wrote in the accompanying letter "Henceforth, depending upon your
service, we will not neglect to reward you, but at this time we shall not
send you against any Crimean camps. The Crimean khan Janibek-Girey
is not at war with our realm, nor do our people attack Crimean settlements."

Despite Sahaidachny's excellent relations with the nobility, the cossacks were not fully reconciled with the Polish realm. The question as to
whether the cossacks should be condoned or annihilated assumed great
urgency. As we have seen, that issue was posed in the treaty concluded
at Smolensk between the Russian Tushinites[47] and King Sigismund.[48] In
1617 peace with the Turks came. Its conditions included a promise from
the Poles to prohibit cossacks from sailing the Black Sea. Just like the
Don Cossacks, the Dnieper Cossacks could not refrain from cannibaliz-
ing Turkish ships since this was, when all was said and done, the source
of their livelihood.[49] Such actions caused them to undermine the existing
peace. That is why the question of whether or not the cossacks should be
allowed to exist as a force was raised once more.

In 1618 the prominent Polish author Palczowski determined to write
a book, *The Cossacks. Should they be Abolished or Not?,* to which the
author responds in the negative. In his opinion to annihilate the cossacks
as a force would be *dishonest, useless* and *impossible. Dishonest,* because
it would mean catering to the demands of the Turkish enemy and destroying a Christian force at a time when Rus was being regarded by the courts
of Europe as the one bulwark protecting the Christian world. *Useless,*
because instead of cossacks as neighbors we would have Turks and
Tatars. Which is preferable? *Impossible,* because as far back as King
Stefan's time the cossacks were threatened with destruction, yet even then
this was impossible, so the project was abandoned. There were far fewer

cossacks then than there are now. "To those who would suggest that they be destroyed just as once the Teutonic knights were destroyed, I say 'Poland struggled with the German Order for two hundred years before it conquered them. Anyone who suggests that we begin a two-hundred-year war with the cossacks to rid ourselves of them should be banished.'"

METROPOLITAN BORETSKY

After Sahaidachny's death religious unrest escalated. The struggle between Uniate and Orthodox bishops, increased persecution of the Orthodox faithful and the murder of their main oppressor Kuntsevich all combined to heighten cossack visibility as a force for the defense of Orthodoxy. This was all the more true after the Orthodox church acquired, in the person of Metropolitan Job Boretsky[50] an energetic leader quite unlike Onisifor Devochka or Mikhail Rogoza. Boretsky appreciated the profound significance of the people's lament which so troubled Sapieha. "Better a Turkish prison than such oppression!" Boretsky of course had no intention of entering a Turkish prison. He had the cossacks at hand and Moscow in sight. At the end of 1624 an uprising erupted in Kiev. The mayor of the city, Fedor [Fedir] Khodyka, and the townsman Sozon took it into their heads to close all Orthodox churches. The metropolitan immediately so informed the Zaporozhian hetman Kolenik Andreev [Kolenyk Andriiv], and the entire Host. The hetman sent the two colonels Yakim Chigirinets [Yakym Chyhyrynets] and Anton Lazarenko to Kiev with instructions to join the local cossacks in the areas around the city, and together proceed thence prepared to defend the Christian faith. The colonels complied. Arriving in Kiev in 1625, immediately after Epiphany, they opened the churches and seized Khodyka along with those townsmen who supported him in his anti-Orthodox designs.

Of course these actions did Boretsky no good in the eyes of the Polish government. Moreover in February 1625 Bishop Isaky of Lutsk arrived in Moscow from the metropolitan of Kiev with a request that the sovereign take Little Russia [Ukraine][51] under his exalted protection and forgive the cossacks for their transgressions. "Your speech indicates," the boyars charged, "that you have not thought this matter through, that all your ideas lack fixation. You claim that there are too few cossacks to withstand the Poles without reinforcements, yet you say that now the Zaporozhian Host has decided to attack the Turks by sea next spring. If you continue to endure religious persecution, and are able to unite and strengthen your resolve against the Poles, then so inform the sovereign and his holiness the patriarch.[52] Both his majesty and his holiness will consider how best to liberate the Orthodox confession, our church and all of you from these heretics."

"Our resolve is strong," Isaky assured the boyars, "we will rejoice in the sovereign's grace and seek his protection. We shall discuss this amongst ourselves, but for the moment we fear that if the Poles move on us any time soon his majesty will be our only hope. If the metropolitan, the bishops and the Zaporozhian Host turn to his majesty for assistance, and pay the sovereign a visit, he should graciously welcome them, not reject or cast them out, for they have nowhere else to turn."

The conduct of the cossacks in Kiev along with their interference in Crimean affairs, where they supported a khan unfriendly to the Turks, and the resulting complaints from the sultan all moved the Polish hetman Stanisław Koniecpolski[53] to enter Rus at the end of September 1625. He arrived with thirty thousand of his own troops and three thousand of the emperor's German soldiers. A rumor spread among the Rus that Koniecpolski came to decimate the cossacks after which he intended to introduce the Roman confession to Kiev and the Lithuanian lands. In Kanev [Kaniv] and Cherkasy the Poles killed many cossacks and razed their towns. Leaving Cherkasy, Koniecpolski moved his forces to within ten versts south of Krylov [Kryliv]. The Zaporozhian Host massed on the opposite bank of the Dnieper where they were joined by about twenty thousand town cossacks,[54] and the colonels Doroshenko, Izmail, Olifer [Olyfer], with Pirsky [Pyrsky], who had been their hetman back in Zaporozhie. Now Izmail assumed that office.[55] On October 26 the Poles routed the cossacks, who retreated to the shores of Lake Kurkove with the Poles once again giving chase. This time there were heavy losses on the Polish side, including a number of prominent individuals, and numerous horses. The cossack defeat had even weightier implications. Seeing no way of holding on, his forces overthrew Izmail, elected Doroshenko hetman and commenced negotiations with Koniecpolski.

POLISH TRIUMPH

A commission headed by Koniecpolski assembled in the woods of Medvezhi Lozy, and accused the cossacks of the following violations. (1) Disobedience to the Polish Commonwealth as demonstrated by the frequent sea raids which provoked the Turks to wage war against Poland. What is more, the cossacks launched a sea raid at the very time the distinguished Polish emissary, the lord equerry of the crown, was assuring the sultan that the cossacks would not disturb him again. (2) Relations and exchanges of envoys with Muscovy which, except for one brief truce, did not give the Poles a reliable peace. The Zaporozhian Host referred to the Muscovite ruler by the title of "tsar," conducted relations with the Crimean Shagin-Girey without the knowledge of the Commonwealth, concluded a truce and rendered him assistance. (3) Receiving ecclesiastical dignitaries (for example the patriarch of Jerusalem) as well as various frauds called Turkish kinglets and Wallachian lordlings.[56] (4) Ignoring royal authority, the cossacks install new metropolitans and bishops while the old ones still live. (5) Subjects of the nobility or royal officials refuse to obey their lords, and join the cossacks to attack their masters as though they were thieves. They usurp their land, seize their wealth and appropriate the profits of prominent people. (6) During a recent cossack raid on Kiev for no reason at all the cossacks murdered a city official, a fine man as well as a priest of their own confession. They threw others into prison, demanded bail for them and seized their property. They maliciously attacked a Kievan monastery, appropriated its property and built a farm on its land. They humiliated a deputy of the Polish provincial administration and subjected people of various ranks, spiritual and secular, citizens and Jews, to unparalleled mortifications.

These accusations elicited the following demands. (1) All commanders in Turkish campaigns during the time that the lord equerry of the crown was negotiating with the Turks, as well as those guilty of the Kiev murders and raids on the homes of nobles in Boguslav and Korsun, were to be executed. (2) Deputies to Moscow be required to reveal under oath the reasons for their journeys there, and turn over to the commissioners their charters from the Muscovite tsar. (3) The cossacks disclose what they did with Tsarik Akhia.[57] (4) The cossacks burn their boats in the presence of the commissioner's representatives. (5) Henceforth not a single Zaporozhian Cossack put out to sea, whether by the Dnieper or the Don. (6) Inasmuch as retainers escape from their landlords and craftsmen from their crafts to join the cossacks, and by their unruly behavior tarnish cossack glory, the king would not condone any increase of their ranks. The names and domiciles of all cossacks were to be recorded in a single register, to be submitted under the supervision of a senior official to the king's exchequer. (7) The cossacks obey the senior officer appointed from amongst them by the crown hetman in accordance with the king's will. For the time being the hetman confirmed Doroshenko. (8) The cossacks not interfere in the management and administration of villages

COSSACK VESSELS

D.I. Evarnytsky, *Istoriia zaporozhskikh kozakov*. Vol. 1, St. Petersburg, 1892

or counties. (9) Cossacks accused of coercion by persons of any rank must immediately be placed on trial. (10) Cossacks charged with a crime to be judged by hundredmen[58] in the presence of a deputy commissioner of the local police, or some other rural official. In the event of a cossack complaint against a non-cossack, the latter is to be tried by a deputy commissioner of the local police, or some other local official, and cossacks tried in their own courts. (11) Cossacks must not meet with foreign rulers, conclude agreements with them, or enter into their service.

To these charges and demands the cossacks responded in this way. (1) While the crown equerry was meeting the Turkish sultan we apprehended and sent to the Sejm for punishment individuals in positions of leadership during the campaign against the Turks even before being instructed to do so. (2) We dispatched our representatives to Moscow in accordance with an old custom, that Moscow might continue to send us funds. As for our relationship with Shagin-Girey, our comrades were cast ashore on the Crimean lands when they sailed to the Don hunting for spoils. Shagin-Girey took these hungry men into his service, and eventually returned them to us along with the Christians taken captive. Moreover Shagin-Girey promised to make peace with the Polish king, and it seemed to us that this matter should not be put off. (3) The king long knew about the patriarch and other clerics, and together with our clergy we already have justified ourselves before him. (4) As for the arrival of kinglets from Turkey and Moscow, and the lordlings from Wallachia, we accept no responsibility for this because people with all kinds of titles have been welcome to come and go to and from this area below the rapids [Zaporozhie] since time immemorial. (5) It is our duty to punish and exact penalties from those accused of plundering and raiding. (6) In light of what is happening in the principality of Lithuania, in Belorussia, in Volhynia and Podolia, the persecution that the churches of our ancient Greek religion endure, what with their priests being forbidden to hold services and driven from their parishes which then are turned over to the Uniates, we respond to the charges made by the mayor of Kiev, the priest and the rest, that we are simply forestalling the possibility of such a fate for ourselves. Incited by that priest, the mayor of Kiev not only sealed churches and appropriated their incomes, he anathematized the metropolitan and us. In view of such occurences should we have endured the suffering? We ask your worships to judge. (7) The land confiscated from the Kiev monastery did not belong to it, rather to the church of St. Basil. (8) In Korsun and Boguslav we avenged the shedding of Christian blood.

(9) Tsarik Akhia came from goodness knows where and went goodness knows where. (10) We are ready to burn our boats as soon as we receive compensation for them. (11) In exchange for gifts [bribes] the noble officials allowed anyone who wished to run away and join us. Thus we accumulated a multitude of tradesmen. At this time we are prepared to disassociate ourselves from those unfit for military combat.

"The commission has determined that henceforth the cossacks shall answer only to the leader comfirmed by the king and crown hetman. If he fails to fulfill his obligations the cossacks will petition the king and crown hetman to have him replaced. They will do the same in the event of his death, but if the cossacks are on a campaign distant from the king and hetman they are allowed to elect a leader from amongst themselves, and turn over all authority to him until such time as the king and crown hetman shall ratify their choice."

The form of the oath of confirmation pronounced by the leaders was as follows. "I, Mikhail Doroshenko, swear to the Almighty God and One in the Trinity that in my office I shall defend with loyalty and obedience his majesty the Polish king Sigismund III, his successors and the republic of Poland in accordance with the will of his majesty, observing all injunctions of the king and the republic, curbing all willfulness and insubordination. That is to say, neither personally nor through others shall I attack or wage war on the Turkish emperor, either by land or by sea, unless his royal highness and the republic so will it. On the contrary, should anyone from the army of his majesty which has been entrusted to me or any outsider decide to do so and I learn of it, I shall apprise his majesty and the crown hetman, and actively rebuff such violators of the king's will. I shall neither summon nor muster any standing battalions without his majesty's authorization but shall pursue such formations as duty requires. Also I and my entire force shall observe in their minutest details all agreements entered in the commission's records at Medvezhi Lozy."

Details of the agreement were these. The number of registered cossacks shall stand at six thousand. They are entitled to all rights guaranteed by the previous Polish rulers and the present King Sigismund. They may earn their livelihood by engaging in trade, fishing and hunting, but without damaging the forests and fields belonging to the administration and its governor. In addition the crown shall pay them sixty thousand zlotys annually. Of the six thousand registered cossacks, one thousand or more shall be stationed beyond the rapids to monitor enemy movements.

If the leader himself goes to Zaporozhie he shall leave someone qualified in his place. Cossacks are not to go out to sea by way of the Dnieper to engage any neighboring power in combat, hence all boats shall be burned in the presence of the commissioners. No cossack may reside on the land of his former landlord unless he is prepared to obey him, otherwise that cossack is given twelve weeks to leave his home and his land. The cossack army shall not interfere in any affairs not under its jurisdiction. Under no circumstances shall cossacks enter into an alliance with a neighboring land, receive any ambassadors or join the service of foreign rulers.

Upon concluding his commission Koniecpolski left for Bar, and the nobles who were with him dispersed to their estates. The crown hetman left Colonel Kazanowski with fifteen thousand troops as his deputy in Rus, stationing them in Vasilkov, Trepolie, Orzhishchy, Staiki, Khvostov and Kiev. Together with the Polish commissioners Doroshenko visited cossack towns, reorganizing troops and reducing their numbers. The town cossacks obeyed Doroshenko because the finest among them supported the hetman. Those denied entry into the restructured ranks planned to petition Tsar Michael Fedorovich to receive them, to assist them with his own troops in their stand against the Poles. They in turn would serve the tsar, and clear the Lithuanian towns in his name in order to preserve their Orthodox faith.

TURKISH PRETENDER

After their defeat at the hands of Koniecpolski the cossacks were too weakened for any major enterprise. Their defeat deprived Job Boretsky of all hope of using the cossacks to foment an Orthodox rebellion in Turkey in the name of the pretender to the Turkish throne. The latter presented himself as prince of the sultan's bloodline and, at the same time, a Christian of the Greek confession. We saw that the Polish commissioners engaged in talks with the cossacks about a certain kinglet Akhia. At the end of 1625 there appeared in Moscow from Zaporozhie a cossack named Ivan Giria. He arrived with some friends and the Macedonian Mark Fedorov. They were dispatched to Tsar Michael from Alexander Akhia, who represented himself as a Turkish prince, the son of Sultan Mohammed. Alexander claimed that he was taken out of Turkey by his Greek mother Elena. He had spent time at the courts of the Byzantine emperor,[59] the duke of Florence and the Spanish king, and now sought the help of the Muscovite sovereign in stirring up the Zaporozhian Cossacks against the Turks.

Alexander informed Michael that during the coming spring he wished to enter Greece by sea and land. There a large military force of one hundred and thirty thousand Orthodox Bulgarians, Serbs, Albanians and Greeks awaited him. The conciliar secretary Gramotin told the emissaries that the sovereign wished Prince Alexander well, and hoped that God would look with favor upon his attempts to reclaim the realm of his fathers. Personally he could be of no help to the prince because Alexander now resided in Lithuania among the Zaporozhian Cherkasy.[60] They owed allegiance to the Polish king, who was no friend to the sovereign. Moreover assistance to a foreign realm was now out of the question. Nor could his majesty approve a charter for Prince Alexander because, if he learned that the prince was seeking help from his majesty, the king would give Alexander no quarter. Nevertheless as a sign of his affection his royal majesty was sending Prince Alexander a gift of sables, foxes and velvet shot with gold thread to the value of one thousand rubles.

In December of 1625 the governor of Putivl informed Moscow that approximately thirty thousand cossacks joined Alexander in Zaporozhie, but as soon as news reached them that Hetman Koniecpolski was marching on Kiev to attack, dissension appeared within the cossack ranks. They left Zaporozhie, scattered to various Lithuanian [sic] towns and began to marshal their forces against Koniecpolski. On September 1 Prince Alexander and four of his followers left Zaporozhie for Lithuanian territory and arrived in Kiev. Metropolitan Job concealed Alexander from the Poles in the Archangel monastery by dressing him in monastic garb, in defiance of Koniecpolski's strict orders that the prince must be found at all costs. In November Job secretly sent Alexander to Muscovy, instructing him to pass himself off as a merchant bound for Putivl.

When the Muscovites discovered that Alexander was in Putivl his majesty [the tsar] demanded that his boyars seriously consider the matter. They debated the matter and responded "This is a new, an unprecedented affair. If we receive Prince Alexander will we not invite retaliation from the Turkish and Crimean peoples? We do not know the prince's motives for going to Putivl. Is he fleeing from the Poles, or have they sent him to sow discord between our sovereign and the ruler of the Turks? Yet to arrest Alexander and turn him over to the Turkish sultan Mohammed in exchange for a permanent peace, simply to avoid attacks on the sovereign's borderlands by the Crimeans, is a dangerous business. For this we risk offending God by sending a Christian man to his death. Nobody can predict God's righteous judgment. What if Alexander does turn out to be a true son of Sultan Mohammed who was baptized in a normal fashion into the Orthodox faith, and spent time in numerous countries where no harm ever came to him? Should we decide to turn him over we can only hope that this will not anger God, or offend the Greeks and all who rely on Alexander, or leave ourselves open to ultimate destruction at the hands of the Turks. We also must consider the potential for reproaches from foreign rulers for turning over a Christian to infidels."

On December 17 the sovereign, with the boyars' concurrence, issued orders to send a nobleman to Putivl. He was to take Alexander to Mtsensk and leave him there for the time being. Ten musketeers would be assigned to guard him.

Patriarch Filaret gave the following instructions to the guards. "If Alexander seeks entry to the church, you may admit him only as far as the refectory, which has not been consecrated. Should he insist upon going into the church itself, you will answer that this is forbidden because, having cultivated a forelock, he now is considered a Pole.[61] In the Russian realm Poles are forbidden to attend our church." Alexander petitioned the tsar for permission to join the Don Cossacks, whence he would journey by way of the Danube to Wallachian territory, Bulgaria and other countries, all of which recognized his sovereignty. He also asked that the tsar instruct the Don Cossacks to give him assistance. If Michael refused him permission to enter the service of the Don Cossacks he asked to be allowed to join the Germans travelling by way of Novgorod or Archangel so that he might eventually reach the duke of Florence.

The tsar issued instructions that Alexander be warned about cossacks living on the Don, who were free and paid scant attention to his commands. They were also small in number, and incapable of waging much of a war on the Turks. Moreover between him and the Turkish sultan there existed love, peace and diplomatic relations. Alexander was sent out of the country by way of Archangel. In 1637 he appeared in Russia once again. He sent a letter to the Don Cossacks inviting them and the Zaporozhian Cossacks to confer with him in Chernigov [Chernihiv]. The rest of his adventure remains shrouded in mystery.

HETMAN DOROSHENKO

In the meantime under Doroshenko's leadership the registered cossacks also showed little inclination to honor the Medvezhi Lozy agreement. Their boats continued to appear on the Black Sea. At the beginning of

1626 the khan of Crimea attacked Ukraine. The Poles demanded that Doroshenko, together with his own retinue, meet with them in a council. Doroshenko had departed already but a deputy from the khan intercepted him in Bolshie Priluki. He reminded the hetman that the cossacks and the Tatars were at peace, cemented by an oath. The cossacks ought not to ally with the Poles. This caused Doroshenko to turn back. For their part Hetman Olifer and his Zaporozhian Cossacks went over to the khan, and together with him campaigned against Poland.

In 1627 the Polish king sent one of his noblemen to Doroshenko, instructing the hetman to have all his cossacks ready by spring for an attack on the Swedish king. The hetman summoned a council in Kanev, during which the cossacks responded to the king's representative "We will not attack the Swedish monarch because the Polish king and his lord councillors have deprived us of all means of income, and have prohibited sea raids. This has impoverished us, leaving us without the necessary resources for an uprising against the king of Sweden." They appointed emissaries to meet with the Polish king and his nobles to request that cossack forces be brought up to a strength of ten thousand, and be issued money and fabric sufficient to outfit these men.

In 1628 Doroshenko was killed in Crimea, where he was involved in local factional strife. Grigory Cherny[62] was appointed to replace him, but because of his pro-Polish sentiments and, according to rumor, his acceptance of the Uniate confession, he did not appeal to the cossacks. In 1630 the [Polish] government posted its troops in and around the district of Kiev. Another rumor, allegedly started by the archimandrite of the Kievan Caves monastery, Peter Mogila, began to circulate, according to which the troops were dispatched to destroy the cossacks and their Orthodox faith. In their outrage over this news the cossacks killed their leader Grigory Cherny, and proclaimed as their new commander one Taras.[63] Koniecpolski decided to attack and engaged them near Pereiaslav.

The course of this war, both in Little Russian [Ukrainian] and Polish reports, has been portrayed somewhat enigmatically. Although the cossacks gained the upper hand over Koniecpolski they chose to surrender Taras to the Poles for execution in Warsaw. The Putivl citizen Gladky, already known to us, described the affair as follows. "Hetman Koniecpolski besieged the cossacks at Pereiaslav. Within a period of three weeks the Poles and Cherkasy fought numerous battles which the cossacks kept winning. In the final battle the cossacks seized the Polish hetman's retinue from his own camp, killed numerous Poles, took over the crossing points on the Dnieper and burned the ferries.

"Following that battle the Rus were reconciled with Koniecpolski. He had marched against them for their disobedience, charging that they willfully stormed Turkish towns. At the same time the entire army took part in the execution of Grishka [Hrytsko] Cherny, whom Koniecpolski earlier named to be their hetman. Having reconciled with the Rus, Koniecpolski appointed another hetman from their midst, Timokha [Tymish] Arandarenko. Koniecpolski himself had eight thousand men, Poles, Germans and the finest of the Zaporozhian Cossacks who had crossed over to the Poles, whereas the Cherkasy [Zaporozhians] numbered only seven thousand." This report yields one important detail with respect to that affair, the presence of the *superior* Rus in the Polish army. It is quite conceivable that it was they who manipulated events in such a way as to cause Taras to be turned over to the Poles, to deprive the rank-and-file of all benefit from the uprising.

COSSACK-POLISH WARS

As early as 1631 the cossacks replaced Arandarenko by electing Ivan Petrizhitsky-Kulaga. Meanwhile they continued to raid the Turkish Black Sea shore. Together with the Muscovites the sultan assembled an army against Poland, but Moscow's defeat at Smolensk convinced him to follow suit and seek an accord with Poland. The ensuing peace stipulated that the Polish government attempt to clear all islands in the Dnieper of cossacks. To facilitate this operation, in 1635 Crown Hetman Koniecpolski constructed the fortress of Kodak on the Dnieper, just below Samara and Kniazhy island [also known as Kniahynyn or Kniaginin].[64] That same year, on their way back from sea under Sulima's leadership, the cossacks destroyed the fortress.[65] With the help of the registered cossacks still loyal to Poland, Sulima was captured and executed.

FERMENT

The following year saw much unrest in Rus, and a protagonist whom we shall encounter frequently henceforth, appeared as a representative of the Polish crown. His name was Adam Kisel [Kisil, Kysil], crown vice-chancellor from Chernigov.[66] He came from a prominent Rus family which still worshipped in the ancient Rus faith. Because of this Kisel inclined towards Rus, towards the Rus people, and opposed church union. Yet as a wealthy and prominent landowner in Rus he viewed the inhabitants of his lands through elitist eyes. He was quite incapable of sympathizing with the cossack rank-and-file. Although they too were defenders of Orthodoxy, their primary loyalty was to the peasants and the serfs, yet many of them rejected the life of rustics and fled to the cossacks. This was something which the nobleman Kisel could not accept easily, so he constantly found himself between two fires.[67] Because he was an Orthodox Rus the Polish government deliberately used him as its commissioner or intermediary in its contacts with the cossacks.

In August of 1636 the cossacks in Pereiaslav were in a state of ferment, driven to exasperation by the son of their Rus governor. They decided to set out for Zaporozhie, and from there to put to sea, but their officers did not rebel and Kisel, the crown's commissioner to the cossacks, sided with the latter. The cossacks confronted their officers, shouting that their pay was sent in May. Now it was August and they had yet to see it. They also shouted that the government oppressed them. Kisel convinced the rank-and-file to wait four weeks, then promptly wrote to the king (on August 6) about the matter, pointing out that in many areas the cossacks indeed were being oppressed.

On August 25 he also wrote to Hetman Koniecpolski listing three things that he considered wrong with the insubordinate cossack army. (1) Notwithstanding their love for the Greek religion and its clergy, when it comes to their religiosity the cossacks behave more like Tatars than Christians. (2) Among the cossacks fear is far more effective than the dispensation of favors. (3) Their rapaciousness.

As a result, Kisel convinced the metropolitan to send two members of the clergy to persuade the cossacks not to rebel against the republic. The officers, added Kisel, needed to be kept in line with gifts, and the rank-and-file by fear.

The spring of 1637 was a time of more ferment, even after the royal commissioners finally arrived with the cossacks' pay, and prepared to administer the oath of loyalty. The rank-and-file declared that they had no intention of swearing such an oath, because they preferred Zaporozhie. The commissioners urged them to reconsider, warning the cossacks that they were endangering themselves. Without a doubt the republic would wipe them off the face of the earth, for its leaders would sooner see wild beasts and a wasteland on the Dnieper than such a mutinous mob. "Your present actions," declared the commissioners, "might begin with obstinacy, but they will not end in rebellion. Go to Zaporozhie if you must, but you cannot take the women and children. Indeed you yourselves will not be able to survive there for long. Once again you will place your heads under the republican saber. Rethink your choices and stop making empty threats about betraying us and moving elsewhere. The Dnieper is your homeland. You will not find another like it. The Don cannot compare with the Dnieper, and the lack of freedom there cannot compare with the freedom that you enjoy here. A cossack without the Dnieper is like a fish without water. You should swear permanent allegiance to him who owns that river."

Listening to these sentiments about the Dnieper, the cossacks burst into tears. Their hetman, Tomilenko, whom the commissioners considered a simple if sober and modest man, refused to continue in office. Nevertheless the cossacks elected him once again, agreed not to abandon the republic, and kissed the cross.

It was an ephemeral peace. Kisel wrote that the situation in Rus was critical, for the cossacks are like a beast without a head (Bellua sine capite), a flock without a shepherd. In his opinion a leader capable of taking charge was indispensable, one able to douse a conflagration that a single spark might ignite. He must be duty bound to avert conflicts between the cossacks and the crown officials, to settle any disturbance the moment it threatened. He must be responsible for distributing the wages, be empowered to strike a rebel from the register and possess the financial means to attract loyal followers, who would oppose rebels. "It is essential," wrote Kisel, "that the cossack leaders be senior officers in name only, that real power belong to such a leader, whatever his title."

REBELLION AND RETRIBUTION

Despite disaffection and unrest among the cossacks there was no uprising in Rus. It flared up in the sparsely settled South Niz, under the leadership of Pavlik [Pavlyk or Pavliuha]. He came secretly from Zaporozhie seizing artillery from Cherkasy along the way.[68] All the rabble in Rus, the grave diggers, the field watchmen, the shepherds, especially those from Prince Wiśniowiecki's lands and from the other side of the Dnieper [the Left Bank], all such folks [pejorative connotation in the original] rose up and joined him. Accusing their hetman Tomilenko of weakness in the face of such license, the registered cossacks convened a council, overthrew him and elected Savva Kononovich.[69] The new hetman's subsequent actions reflected the spirit of the men who elected him, and paralleled those of the government. He tried to persuade the rebels to suspend their rebellions. Then Pavlik and the other leader of the uprising,

Skidan,[70] appeared in Pereiaslav. They convened an assembly and, taking advantage of their majority, murdered Savva Kononovich. Not wishing to break openly with the government, once more they appealed to Koniecpolski to persuade the crown to set aside anger. They described Kononovich as someone unfit for the office of hetman, a foreigner, indeed a Muscovite. "Obey the leader whom the king assigns to you," Koniecpolski replied, "not one who would assume that privilege on his own. Burn all boats and suspend the sea raids. Only thus shall you win back the king's favor."

Such exhortations did not find favor with Pavlik and his cossack followers. On October 11, 1637 there appeared a manifesto calling on the Rus to rise up. It stated that the enemies of Rus and their ancient Greek faith, that is the Liakhs, were coming to Rus to exterminate the army [the cossacks] and all subjects of the king, of the princes and the nobles, to defile women and enslave children. Indeed the Poles did appear from Bratslav province under the leadership of Governor Potocki.[71] They engaged the cossacks near Kumeiki on December 8. Despite their desperate valor the Cossacks were routed. About three thousand were slaughtered in their field camp, yet not one pleaded for mercy, shouting instead that they were prepared to die for one another. Whenever a Pole fell from his horse, cossacks descended upon his corpse and hacked it to bits.

During the night Pavlik and Skidan escaped, but when morning came Potocki caught up with them in Borovitsa. He surrounded them and opened fire. For his part Adam Kisel [still acting as mediator] advised the cossacks to surrender Pavlik and other instigators of the rebellion, promising amnesty for the rest. Pavlik and Tomilenko were turned over to the Poles while Skidan escaped. Once Pavlik was surrendered to the Poles, the cossacks elected a new hetman, whereupon Potocki made it clear to them that their rebellion had cost them everything. He issued orders for the newly-elected hetman to relinquish his mace, staff and seal, insisting that the existing colonels be discharged, and replacements appointed. Iliash Karaimovich became the new leader.[72] In addition to the main army, which had been under Pavlik's command, there remained a detachment led by Kizimenko[73] who took Lubny, butchered a few nobles and some Bernardine monks, then threw their corpses to the dogs. Kizimenko was captured by Potocki who ordered him impaled "because," as he wrote from Nezhin on January 8, 1638, "there is no point in taking any of them to Warsaw simply to stage a pageant. Better to execute them here, where they committed their crimes." In the end, over the protests of Kisel, Pavlik and four of his companions were taken to Warsaw, where they were put to death.[74] The cossacks' principal town of Terekhtimirov [Terekhtymyriv] was confiscated as well, and the hetmans instructed to root out all cossacks who might object to the Sejm's resolution on recruiting a new army of six thousand cossacks led by government-appointed officers.

NEW REBELS

Implementation of the Sejm's decree had to be postponed until after a new and desperate battle costing the Poles dearly had been fought. In April 1638 yet another cossack rebellion broke out in Zaporozhie. It was led by Ostranin, wishing to avenge his father whom the Poles tortured to death.[75] Skidan also re-emerged on the scene at this point. The majority of the unregistered cossacks, together with their leader Iliash [Karaimovych], fought with the Poles against Ostranin's cossacks. This was an extraordinary war because the rebellious cossacks regarded the left bank of the Dnieper, the Muscovite side, a safe haven [for escapees] in the event of an unsuccessful military engagement. Having defeated the Poles at Goltva on May 5, only to be routed at Zhovnin on June 13, Ostranin left for Muscovy, to which he had carted off his wife already.[76]

Ostranin's flight did nothing to destroy the spirit of the cossacks. They elected a new leader by the name of Gunia [Hunia],[77] built fortifications on the estuary of the Staritsa [Starytsia] river, which flows into the Dnieper, and defended themselves to the end against an enemy which exceeded them in both men and artillery. Finally a shortage of provisions forced them to accede to the Sejm's resolution. For their part the Poles failed to live up to their pledge not to harry the cossacks as they made their way homeward. At the end of the year a cossack council met at a location near Maslovy Stav[78] to hear the decision of the Polish king depriving the cossacks of the right to elect their own leaders. Instead they were to receive a crown appointee, the commissioner Piotr Komarowski, who was authorized to assign the colonels. Korsun was designated as the cossacks' main city and the commissioner's place of residence. The government also ordered the return of their former lands to the cossacks, to be farmed in perpetuity, but the Polish hetman Potocki and his aides named to assist in settling this task declared that it would be hopeless to attempt to establish boundaries. A fresh snowfall obscured the markers, embankments, streams, roads and marshes, making it virtually impossible to parcel out the land. In the presence of Potocki and other officials the cossacks were required once again to swear the oath of allegiance to king and republic. All arms were piled together, and standards, maces and armor were laid at the feet of the commissioners, representing Poland. The cossacks sighed heavily in the face of this demeaning procedure, and Potocki mistook these sighs as a sign of sincere repentance.

COSSACKS LOSE LIBERTIES

A Little Russian chronicler recorded the following atrocities. "From this moment on the cossacks were deprived of all liberties. They faced extraordinarily heavy and unusual tax burdens. Access to their churches and religious rituals was contracted out to the Jews. Cossack children were boiled in cauldrons, and women's breasts were squeezed between two pieces of wood." A Polish chronicler, on the other hand, wrote "In February of 1640 the Crimean Tatars devastated the length and breadth of the lands of Pereiaslav, Korsun and the surrounding territories owned by the princes Wiśniowiecki. They captured people and cattle, and in the absence of cossack guards returned home with no one in pursuit. Such was the advantage which destruction of the cossacks brought to the republic, all of this simply because the [Polish] governors and Rus nobility sought to enrich themselves. They brought the Jews into everything, leased out everything to them, even the churches, to which the Jews were given the keys. Anyone wishing to marry or to baptize children was forced to pay them because they held the contracts for the privilege of receiving these sacraments."

In addition to such unsuccessful cossack battles the Rus tried other ways of defending their faith and national identity. So determined did Orthodox resistance remain that, in 1624, the Uniates proposed creating a separate patriarchate, as was done in Muscovy. The agreement came to nothing because, first and foremost, it required the proposed new patriarch to clarify his stance towards the Uniates and the Pope. Meanwhile the Orthodox increasingly augmented the moral arsenal to be used in their anti-Uniate struggle.

BROTHERHOOD SCHOOLS

The Epiphany Brotherhood in Kiev had a school as early as 1594. When fire destroyed it in 1614 Anna [Galsha] Gulevich [Halshka Hulevych],[79] wife of a marshal named Lozka from the town of Mozyr, donated land and buildings for a brotherhood school, a monastery and a hostel for foreign Orthodox clergy.[80] In 1617 the Lutsk brotherhood was founded. In 1619 the nobles in the province of Volhynia [evidently having joined the brotherhood] issued a charter for the residence of Lutsk, charging them to supervise and look after brotherhood affairs. "Because we do not reside in the city," they explained, "and distance makes frequent visits impractical, we turn over all supervision and duties to our junior lords, the brethren and Lutsk town dwellers on condition they confer in all things with us as their seniors. As their elder brothers we are obliged to assist them, to support them in all matters and on all occasions."

The brotherhood established a school based on the following regulations. (1) Anyone wishing to enroll a pupil first must meet with the rector elected by the monks.[81] For three days prospective pupils were to observe the teaching process and study the school regulations.[82] Indigent pupils were to be trained how to earn their keep.[83] This procedure was designed to prevent pupils from leaving because of insufficient knowledge of the school's requirements. A condition of acceptance was the assumption that a full program of study was to be completed.[84] (2) If a candidate decided not to enroll he would depart with the brotherhood's blessing. If he agreed to observe the rules and regulations the incoming pupil must so inform the monitor in charge and pay a fee of four groshas. This completed the registration process.[85] (3) The pupil was absolutely and unequivocally to obey either the one in charge or his designee. (4) Once enrolled, the pupil was to consult the school supervisor about the course of study, and carefully follow his instructions. Pupils whose parents or guardians had designed a course of study for them in advance were to be exempted from the prescribed program. (5) There were to be no commercial transactions made either in or out of school. No trading, purchases or sales of any kind without the knowledge of the teacher were condoned. (6) Nothing said within the confines of the school was to be repeated beyond its premises. (7) No pupils were to keep military equipment, or any tool or instrument of trade, except those belonging to the school. Heretical works and those of other creeds were prohibited.[86]

The curriculum was established as follows. To begin with, pupils must learn to write. Then they were to study grammar, church regulations, reading and singing. Each day they were to ask each other questions in Greek and respond in Slavonic, or ask questions in Slavonic and reply in the vernacular Rus language.[87] In general pupils were not encouraged to converse exclusively in the Rus tongue, but also in Slavonic and Greek.

Once these subjects were mastered , pupils would proceed to higher stud-ies, to dialectics and rhetoric, which were to be taught in Slavonic.[88]

DEFECTION TO ROME

In 1625 Peter Mogila, son of a Moldavian ruler [hospodar], became a monk at the Caves monastery in Kiev. In 1626 he was elevated to the position of archimandrite. At his own expense Mogila sent a number of young people, monks and laymen, abroad to academies in Lvov, Rome and elsewhere. When they returned to their homeland four years later Mogila conceived the notion of founding a school attached to the Caves monastery hospital. The members of the Epiphany Brotherhood [in Kiev] begged him not to found a separate school, proposing instead to merge with the older brotherhood school. Hetman Ivan Petrizhitsky and the Zaporozhian Host swore to defend the brotherhood school from its enemies and oppressors, even if it involved bloodshed. The nobles promised an annual collection among their leaders for its maintenance. On behalf of the entire clergy Boretsky's successor, Metropolitan Isaiah Kopinsky,[89] named Mogila as the senior brother of the Epiphany Brotherhood, as well as guardian, supervisor and defender of the brotherhood school. In accepting the appointment, Mogila substantially augmented its assets.

At the very moment the Kievan school, which Mogila so greatly en-hanced, was busy training new champions of the Rus faith, Orthodox Rus lost the mightiest of them all in the person of Melety Smotritsky.[90] The murder of his Uniate rival Josaphat Kuntsevich, and subsequent charges that Melety was both an accomplice and agitator of his people, caused him to leave for the East for more thorough training in the Eastern faith and the church, as Melety himself explained it. Instead of drawing closer to the beleaguered church, whose suffering he so powerfully portrayed earlier in his *Threnos*, Melety returned to his native [Belarusian] land convinced that the Eastern church was tainted by Protestantism. In 1628 in Lvov he published a defense of his journey to the East in his *Apology for Peregrinations to Eastern Parts*, in which he presented his reconsidered view of the Eastern church, suggesting that the Orthodox Rus accept church union. At the Orthodox council in Kiev that same year he was constrained to renounce his ideas and beg forgiveness.[91] The moment he departed Kiev Melety wrote a *Protest* against the council,[92] declaring that he was forced to renounce his sincere and correct convictions. The Orthodox archpriest Andrei Muzhilovsky wrote a rebuttal to the apology in his *Antidotum* (Remedy), published in 1629.That same year in Lvov Smotritsky issued his response in a book entitled *Exethesis* (Explanation),which elicited the Orthodox rejoinder *Apologiia pogibel'* (from the Greek *apollimi*, "I perish," and not from *apologeo*, "I defend").

RECONCILIATION ATTEMPTS

King Sigismund died in April 1632. He was laid out on the ceremonial bed wearing a cap robbed from the Muscovite tsar's treasury [during the Time of Troubles]. That same day (June 18), as Kiev's Uniate metropolitan Veniamin Rutsky celebrated mass in Slavonic over the body of the king, the Senate received cossack deputies who asked (1) for a voice in the election of the king inasmuch as the cossacks were also part of the republic. (2) That the Uniates leave the Greek religion in peace. (3) That the size of their army and their salary be increased.

The cossacks were informed that they were indeed part of the republic, but only one that can be likened to the hair or toenails of a human body. Whenever hair or toenails grow too long they need to be clipped. The same was true of the cossacks. As long as their numbers were moderate they might serve as defenders of the republic, when they began to multiply there was a danger that these peasants would rise up against their masters.

Both Orthodox and Protestants demanded an end to repression endured during the reign of the deceased king. Now Sigismund's inflexibility generated its own consequences. A strong group of Catholics formed which tolerated no concessions to the dissidents. Reaction to Sigismund's system was strongest of all in the family of the deceased king, in his eldest son Władysław. Small wonder that the cossacks supported him. Władysław accepted the challenge of a Uniate-Orthodox reconciliation, yet for five uninterrupted hours negotiated with them in vain. The two went away hating each other more than ever. Władysław persisted and ultimately bargaining ended with both agreeing to several conditions. (1) There were to be two metropolitans, one Orthodox and the other Uniate. (2) The Polotsk eparchy was to have two bishops, an Orthodox in Polotsk and a Uniate in Mstislav. The eparchies at Lvov, Lutsk and Peremyshl, as well as the Caves monastery in Kiev, were to be reserved for the Orthodox.

POLEMICS CONTINUE

The struggle which led up to these concessions could not sidestep polemics and polemical writings. In 1632 by way of an historical legitimization of their demands the Orthodox issued *Synopsis*, a collection of rights and privilege granted through the years to the Rus people [or nation] by the Polish kings.[93] This was followed by a supplement to the *Synopsis* published in Wilno in 1632. That same year the Uniates responded with works on (1) the rights and privileges granted by Polish kings to the inhabitants of Crown Poland and the grand principality of Lithuania who were united with the Roman church and[94] (2) the holy union of Eastern and Western churches. In these works they attempted to prove that a union actually existed in the Rus church since the days of St. Vladimir [in the tenth century].

In 1633 in Cracow the Uniates published *Rus Deviations*, in which they detailed all of the coercive measures used by the Orthodox against Uniates, namely "On August 11, 1600 a scoundrel attacked the metropolitan Ipaty Potey with a saber, striking him on the neck. Although he failed to kill him, he cut off two fingers of the left hand. In 1618 the Orthodox seized a Uniate archimandrite named Anton Grekovich (Antin Hrekovych] in the Vydubets monastery, and drowned him in the Dnieper. In 1622 they killed a Uniate archpriest in Shargrad, and murdered the mayor and a priest in Kiev. In 1623 in Podgorie [Pidhiria] they killed a Uniate monk called Anton Butsky. Finally, on Easter Sunday 1623 they killed Kuntsevich. For a long time the king refused to believe that such acts were committed by his subjects, attributing them instead to Muscovites living near the border."

WŁADYSŁAW IV

Władysław was elected king and Peter Mogila became the Orthodox metropolitan. His office was now legitimate in the eyes of the Polish government. In his chronicle the Orthodox noble Yerlich [Joachim Jerlicz, a Pole by birth] described Mogila. "Peter Mogila conducted himself in a pious, sober, exemplary manner and constantly worked at maintaining the integrity of God's church, yet this did not dampen his enthusiasm for the glories of this world as well. When Władysław ascended the throne Mogila represented Metropolitan Isaiah Kopinsky and the rest of the clergy at the coronation. Owing to illness the metropolitan could not make the journey. Mogila obtained a royal charter naming him to the metropolitan see, then journeyed to Lvov, where he was consecrated by the Wallachian metropolitan and bishops. Returning to Kiev he seized the lands and property belonging to the metropolitan see, overthrew Kopinsky and dismissed the priests appointed by him. As if that was not enough, he sent the ailing old man away from St. Michael's monastery wearing only a hair shirt, forcing him to live out his days in dire poverty.

Later as metropolitan he accepted money to take an armed detachment to the St. Nicholas hermitage, which he attacked with small arms and canon. Although the abbot escaped, Mogila had the monks whipped until they disclosed where the money and silver were concealed. Expelled from the hermitage, a number of monks went over to the Uniate church, while others wandered in various towns without refuge. He sent some of the monks, whom he labelled Uniates, in shackles from the Caves monastery to the cossacks. The cause of Mogila's hostility toward that monastery was the school, in the interest of which he evicted the monks of the Trinity monastery, even those being treated in the infirmary, as well as the blind and the lame. The blind abbot of the Trinity monastery, Arseny, was beaten so severely that he died within a few weeks."[95]

If accurate, this account indicates that society in Mogila's time differed little from the days of Kraseński and Lazovsky, when the powerful resorted to the same kinds of brutal tactics. It leaves the impression that they were people with equally ruthless characters, equally wealthy and equally remarkable in promoting the welfare of society, people who shrank at nothing to achieve their objectives. Given this state of society, we really have no right to expect that any agreement between Orthodox and Uniates would produce a tranquil Orthodox church, or that its mighty enemies would resist the temptation to make their power felt.

MORE PERSECUTION

On May 24, 1624 during a procession in Lutsk of the Catholic clergy with their sacraments, brandishing sabers, daggers, rifles or merely sticks and stones, about one hundred Jesuits, servants in the Jesuit collegium, pupils and various artisans broke into the courtyard of the Orthodox brotherhood church, the chambers of the clergy and the almshouse. They began to seize and attempted to break down the church doors. Because the doors were so securely bolted from the inside this proved impossible, then they climbed into the belfry and began ringing the bells. When bells attracted even more fanatics they broke into the church, overturned the candle

holders and benches and tore up the rugs and wall hangings. Others ran
around the courtyard with sticks, swords and other weapons, chased away
the schoolchildren with blows, beat up and tortured the poor souls in the
almshouse, old men and women. They responded with sticks and stones
to the holy people who emerged from their cells to admonish them, used
whatever was to hand to beat anybody who got in their way, provided
they were Rus, broke open two chests and took the money, smashed all
the windows, damaged the roof, then went away.

The Jesuits, whose collegium was located in the Podol [artisan] sec-
tion of Kiev [as was Peter Mogila's] could not accept with equanimity
the flowering of Mogila's Orthodox collegium. They tried to convince the
Orthodox faithful that the collegium's preceptors were not Orthodox, that
having received their higher education in Roman, Polish and German
academies they were infected with various heresies. That is why the language of instruction was not Greek, as would befit an Orthodox institution, but Latin.

In 1635 Sylvester Kosov,[96] one of the preceptors in Mogila's collegium at the time, published in Kiev a book in defense of his colleagues
entitled *Exegesis* in which he states "It was a time when we, having gone
to confession, simply waited for the nobility to begin feeding us to the
sturgeon in the Dnieper. Some they sent to their Maker by fire, others
with the sword. In the end the One who knows the heart of God, observing our innocence and the great need for useful learning among our Rus
people, dispersed the cloud of false ideas, and enlightened the hearts of
all who saw in us true sons of the Eastern church. As a result the inhabitants of Kiev and other region began not only to fill up our *Horrea Apol-
linea* [Halls of Apollo] with their children, like ants, in greater numbers
than before the tenure of our predecessors, but to glorify our educational
institution by calling it the Helicon[97] and Parnassus and boast about it."

Mogila wanted formal education to spread to Muscovy as well. In
1640 he asked Tsar Michael to found a monastery in Moscow in which
the senior monks of the Caves monastery would instruct gentry and com-
moners in Greek and Slavonic. That same year Peter Mogila announced
that he would convene a council to address the problem of increasing
oppression. The Muscovite expatriate Pavel Saltykov requested the king's
permission to build an Orthodox church in Smolensk, dedicated to St.
Boris and St. Gleb. "If we are not permitted to build a holy church in
Smolensk," he declared, "then we, the entire Orthodox gentry from

Smolensk and Dorogobuzh, from petty to great, must move to a place where Orthodoxy is free."

In spite of this threat no permission was granted. Meanwhile a recent convert to the Uniate confession, the archbishop of Smolensk Andrei Zoloty-Kvashnin, tried to rouse both king and gentry against Orthodoxy. He swore that he would bring into the Uniate confession all the Orthodox inhabitants of Smolensk, Dorogobuzh, Chernigov and Starodub.

RELOCATION TO MOSCOW

Monks and nuns relocated entire monasteries and convents to Muscovy. Hence in 1639 the abbot Vasily and seventy brethren from the Gustin monastery in Priluki, and the mother superior Elizaveta, together with thirty-five senior nuns of the Intercession convent in the same town, arrived in Muscovy. We also have observed that, like the monks and nuns, cossacks too escaped to Muscovy. In December 1638 Potocki wrote to Koniecpolski "More than once I have written to you requesting that you remind his majesty to apprehend all traitors who flee to Moscow, for it is well known that the thief will not steal if he has nowhere to run. I am confident that this proposal will end all such anarchy." In 1639 Koniecpolski wrote to the king "The commissioner informed me that Gunia, who led those hooligans against your army, together with several other leaders and three hundred horses, went to Ostranin in Muscovy. If we continue to ignore these flights, as long as the fugitives have such ready asylum we can never expect peace in Rus." As we know, Tsar Michael did not betray the cossacks. Presently we shall see that neither would Michael's successor.

III

REIGN OF ALEXIS MIKHAILOVICH

THE TSAR'S CHARACTER

The new tsar resembled his father in goodness, gentleness and talent for forming strong bonds with his intimates, but his intelligence and character were livelier. Moreover, he received an education more in keeping with his calling. As already noted, his tutor was the boyar Boris Ivanovich Morozov, with whom Alexis already had spent thirteen inseparable years.[1] The young tsarevich was strongly attached to him, and with the passing of his mother Tsaritsa Evdokia Lukianova shortly after his father's death (August 18, 1545), leaving Alexis orphaned, Morozov's influence over the sovereign, and ultimately on the realm, was unmatched. He was intelligent, canny, well educated by the standards of that time, and he understood the new demands of government. Yet he could not rise above his need to be a favorite, nor could he resist exploiting his position for personal advantage. Next to Morozov the conciliar secretary Nazar Chistoy [also known as Chistov], a former merchant from Yaroslavl, exerted the greatest influence in public affairs. As far as his character is concerned, recalling the history of his dealings with the emissaries from Holstein during the preceding reign will make it clear that Chistoy's seeming selflessness did not overcome personal advantage.[2] It is said that Morozov and Chistoy benefited from the advice of the foreign mill owner Vinius, whom we have met. He was the first foreigner to exert his influence in governmental affairs.[3]

VALDEMAR AND LUBA

From the very beginning of the reign it was obvious that the helm of government was in the hands of a strong man, capable of taking charge wisely and with dignity. Two serious issues left over from the preceding regime were resolved at the outset of the reign, Prince Valdemar [son of the Danish king] and Luba.[4] On July 17 the prince was on hand to greet the new sovereign. Alexis Mikhailovich began the conversation by broaching the question of baptism,[5] at which the prince responded as he had done earlier, with a resolute refusal. That same day he and the Danish emissaries petitioned the tsar for permission to return home. In August Tsar Alexis notified King Christian [IV] of his recent accession to the throne, assuring him that he wished to dwell with the king in brotherly friendship and love. He promised Christian that his son Prince Valdemar, together with his emissaries, shortly would be free to go. He was as good as his word. On August 17 they were given permission to leave. The sovereign informed Valdemar that because of his refusal to convert to the tsar's religion and his petition to be allowed to return to his father the king, he would be released as honorably as he was received.

Following his departure the prince wrote to Tsar Alexis Mikhailovich from Viazma, thanking him for the great love and sincere devotion which the tsar consistently showed him, and recently emphasized by releasing him and the royal emissaries with all honors. In conclusion, he requested that the tsar receive Peter Marselis.[6] News of the prince's release from Moscow preceded the arrival in Denmark of the messenger to the king, Apraksin. Accepting the tsar's letter, the king did not inquire after his health, nor did he extend his hand to the messenger or invite him to dine. Moreover the king sent his reply through his secretary, over the protestations of Apraksin, who requested that his majesty personally dismiss him. "Although we have such cause for bitterness," wrote King Christian, "over the collapse of our agreement on the marriage of our son and your sister, in view of your father's recent demise we are prepared to forget the matter, and abide with you in the same spirit of friendship that distinguished our relationship with your forebears."

The Polish king, Władysław, also sent a letter to Tsar Michael to request that Prince Valdemar be released and sent to Poland. He gave his word that the Danish king would not quarrel over his son's detention in Moscow. In a second letter the king, testifying to Luba's innocence, promised not to recognize him or any other pretender to the Muscovite throne, and to prosecute any one who dared to make such a claim. To reinforce his pledge he affixed his seal to the letter and wrote on the reverse side "Wishes of fortitude for his majesty the tsar from his majesty the king." The lord councillors sent a virtually identical epistle."

TEMPEST OVER PROTOCOL

In their reply the boyars raised some old grievances about the improper use of titles. Instead of the sovereign of Pskov, the Poles wrote tsar of Pskov. They wrote "autocrats" instead of "autocrat,"[7] and "Igorskoy" instead of

"Iugorskoy".[8] "His majesty the king," the boyars complained, "conducts this new matter in a manner inconsistent with the terms of the Eternal Peace,[9] in accordance with some mysterious custom, seemingly designed ᶦɔ violate our brotherly friendship and love. We have only one autocrat. To render the title in the plural is unseemly." They insisted that the emissary offer some assurance that those responsible for the incorrectly written titles be punished relentlessly. The emissary replied that he would so inform his king, who was sure to express regret and punish the guilty.

Next the boyars complained about robberies along the border, and the language that the brigands used. The emissary assured them that his king also would punish anyone found guilty of that crime, prompting the boyars to ask "What if he should turn out to be a gentleman or some other honorable person, or even a chancellor, would he too be punished?" The emissary assured them that he would be. To this the boyars responded "You yourself, high emissary, when you came from the Danish prince Valdemar, son of Christian, made insulting speeches in the presence of our guards. You assured them that you are not yet so weary, and your sabers not yet so dull, as to be incapable of cutting the Muscovites to ribbons. It is both inappropriate and embarrassing for plenipotentiaries to speak and behave thus. Besides, your sabers do not frighten the Muscovites." The ambassador did not deny this charge. His words, he pointed out, rose from the heart in anger, for some musketeers had just beaten two Lithuanians. With his own eyes he saw them covered with blood, so he spoke out of anger "having drunk a little." It was the wine talking. Yet nobody investigated the incident. Then the emissary broached the subject of an alliance against the Turks, without receiving a response.

STEMPKOWSKI'S DISMISSAL

On July 23 Stempkowski presented his credentials to the new tsar, and spoke at length about the fragility of human life. "We have a fresh portrayal of this in the blessed and eternal memory of the great sovereign Tsar Michael Fedorovich, who ruled successfully over his subjects for thirty-two years. He reigned in sanctity and righteousness, protected his realm from neighbors near and far, and saw it flourish and blessed with a bountiful peace, in which he should have continued to dwell with his subjects. Then suddenly, from a throne surrounded by so much glory and wealth, he was removed to a terrestrial cave." In conclusion, the emissary greeted the new sovereign on his accession to the throne in the name of the king, and assured him that his majesty also was prepared to show the present tsar brotherly affection and friendship. Answering in the tsar's name, the conciliar secretary declared that his sovereign too wished to abide with the king in a powerful bond of fraternal love, friendship and unity, as was written in the text of the Eternal Peace.

To demonstrate his sincerity the tsar ordered the release of Luba, whereupon Stempkowski promised, in the name of the king and the lord councillors, that Luba would never lay claim to the Muscovite realm, nor ever title himself tsar. Instead, he would live in a large fortified place and never again be allowed to leave Poland or Lithuania for another country. Anyone attempting to create a disturbance in his name faced the death penalty. All of this was to be written into the constitution at the next Sejm, and a letter of confirmation signed and sealed by the king would be delivered to the tsar. The lord councillors and the district representatives would add their confirmations. The emissary further was required to promise in writing that Lithuanian merchants no longer would travel to the Muscovite realm with wine and tobacco. Stempkowski requested that both sides exchange agents, that the Polish king's agent in Moscow be empowered to judge the Polish and Lithuanian merchants in all their dealings, and see to it that they did no harm. To this the Muscovites replied that such an exchange was impossible, for nothing was mentioned about agents in the Eternal Peace, and there was no established procedure for this. They did agree to refer to the king as "most illustrious."

The emissary then requested a dinner invitation from the tsar, otherwise he must feel slighted at receiving a less honorable reception than was accorded his predecessors. The Muscovites replied that owing to the recent demise of their tsar Michael there would be no dinner of this kind, to which the emissary responded that the high Muscovite emissaries dined with the king even though his queen had just passed away. "Those are two different matters," the Muscovites explained. "The tsar lost his one and only father, whereas a second or even a third wife may be taken. Mourning for a wife lasts only until the subsequent marriage." The emissary declared that he would wait for Tsar Michael's forty-day period of mourning to end. If the tsar had not changed his mind by then, he should give his reason in writing, that the emissary not lose face with his peers.

Before Stempkowski's departure an incident occurred which demonstrated what the prevailing lawlessness allowed members of such an emissary's retinue to do with impunity in those days. On the road between Moscow and Novgorod the brigand Yakim Danilovets and his companions murdered five people, stole furs from them belonging to a

Dutch trader and took their loot to the village of Molochino, in the district of Staritsa. Stempkowski's butler, the Pole Samoil, made a deal with the brigands. He would go from Moscow to Molochino, take the stolen furs over the border to Lithuania where, after selling them, he would pay the brigands half the proceeds and keep the remainder for his trouble. Samoil did in fact leave Moscow with the tsar's charter permitting him to travel to Viazma, but instead he went to Molochino. At the Zubtsov checkpoint he was apprehended along with the brigands and sent to Stempkowski with the demand that the emissary reimburse the Dutchman for the robbery and execute the butler. He did neither.

PRETENDER TO THE THRONE

Although this marked the end of the Luba affair, the procession of pretenders did not abate. In 1646 this denunciation appeared. "Your majesty, your orphan son of Chulka bows before you and denounces Alexander Nashchokin, son of Fedor, nicknamed Sobaka [Russian for dog], charging that this Alexander plans to violate his oath, and betray you, his just ruler, by going to another land with all his kin. He calls himself a member of the tsar's family and wishes to oppose you. Just as Fedor Nashchokin, son of Ivan, took the tsar's staff from the hand of Tsar Vasily Ivanovich Shuisky, so now Alexander Nashchokin boasts of the same devious intent towards you, the just tsar, threatening to create trouble in your Muscovite realm." All chancellery officials were questioned as to whether they had ever seen, or possessed, certificates or records pertaining to this claim, perhaps in their documents, in copies of town registers, or in petitions. They concurred that there was no such record or certificate, and that none had ever existed. Thus the matter was laid to rest. Just then, two more pretenders unexpectedly appeared in Turkey.

At the beginning of 1646 Muscovite emissaries, the noble Telepnev and a high official from Kaffa named Kuzovlev, learned that Archimandrite Joachim had arrived in that city from the Savior monastery, on the Sacred Mountain in Tsargrad [Constantinople]. The emissaries quickly sent a translator to meet with him, and to learn from the archimandrite what was happening in Constantinople. This is what he told them. While in a Jewish town in Crimea he was approached by a stranger who passed there for the Muscovite tsarevich Dolgoruky, son of Dmitry. That individual claimed to be the tsarevich, and complained that he had asked the khan for an army to help him enter the Muscovite realm, but the khan deceived him. He did not provide the army or send him to the sultan.

Whereupon the man said to the archimandrite "Take my letter of authorization with you. Use it when you call on the border town and Kaluga.
They will honor it there, and when I reach the Muscovite realm I shall
reward you with the revenues from Kaluga."

Emissaries Telepnev and Kuzovlev received other news as well. A
captured Ukrainian cossack from the city of Poltava, Ivashka [diminutive
of Ivan] Romanov related "I know this felon who calls himself the son
of Dmitry. His home town is Lubny, he comes from a cossack family and
is called Ivashka Vergunënok [Little Vergun],[10] because his father's name
was Vergun. In Lubny, after the death of his father, Ivashka beat his
mother, so she threw him out. He came to Poltava and hired himself out
to me. Ivashka lived in my house and was in my service for about a year.
When I left Poltava for the Don region, Vergunënok remained behind.
Some time later he too quit Poltava and came to the Northern Donets
region near Sacred Mountain, where he consorted with the Zaporozhian
and Don cossacks. From the Donets he moved to the Don, where he spent
about half a year, and started to steal, a crime for which he frequently was
beaten. Then he and three others rode to the open country to roam around
with shotguns, and hunt wild boars. The Tatars captured them on the
Mius river about six years ago, and sold Ivashka to a Jew in Kaffa, but
the felon told the Jew that he was the son of the Muscovite tsar, whereupon the Jew began to show him respect.

"While this felon lived with the Jew in Kaffa he had a sign made on
his body. He paid a Russian woman to brand him with a crescent and star
between his shoulder blades. Vergunënok showed this mark to many of
the captives, telling them that he was the tsar's son, that as soon as he
captured the Muscovite realm he would reward them. Believing the
felon's lies, the Russians visited him in the Jew's courtyard, bringing him
food and drink. The Crimean khan heard about this trickster, sent for him
about three years ago and had him brought to Crimea, where he ordered
the Jews to guard him. They have put him in chains, feed and care for
him" Thus was revealed the identity of this tsarevich, about whose whereabouts Constantinople informed Tsar Michael.

The emissaries discovered one felon in Crimea, and two more in Constantinople. Two Russians turned up in the vizier's court. One called
himself the son of Tsar Vasily Ivanovich Shuisky [reigned 1606-1610],
sent from Moldavia by the hospodar [governor] Vasily, claiming to have
served Tsar Michael Fedorovich as a government clerk. The vizier
wanted to know why he had not identified himself in Moscow. The felon

replied that it was because he feared imprisonment and left to serve in Lithuania instead. The Lithuanian king failed to receive him as befitted his dignity, so he moved on to Moldavia. The vizier inquired whether he wished to convert to the Muslim faith, to which the felon replied "If his majesty the sultan will accord me the dignity of my stature, I am prepared to convert."

Eventually the Crimean khan sent the second felon, and the emissaries dispatched an interpreter and an official to interrogate him. It turned out that the felon [from Crimea] was the very one of whom they had heard in Kaffa. The official explained that he knew the second one when he was employed in the Chancellery of the New Quarter.[11] The man's name was Timoshka [diminutive of Timofey], and he was called Akundinov from Vologda. He was the son of a musketeer, who burned his homestead and his wife in it, then secretly fled Moscow. Subsequently he appeared in Lithuania as Prince Timofey of Great Perm. Also with Timoshka in the vizier's court was a young official of the New Quarter named Kostka,[12] who called himself Timoshka's man.

After this the emissaries informed the vizier that felons were hiding at his court, and cautioned him never to believe anything they said. Instead they would question them carefully to get at the truth of the matter, whereupon the vizier summoned Timoshka. A Russian interpreter and translator provided by Telepnev interrogated him in an attempt to establish his guilt. The felon refused to talk to them, demanding that the vizier allow him to confront the emissaries in person. "The emissaries will simply confirm what I said," he declared, then turned to the translator and asked "How long has it been since Tsar Vasily passed away?" The translator replied that his death had occurred nearly forty years ago, whereas the little felon was not yet thirty. A Turk was standing before the vizier, an old man who noted "The sultan's records indicate that Tsar Vasily died thirty-seven years ago." The vizier dismissed the felon and remarked to the translator "This is a cunning man. His responses lack consistency, he makes numerous unreasonable demands and promises the sultan much. As for the one sent to us from Crimea, I am convinced that he is the legitimate son of the tsar. The Crimean khan wrote that he made inquiries about him among the Russians, who informed him that this was indeed Tsar Dmitry's legitimate son, and that Urak-Murza had murdered his father." "It was not Tsar Dmitry whom Urak-Murza ordered killed," the translator replied, "but another felon called Petrushka (?)."[13] To which the vizier responded "Tell the emissaries that this is none of their affair. They were not sent here for this purpose, and I have nothing to do with the matter."

Then Zelfikar-Aga, already well known to us,[14] and the archimandrite Amfilokhy met secretly with the emissaries. They learned that "the felon Timoshka told the vizier that the sultan must provide him with armed men and instruct his soldiers to accompany him to the Muscovite border, where the people would not oppose him. Instead they would pay him homage. He also promised Astrakhan and its hinterland to the sultan. The vizier made no comment." Then the emissaries inquired of Zelfikar-Aga and the archimandrite how the felons might be apprehended, to which their guests replied "The vizier cannot act alone. Perhaps a substantial amount of money would do it? We hope that all such money is not wasted, because our people are neither taciturn nor discreet. Indeed, it would be more prudent simply to forget the whole thing. Roving and prowling about, the felons eventually will vanish from sight, or they might be conscripted and sent to serve in distant towns, or perhaps even end up as galley slaves. Meanwhile your continued inquiries will draw attention to them, and facilitate the process of establishing their true identities."

The archimandrite also revealed that the felon Timoshka gave the vizier a document which he asked the archimandrite to translate. Its contents suggested that Timoshka was the son of Tsar Vasily who, when his father was sent to Lithuania, remained behind for six months. Vasily instructed those who had served him loyally to care for Timoshka, and they raised him. When Michael Fedorovich became tsar he ordered Timoshka to appear before him and gave him the appanage of Great Perm, together with its environs. Timoshka quickly grew bored there, then he came to Moscow, where the sovereign placed him under guard. Tsar Vasily's former retainers freed him and got him safely out of the city. Then Hospodar Vasily of Moldavia robbed Timoshka. He removed his father's priceless cross, set with sapphires and emeralds, and helped himself to many other valuables. Vasily also tried to kill Timoshka, just as earlier he had killed his older brother, then sent his head and skin to Moscow. The sovereign had the skin covered with gold and precious jewels, and returned it to the governor as a token of his gratitude.

In October 1646 Archimandrite Amfilokhy informed the emissaries that the felon sent from Crimea was imprisoned in the castle of the Seven Turrets. The felon Timoshka complained to the vizier about the archimandrite, charging that the priest frequented the emissaries' court where he spread various pieces of news, for which the vizier threatened to condemn Amfilokhy to penal servitude for life. Meanwhile the archimandrite sent word to the emissaries that their people should visit him after dark, stay the night and be gone before daybreak. The reason for such drastic measures was the news of Russian troop movements in the vicinity of Azov. They began locking up the emissaries and in November the oldest of them, Telepnev, passed away. His colleague Kuzovlev wrote to the sovereign that the felon Vergunënok was incarcerated in the town of Kozan, located on the banks of the Black Sea, about three versts from Constantinople. He was imprisoned there because when left at liberty to move about he drank and fought with the Muslims. Timoshka Akundinov was evicted from the vizier's court, and ordered to live behind his residence. His food was sent by the vizier. Very soon Kuzovlev had more important things to think about than Timoshka.

THE CRIMEAN AFFAIR

Under torture a captive cossack from the Don revealed that the cossacks had three hundred boats in Cherkasy, while in Voronezh, Yelets and other borderland towns five hundred more boats were being readied for spring. The sovereign had instructed the cossacks to take those boats by sea to Crimea, to various Crimean settlements. On January 27, 1647 the vizier Azem-Salikh-Pasha requested that the emissary send him some translators, to whom he made the following speech. "The instant the Don Cossacks enter Black Sea waters, and the sultan learns of it, I will be disgraced, perhaps even lose my head. Nor will you and your emissary keep yours. I will be accused of lying, for no other reason than because I made a good word for you to the sultan. You barely made it alive during last summer's quarrel after the sultan ordered you all killed. If I do survive, and something bad happens to me, I will have you and your emissary roasted on spits. Tell him this and let him consider well how I, he and you can avoid such misfortune. The best way for him not to come to grief is to send messengers to the Don at once, to prevent the cossacks' venturing out to sea. I personally will grant them safe passage to Azov."

Kuzovlev replied that the cossacks long were barred from sailing on the Black Sea, and his majesty the sultan knew the Don Cossacks to be traitorous thieves. They ignored the tsar's edicts in the past, consequently there was no point in dispatching emissaries to tell them to curb their larceny now. "You will not talk your way out of this with your fine speeches," the vizier warned Kuzovlev. "The moment any cossacks are sighted on the Black Sea, no matter how few, I will burn you to a cinder. Send the messengers if you want to live." Kuzovlev replied as before that it was pointless to send them. "No realm so dishonors emissaries it receives, and heretofore neither had Constantinople. They are locked up and forbidden to leave the court, denied subsistence, and for reasons unknown to us are not returned to their sovereign." The vizier was silent for a while. In a private interview he said to Kuzovlev "The moment the Don Cossacks appear on the Black Sea, you and I are in serious trouble. Together we favor both sides, therefore we will share a common fate in everything, good or bad. You must convince the cossacks to turn back. If not, you will render them defenseless. Without you they would have perished long ago." Things did go badly for the vizier. He was given the death penalty. Meanwhile the Don Cossacks caroused on the Black Sea, eventually showing up near Trebizond and Sinop.[15]

TIMOSHKA'S FATE

Timoshka Akundinov grew bored in Constantinople, where no one paid him the slightest attention. He attempted to flee to Moldavia, was apprehended and returned to Constantinople to face severe punishment. This the felon evaded by giving his word that he would convert to Islam, and saying an Islamic prayer before the vizier, although he did request that the circumcision be postponed.[16] He was released and dressed in a turban, but then Akundinov put on Greek attire and left once more, setting out for Mount Athos with a Russian captive. Again he was captured and sentenced to execution, and again offered to become a Muslim. This time Akundinov was taken at his word, circumcised and placed under guard.

The Muscovite government now might rest easy with respect to the pretender in Constantinople. Still, the sultan demanded the recall of the Don Cossacks from the town of Cherkasy, and insisted that the tsar continue to communicate with the Crimean khan, as in the past. Once again Tsar Michael responded that the Don Cossacks paid no attention to his decrees. To the khan the sovereign suggested that for the sake of the sultan's friendship he had begun to establish good relations with the Crimean Tatars. Even so, should the khan violate his oath one more time, the Muscovites would lose patience with him.

This was no empty threat. The Muscovite boyars resolved not to grant any further concessions to the Crimean Tatars, who at the end of 1645 greeted the new tsar with the invasion of Muscovite lands. The cutthroats met the Muscovite military commanders[17] in the Rylsk district near Gorodensk, and after the battle returned along the same route by which they

came. In the spring of 1646 a decision was made in Moscow to launch
an offensive. The tsar ordered Prince Semeon Romanovich Pozharsky to
gather the local inhabitants of Astrakhan, the Nogay murzas [Tatar no-
bility] and the Circassians. They were to proceed to the Don where they
would join the military commander Kondyrev, who was to arrive from
Voronezh. Together they were to march to the vicinity of Azov. In the
Ukrainian towns Kondyrev collected three thousand volunteers willing to
assist the Don Cossacks, but was repulsed and sustained heavy losses. At
the same time talks of an anti-Crimean alliance were being concluded
with Poland. In January 1646 influential plenipotentiaries, the boyar
Vasily Ivanovich Streshnev (a relative of the tsar), and the earlier-men-
tioned aristocratic official Stefan Matveevich Proestev, were dispatched
to King Władysław to congratulate him on his marriage to Louise-Marie
of Mantua, and to strengthen the Treaty of Polianovka.[18]

MORE ON PROTOCOL

On March 10 the emissaries presented themselves to the Polish king, who
lay ill in bed supported by pillows. The emissaries protested, because at
the sound of the tsar's name the king failed to rise, or order his attendants
to raise him. The king motioned them to his bedside, saying "Bearing in
mind the eternal peace, my sovereign affirmation of it, and that of the
father of your great sovereign, Michael Fedorovich, I wish my brother
Tsar Alexis Mikhailovich many years of good health and a happy life.
Your sovereign's honor shall always come before my own, still there is
no way for me to rise or even sit up because I am extremely ill. I cannot
use my hands or my feet, much less arise from my bed. The Lord knows
this is no deception. If it is a deception, may the Good Lord deprive me
of my hands and feet altogether. You emissaries can see for yourselves
how truly ill I am." They were satisfied, and from the king went to the
young queen who, to their delight, stood as she inquired after the health
of their tsar.

In an exchange with the lord councillors the emissaries raised the old
issue of a number of errors in the tsar's title, and noted some new offenses.
The land surveyor Abramovich sent his majesty the tsar a letter in which
he carelessly used the term "with that," yet when the tsar and king exchange letters they never use such a term, they insisted. As earlier, the
emissaries demanded that anyone found guilty of such breaches in eti-
quette be executed, whereas those who committed lesser mistakes must
be severely punished. In this way the king might prove his brotherly

friendship and love for his majesty the tsar. They also demanded that the king issue instructions for the proper use of the tsar's title to be written into the constitution of the Sejm, that henceforth, on pain of death, no excuse remained for such diminution of his title.

The emissaries turned their attention to the second matter. "Our great sovereign has learned that Venetian soldiers are responsible for the serious decline, devastation and overcrowding among the soldiers of the Turkish sultan Ibrahim, persecutor of all Christians. On the isle of Crete the foreigners[19]have his people under siege.[20] They are dying of hunger and thirst, and it is impossible to send aid from Constantinople. Sultan Ibrahim has ordered the construction of one hundred galleys, and has begun to consider sources for galley slaves to fill them. He sent a messenger to the Crimean khan with a missive instructing him to move against the Muscovite, Polish and Lithuanian realms without delay to take captives to man the oars of the new galleys. The moment has arrived for the great Christian sovereigns to rise up against the Crimean infidel in defense of the Christian faith. It would be most timely. Our own great sovereign is seriously contemplating an alliance with your great sovereign against the pagan sons of Hagar.[21]

"For the protection of his borderlands he sent a large army led by the boyars Prince Nikita Ivanovich Odoevsky and Vasily Petrovich Sheremetev. In the interest of the fraternal love and friendship which our sovereign feels for the Polish king he has instructed his military commanders to assist the soldiers of his majesty in the event of a Tatar attack on his borderlands. You lord councillors should consider this, and encourage your king to think about it, that in this most propitious time his royal majesty might order the Dnieper opened up. He should permit the Dnieper Cossacks, together with the Don Cossacks, to raid the Crimean settlements in the name of preserving the Christian faith. He needs to instruct his hetman to bring his troops to battle readiness in Ukrainian lands, and to confer with the tsar's military commanders on all matters of war, their manner of opposing the Crimean Tatars, and the towns in which they meet."

"We welcome this with all our hearts," the Polish lords responded, " and beg Almighty God to unite the hands of the two great sovereigns in common retribution against the Muslims. As for the errors in the tsar's title, we declare in all truthfulness and with a sincerity that comes from the heart they were unintended, indeed were made without guile. Our scribes' unfamiliarity with the Russian language is responsible for the errors. The Almighty God bears witness from above that errors occurred without any intent to deceive. Even so, our king has ordered the guilty to appear before the Sejm. You of course are aware that neither the king nor we can punish anyone, be he nobleman or commoner, without the Sejm's approval."

The king ought to have seen to this matter long ago, the emissaries charged. At the same time they handed the lords a royal letter, and the place in the title of the address where the word "autocrats" instead of "autocrat" was inserted.[22] "We have assured you that 'autocrat' and 'autocrats' are undifferentiated forms in Polish," the lords declared, "that no disrespect was intended towards your majesty, nor indeed did any true error occur."

"Do you lords feel no shame in speaking thus?' the emissaries asked. "Not just you, but ordinary folk easily can understand and grasp this matter. To write and to say 'autocrat' is to refer to a single individual. The form 'autocrats' connotes more than one. For all the territories in the Russian realm there is only one autocrat, and so shall it always be. It is pointless to delay this matter until the Sejm meets. According to the mutual agreement reached by our emissaries, people who render the title thus, in flagrant disregard of the treaty about our mutual relations, are condemned to lose their honor, their goods and their lives, as provided by royal decree and the code of the Sejm."

"We swear to God," the lords declared, "in Polish there is no distinction made between 'autocrat' and 'autocrats.' If this is not the case in Russian henceforth we shall be extremely careful. Indeed, henceforth our sovereign would do well to write his letters to his majesty the tsar in Polish, and should do likewise in his ordinary dispatches to the border towns. This practice would forestall all such errors." "It is an old custom," the emissaries responded, "for the king to write letters to our great sovereign in the Belarusian language,[23] and it appears unseemly to disregard this tradition by starting to write them in Polish. Moreover the governors in your towns lack translators." Requesting that the emissaries lay to rest the issue of errors in the tsar's title, all the more so because it was unnecessary to persecute people for their alleged guilt towards a now-deceased tsar, and promising to observe strictly the proper form of address to the reigning tsar, the Polish lords turned to the more important matter of an anti-Crimean alliance.

ANTI-CRIMEAN ALLIANCE

The same lords announced that the king had ordered Hetman Potocki to confer with the tsar's military commanders on the matter of defense against an infidel onslaught. In point of fact the hetman was prepared to assist the Muscovite commanders as early as the previous winter, but terrible frosts intervened. This summer his majesty the king wished to deploy his troops only to Ukraine, to defend the country against the infidels, and to postpone the further and far weightier matter to a later date. Notwithstanding other obstacles it would be impossible for the Zaporozhian Cossacks to put to sea any time soon because their boats had been burned, and at present they lacked the capacity to build new "seagulls."[24] The king believed that the best time to wage war with the Tatars was after the sultan dispersed them from his service. Because Poland and Turkey had concluded a treaty of eternal peace, his majesty the king could not permit the Zaporozhian Cossacks to proceed to Crimea without the approval of the Sejm.

Finally the matter of Luba came up. The emissaries pointed out that his majesty the tsar, having no desire to witness bloodshed, and responding to the request of his brother the king, had permitted Luba to proceed to Poland. Everywhere along the way, in Minsk and other cities, Luba styled himself the Muscovite tsarevich, as he did in the past, claiming that he was sent to Moscow for confirmation as tsarevich, and that his majesty himself acknowledged him as the rightful heir of the Renegade Monk.[25] We will recall that the emissary Stempkowski gave his word that Luba would be closely guarded, yet not only was he at liberty, the king made him an officer in his infantry and paid him a salary. The Muscovites were adamant in their insistence that the agreement between the emissaries on both sides required the Polish king and his lord councillors to execute Luba in their presence because he refused to stop styling himself the Muscovite tsarevich. The Polish lords promised "If you find that Luba is indeed styling himself the Muscovite tsarevich, he shall be executed. But we are telling you the truth when we say that he has been turned over for safekeeping to the infantry under Captain Jan Osiński. We have assigned men to guard him, he is closely watched and receives neither salary nor rank from the king." Whereupon the emissaries demanded proof of this in accordance with Stempkowski's pledge. The lords agreed to provide such proof from both the king and themselves, but refused to do this on behalf of the district representatives.

As for the anti-Crimean alliance and the towns around Putivl[26] (Nedrigailov [Nedryhailiv], Gorodets [Horodets], Kamiane, Akhtyr, Olshana) promised to the Muscovites, the lords pledged that special royal emissaries were to be sent to Moscow to settle the matter. The towns around Putivl could not be handed over to the Muscovites immediately because they were essential for waging the Crimean war. "Your sovereign," the emissaries said, "acts in this matter in flagrant disregard of any vestiges of truth. The Almighty God sees your duplicity from above, and will help our sovereign achieve justice. His majesty the tsar shall never relinquish his right to the towns of Putivl and their lands. He will insist on what is rightfully his."

For their part the lords complained bitterly against the practice of luring peasants across the border from Lithuania to the Muscovite side. This, they insisted, resulted in severe losses for them.

THE CASTELLAN OF KIEV[27]

Streshnev returned to Moscow with confirmation of the Treaty of Polianovka, and Stempkowski's pledge concerning Luba. In the summer of 1646 the king's plenipotentiary, Adam Kisel, castellan of Kiev, arrived in Moscow. He delivered the a message to the tsar. "The mighty Polish kingdom, together with its great principalities, and the great Russian realm, are like two great Lebanon cedars growing from a single root. The right hand of the Almighty Lord created them thus from the same Slavic blood, and the common language of one Slavic people. Greek and Latin chroniclers and historians attest to this. The most credible witness here is the language itself, common to and indispensable for both great states, for they comprise a single people. This is why for you great sovereigns, and for all of us inhabitants of two mighty realms, products of a single Slavic blood, the words pronounced by the Holy Ghost testify 'Behold how good it is for brethren to dwell in unity!'[28] Adhering to this spiritual guidance, the late great sovereign Michael Fedorovich of blessed memory forged an eternal union of brotherhood with the great sovereign, my lord. The star of depredation, bloodshed and internecine strife was extinguished. In its place arose and now shines a sun that never sets, the sun of eternal peace, friendship and brotherly love. It dimmed when the great sovereign Michael Fedorovich departed this world to heaven above, causing my lord the king to weep as though for his own brother. Yet when God granted your majesty the throne and scepters of your father's reign, my lord and king went from grief to joy. The once-dimmed sun shone as brightly as before. Even as your majesty, on your accession to the throne, instructed your emissaries to reveal your love for my lord the king, his highness returns your brotherly love with which I now greet you. Rejoice in grace, O great sovereign, Tsar and Grand Prince Alexis Mikhailovich, autocrat of All Russia! Rejoice O brother of my mighty sovereign, heir to great domains and the great union of brotherly love. Long and happily may you dwell in your mighty realm. After many years of a long life, may the Good Lord grant you the vision of an eternal blessing, allowing you to behold a successor to your tsardom, and may Almighty God permit you to anticipate your own journey from this world to the next with great joy."

In addition to such flowers of eloquence Kisel displayed some impressive historical knowledge. For Tsar Alexis Mikhailovich and his boyars he laid out a tripartite scheme of Slavic history. (1) The happy period, a time when the Slavs with their unified forces won glory throughout the world. Both the ancient and the new Rome testify to their mighty deeds. (2) The era of misfortune, when internecine strife caused the Slavs, through bloodshed and various acts of destruction, to be separated from one another, and tore their brotherly love to shreds. At that time foreign and infidel nations ruled over many of our ancestral lands. The city where St. Vladimir accepted baptism, Kherson or Korsun, is now Perekop, where the Tatar horde lives. In the former Polovetsian seats, vanquished by the sword of our own ancestors, and relegated to oblivion along with their very name, the Crimean horde has settled and multiplies as a result of the unfortunate internecine wars between our two great realms. (3) Now, by the grace of God, a third era is upon us, a time of eternal peace and brotherly love between your majesties and our two realms. It is as if we have returned to that first period of common genesis and fraternal union of love."

After these flowers of eloquence the talks commenced, but thorns soon appeared. Kisel suggested that if any letter contained an error in the tsar's title it should be rejected and returned. This would result in considerable disgrace for its author. "You are a lord in the Sejm and a very knowledgeable man," the boyars answered, "yet you have written something to cause even a commoner to blush, and to tremble before God. It is dangerous for you lords of the Sejm to safeguard our eternal peace, still you treat the tsar's honor as if it were nothing, seeking to justify the guilty by refusing to punish or execute them. If the letters are not to be accepted, are returned to the sender, how shall we know the guilty party, and of what is he to be convicted?"

"I have not spoken in my own name," Kisel responded, "rather upon the instructions of the king and the Polish-Lithuanian Commonwealth. The king and the entire Commonwealth have talked about how these errors in the tsar's title might be avoided, because in the Muscovite realm this is considered a grievous transgression. Here we frequently omit even the king's full title. A good man does things correctly, whereas a fool does them in a stupid way. Thus we decided that carelessly addressed letters, especially petitions, simply are unacceptable. Once people learn that such petitions are rejected, that nothing comes of them, in time they learn to render them properly." "We are surprised," the boyars retorted, "that after so many years they have not yet learned to write properly. Indeed you lords of the council often call your people stupid because they cannot learn the appropriate forms of address. Why even the infidel Muslims write the tsar's titles correctly, while from the German states there is never a slip of the pen." "If this solution does not suit his majesty the tsar," responded Kisel, "we can explore other avenues." In the end they agreed that errors made in the tsar's titles would be punishable by execution.

PEASANT FUGITIVES

Kisel's next move was to demand the return of runaway peasants to their rightful owners. "They depopulate our realm. What sort of brotherly love can there be when you welcome fugitive field peasants? In the most recent incident the peasants in Olshana murdered a deputy mayor, then fled to the tsar. Is this not a serious grievance?"

For their part the boyars charged "Ivan Volkov, the tsar's table attendant and an honorable man, was murdered by his own people, who then fled to the king's domain. It was in vain that we wrote requesting their return. Also many Cherkasy have run to the king's lands, yet no one insisted they be returned. Not a single word was uttered." "The Cherkasy are free and can live where they please," Kisel retorted, "field peasants are indentured slaves." "The eternal peace," the boyars pointed out, "contains nothing about runaways, it is inappropriate to raise the issue at this time." Kisel in his turn replied "I am not inquiring about earlier events. What is needed now is to reach a new agreement and to ratify it, so that fugitive serfs no longer are harbored. Otherwise it will go against God, against brotherly love and solidarity. Recently approximately one thousand peasants belonging to Koniecpolski, Wiśniowiecki and others fled to the tsar's lands. Together the three of us have lost about fifteen thousand. Would it be pleasing were we to bring back all these peasants from your lands and beat them? Choosing to keep our peasants, you must not genuinely desire friendship."

The district representatives informed the king that their peasants were fleeing, and suggested that his majesty issue instructions making this matter part of the first article of the treaty. "Whatever has not been written into the eternal peace cannot be added now," the boyars replied. "From the domains of his majesty the tsar, that is from the Briansk and Komaritsk districts, as well as from Velikie Luki, numerous field peasants have fled to the king's land and are now doing this routinely. This year Artiushka, a peasant belonging to Kolychov from Briansk, ran away to the king's domain. Upon his return from your land he stabbed his landowner with a spear. The tsar decreed that he be handed to the governor of Mstislav for execution. The peasant was not placed under the tsar's jurisdiction. You are a plenipotentiary and defender of the Christian faith. These devout field peasants, born into a no less pious faith than yours, live in your lands among people of various confessions. If such are turned over to you, does this imply that they will be released to Catholics or Lutherans for torture? Is this the Christian way? Finding himself in such bondage, the poor peasant might even lose his faith." "What do the muzhiks know?" Kisel responded. "They have no attachment to religion. They flee because they have no desire to pay their master even a small quitrent. When the peasant runs away to some distant town it is not too insulting because his master never need see him again. When he goes only as far as a nearby border town to live, think of the chagrin of a master who encounters him there. We all must agree that no border town shall harbor a fugitive peasant. Any fugitive living near the border, on either side, can be captured and returned to his rightful master." Speaking in the tsar's name the boyars categorically refused to consider any such article.

ALLIANCE NEGOTIATIONS

The matter of the alliance against the Crimea also stalled. Kisel attempted to come to an agreement on how and where the allied armies might meet to repulse the Tatars. "If soldiers from either side spend too much time in the steppe doing nothing," the boyars cautioned, "they will grow bored. Meanwhile once the Crimeans learn of our alliance they simply will stay away. It would be better to unite our armies and move directly on the Crimea." Kisel replied that the Polish gentry had made it clear to the Sejm that they entertained no desire to move against the Turks, who had given no grounds for war. Hence nothing more than a defensive alliance against the Tatars was appropriate at the moment. "Perhaps," the boyars suggested, "we might send the Crimean Tatars a little something at this time so as to confuse them slightly and in the meantime take two or three years to prepare for a Crimean campaign. The tsar's troops can be garrisoned in the border towns to defend Ukrainian territory. Should the Tatars decide to march on Poland, these troops can assist the Polish forces and pursue the Tatars all the way to the Dnieper. In the event the Tatars attack the tsar's border territories Polish soldiers will assist the Russian military. Each must have a standing army of five thousand men, or more if reports suggest such a need." Kisel responded that were the tsar's troops to proceed only as far as the Dnieper they would be of no use at all because the Tatars never attack the Poles on the Left Bank. Muscovites were needed along the Dnieper as far as the Black Sea route. For their part the Poles would assist the Russians as far as Belgorod. The boyars observed that if they were indeed to proceed along the river they would never arrive in time, but Kisel reassured them by indicating that the Polish commanders had spies in the Crimea. They were to inform the Poles at the first sign the Crimean khan was preparing to mount an offensive.

In the end it was agreed that Polish hetmans and the Muscovite commanders maintain contact in order to keep the Tatars out of their lands, thereby acting in accord against the common enemy. Should the Tatars exhibit unusual enmity, their majesties would consider what to do. For the present, both sovereigns were prepared to treat the Crimeans according to ancient custom, to avoid giving them any cause for open aggression. Thus it proved impossible for the new Muscovite leaders to convince the Poles of any need for an offensive alliance against the Crimeans. The Poles feared that a Crimean war would draw in Turkey which, owing to the proximity of borders, was far more dangerous for them than for the Muscovites. For Moscow, on the other hand, even a defensive alliance against the brigands was crucial.

DOMESTIC ECONOMY

Although at the time Muscovy's external affairs were proceeding smoothly, the domestic situation was far from satisfactory. The people were exhausted by the high tax burden, which also impoverished the merchants. Natural disasters, crop failure and massive losses of cattle to disease, added to the overall misfortune. A malfunctioning justice system exacerbated the situation. As was their custom, the Muscovite merchants blamed foreign traders for their adversity. In 1646 they presented their grievances to the new tsar. "After the destruction of Muscovy," they complained, "when your father came to the throne, knowing that their trade with the Muscovite realm produced huge profits, and wishing to monopolize it, English foreigners bribed the conciliar secretary Peter Tretiakov with lavish promises. In return they received a charter of privileges from the Chancellery for Foreign Affairs, permitting twenty-three English merchants to trade in Archangel and other Muscovite towns. We, of course, could never match their gifts, because we were all ruined and spent our time wandering in other towns. When the foreigners secured their charter from the Chancellery for Foreign Affairs, sixty, seventy or more Englishmen came to Muscovy. In Archangel, Kholmogory, Vologda, Yaroslavl, Moscow and other cities they purchased properties, bought homesteads and constructed warehouses, built mansions with stone cellars, and took permanent residence within the Muscovite realm.

"In Archangel they have stopped selling their customary wares to the Russians, or trading them for Russian goods. Instead they bring in all sorts of other merchandise for trade in Moscow and other cities. Whatever commodity rises in price they offer for sale, and what is cheap and not in demand they store in their residences for two or three years. When the prices of these goods climb they bring them out for sale. Russian merchandise exchanged for theirs in the past they now buy outright, naming their own price. They also commission additional goods from various cities and districts, indebting and enslaving decent Russian people. Once the foreign merchants have completed their purchases, Russians deliver their goods to them. The foreigners then transport them to their own lands, where they are sold without any customs duties being paid. English traders sell other Russian wares for cash in Archangel to merchants on Dutch, Brabançon and Hamburg ships. Thus they steal your sovereign's customs duties. Foreigners monopolize the sale of all goods in which we have traded since time immemorial, causing us to lose our markets, and forcing us to suspend our visits to Archangel.

"Not only do these foreign traders deprive us of our livelihood, they impoverish the entire Muscovite realm. Purchasing meat, grain and various other victuals in Moscow and other cities, they export these commodities to their own countries. When their ships dock in Archangel no one is permitted to examine their cargo. If customs and tax officials were to inspect their wares in all of our cities the way they do ours, and assess duties and taxes as they do for us, foreigners would pay thirty thousand rubles more each in duties and taxes. Their charters of privilege stipulated that they were issued to merchants at the request of their king, Charles, yet the English traders no longer support him. They separated from King Charles and are now in their fourth year of fighting with him.[29] English merchants such as Merrick and his friends,[30] who were issued our majesty's charters of privilege for trade in response to a request from King Charles, never set foot here. They sold their charters to others, and now new merchants arrive with these documents.

"Foreigners bring various and sundry goods, all inferior to those in which they traded earlier. They also resell other people's merchandise. Previously the English traded in foreign wares secretly, now they do it openly. The clever Hamburg, Brabançon and Dutch foreigners dispense numerous bribes and gifts when they arrive here each year, in violation of your sovereign decrees. In other cities and towns they present your majesty's charters of privileges, obtained from the Chancellery for Foreign Affairs by means of fraudulent petitions, and distribute generous bribes and gifts to conciliar secretaries like Peter Tretiakov and Ivan Gramotin, and some foreigners trade without benefit of charters.

"After purchasing a property in Moscow, on which he built a large house, David Nikolaev [evidently a Dutchman][31] proceeded to sell all kinds of goods at retail in his own courtyard, just as they are sold in stalls at the market, without a charter of privilege, and in violation of your ordinance. The foreigners who live in Moscow and other towns travel by way of Novgorod and Pskov to their own lands, four, even five times a year with news of what is happening in the Muscovite realm, and how much things cost. Whatever yields a high price in Moscow, they bring in and offer for sale. They govern their actions by the most current written information available, and arrange their business affairs in concert. Whenever they come to the trade fair in the town of Archangel they can tell you all there is to know about prevailing prices on everything. They select the best of the wares coming from overseas and buy them for cash, or offer Russian goods in barter for them. Conspiring amongst themselves, they act as one in refusing to purchase our merchandise. At the same time they deliberately inflate the prices of overseas goods, thereby making them inaccessible to us, to prevent our participation in future trade fairs. The result is that we are forced to take our pathetic little goods out of Archangel, although some might leave them behind for the following year. Poor folk shed copious tears over being forced to hand over their entire inventories for a pittance because they are so indebted. These various plots and designs have caused us to end our visits to Archangel because we sustained such huge losses and lost our markets. Meanwhile your customs duties are falling further and further into arrears.

"Thus the foreigners Peter Marselis and Jeremiah Felz cunningly bought up all the blubber so that your subjects, traders from Kholmogory and the maritime processors of blubber are prevented from selling it without their knowledge, either to other foreigners or to Russians. They pay their traders half, a third or even a quarter of its value, and succeed because nobody else is in any position to make these purchases. Because of this many people from Kholmogory, not to mention the entire maritime region, who used to go out to sea to fish, are now impoverished and, one by one, are leaving for other parts. Meanwhile your sovereign patrimony, the town of Archangel, the district of Kholmogory, and all the maritime region are gradually turning into wastelands. When it was still possible for us to trade in blubber with various foreigners and people of diverse ranks you earned four or five thousand and more in customs duties from our commercial activity. The fishing industry provided a good living for merchants, and they were satisfied. Now the customs duties the merchants once paid have dwindled to nothing. People are too impoverished to pay taxes, and maritime regions have fallen into neglect. The fishing industry does not even bring in two hundred rubles a year.

"Let us enlighten you, our just tsar, about this foreign thievery. When your father sat on the throne the merchant Anton Laptev of Yaroslavl travelled with his wares through Riga to Amsterdam in Holland. He took sable, fox and squirrel pelts to sell there, and this enabled him to buy Dutch goods. Anton went to all three of their foreign lands [Holland, Brabant and England], yet the merchants conspired not to purchase a single item from him, not one ruble's worth. So he left these lands in their company, journeying on a foreign ship to Archangel. When they arrived the foreigners purchased his entire inventory at a higher price. Without mincing words the Muscovite traders who were present at the fair accused the foreigners, asking 'Where is justice when our sovereign's subject, a trader, came to your realm with his goods and conferring amongst yourselves you purchased nothing from him, almost causing him to starve? You bargained with him and offered much lower prices, about half what the pelts were worth in your own country, yet purchased them all for a higher sum when he came here? Meanwhile, by the grace of our sovereign, foreign merchants trade freely in a variety of goods within the Muscovite realm, without our traders boycotting their commercial activities.

Our sovereign's kindness towards you will not permit us to indulge in such unethical practices. In gratitude for our sovereign's grace it behooves you to be equally honorable and guileless in your transactions with us.'

"The foreigners justified their decision not to purchase Anton Laptev's goods by their intent to teach other Russian merchants to abandon trading in their countries. 'Were the Russian merchants to trade in our countries as we do in yours, we would lose our livelihood and become as impoverished as you. We discouraged the Persian traders in the same way, and you should consider it your great good fortune that we did not actually starve Anton Laptev.' This, O sovereign, is how they ridicule us.

"In the past year, that is 1645, just over nine hundred puds of raw silk were sold to the foreigners on orders from the state treasury. In accordance with previously agreed terms they were charged seventy-seven efimoks per pud.[32] [This year,] noting that the foreigners earlier purchased your raw silk at the wharves before they bought anything else, we successfully petitioned for permission to purchase silk [before it reached the wharves] for sale at the fair in Archangel. It would have brought your majesty a profit much higher than the price of the silk itself, approximately eight thousand efimoks. When we brought it to the fair the foreign traders schemed not to purchase even one grivna's worth from us, saying 'We shall cause the Muscovite merchants to be beaten for indebtedness, so that in future they will trade in bast shoes and forget all about buying merchandise before we do!' Gracious sovereign! Take pity on us your humble servants and orphans,[33] the merchants throughout your realm. Look upon us, poor souls, and do not let us orphans, servants of their righteous sovereign, suffer constant deprivation at the hands of these heretics. Do not deprive us poor people of the humble trades in which we have engaged since time immemorial."

Their request was denied, as was during Tsar Michael's reign, although then there was no one to blame. Now, with a young sovereign on the throne, Morozov was in charge of business affairs. He was well known for his attachment to foreigners and proclivity for all things foreign. For their part foreigners claimed that Vinius [the Dutch mill owner] was more interested in the welfare of the Russians than he was in that of his own people. Naturally the Russians disagreed. Vinius probably deserved this reproach from foreigners because customs duties were doubled in Muscovy on all foreign goods, not excluding those of the

English, in order "to replenish the military." At the same time the government became conciliatory towards the foreign merchants, suggesting that they might recover this money quickly from the Russians by raising their prices.

TAXES AND SERVICES

Foreign conspiracies in Muscovite cities were not the only reason their inhabitants were impoverished. Many sought to abandon their communities as a way of evading their communal responsibilities. In a petition dated March 1648 the townsmen of Novgorod charged that the destruction of their city [during the Time of Troubles and Swedish occupation] left it with very few inhabitants. Some were dispersed, others passed away and no new settlers arrived. The small number of individuals who remained were called upon to collect money, to act as toll collectors for the customs service, to perform numerous petty duties and the various crown services mandated by the city. The people themselves were systematically reduced to penury and impoverishment. Soon there would be no one to perform these services. Besides, numerous cossacks, musketeers, the metropolitan's people, monastery people and non-taxable individuals from diverse ranks sold a variety of merchandise in Novgorod and surrounding districts. They were temporary residents who kept shops, engaged in unlicensed commerce, paid no city taxes and performed none of the public services required of regular tradesmen. Some of their own merchants and tradesmen also evaded their fiscal responsibilities by becoming musketeers or cossacks.[34] Or else they entered various other ranks in which they could work as the metropolitan's bailiffs, clerks or even peasants. Meanwhile Novgorod increasingly was deserted. Non-tax-paying people of all ranks became officials of taxable units of major economic significance, which then became non-taxable. Hence the taxes and service obligations for which they would otherwise be liable fell disproportionately upon the remaining town dwellers.

In the aftermath of this petition the government ordered all defaulters to fulfill their crown service and tax obligations and, among other things, issued instructions like the following. "If children of the priests, deacons, officials and monastery people, or the priests, deacons and officials themselves engage in major trading, or become proprietors of shops, they must move their commercial activity to the market square, and register their shops as taxable municipal enterprises. Cossacks and gunners, or musketeers, who engage in major trade to the value of fifty rubles or more shall reside in the artisan quarter in towns, pay taxes and perform services, together with the regular tradesmen.[35] Those who choose to live outside of town, and continue to engage in commercial activity yielding more than fifty rubles, shall perform military service without monetary compensation from the sovereign. Merchants who serve, and realize a turnover of less than fifty rubles shall receive a salary in money, not the customary compensation in grain."

The peasants also had a tendency to avoid their fiscal obligations, to the detriment of the community. In accordance with Tsar Michael's edict to Cherdyn, for example, the town dwellers and regional elected officials compiled a register for the plow tax there, assessing five and a half plowlands, the homesteaders to record who lived close to whom.[36] After the tax roll was compiled many of the more substantial peasants conspired among their kin, clan and families, according to a petition signed by the governor, not to be included in the tax roll with the middling and lesser peasantry. They sought a light tax on homesteads, not the given assessment. Put another way, they enjoyed tax relief in comparison to middle and poor peasants. The latter found it increasingly difficult to bear the disproportionate tax burden, were impoverished and accumulated huge arrears. This arrangement moved Tsar Michael to order the prosperous peasants to pay their fair share of taxes, to forego Siberian tax exemptions just as the middle and poor peasants were required to do, to share a common burden devoid of tax privileges, to register and pay taxes according to their proper [peasant] category. Thus one peasant category would not bear the burden of another peasant category. This was possible because wealthy peasants were taxed separately from the poor and middle peasants. Nonetheless some refused to abide by the tsar's decree, and it turned out that they were powerful indeed. They bribed governors and their bullying caused many town dwellers and free peasants to leave. Meanwhile influential men continued to live tax-free lives. Tsar Alexis reissued his father's decree.

These machinations demonstrate how town dwellers and wealthier peasants sought to acquire power over the peasant commune, while the weaker peasants pledged themselves to the wealthier, under whose protection they too might avoid communal tax obligations. In addition, among the powerful service gentry the stronger continued to ruin the weak by enticing away their peasants. Gentry and junior boyars stated in a petition that the war, powerful people, boyars, courtiers, privy councillors and ecclesiastical authorities had combined to ruin them utterly. They requested that the free years[37] be cancelled, and no time limit be placed upon the return of fugitive peasants whose names appeared in the cadasters.[38] Landowners must be required to relinquish all fugitives the moment their rightful masters appeared to claim them. The ten-year time limit for tracking down old runaways was not rescinded. There was, however, a promise to delay the matter of the fixed period until peasants and their homesteads could be recorded accurately. "Once the names of peasants, cotters, their children, siblings and nephews were noted, and their status firmly established, there no longer would be free years."[39]

The manner in which the census was conducted gave rise to other complaints. Some entries on homesteads, peasants and cotters, taken according to oral declarations, were incomplete. To conceal actual numbers during census taking peasants from two and three homesteads often combined into one household. Several dwellings might also be fenced together, with a newly constructed gate serving all of them. Dwellings of peasants and landless laborers were listed as those of servants, inhabited dwellings as being vacant, and new settlements omitted altogether. In due course the lesser service people received yet another concession. In 1647 the ten-year time limit for the recovery of runaway peasants was increased to fifteen. The struggle between the interests of large and small landowners continued in this way, but once all peasants were registered the interests of the small landowners were in fact secured. Free years were no longer an issue.

Because town dwellers and peasants alike attempted to avoid onerous taxes a new method was devised to mitigate the evil of disproportionate fiscal obligations. On March 18, 1646 a new salt tax was imposed at the rate of two grivnas on every pud. "It is decreed," stated the edict, "that all minor duties, the previous salt tax, and the transit dues shall be rescinded everywhere. Henceforth no one anywhere shall be hurt by salt taxes. When the new salt tax is fully collected and is safely in our coffers it will constitute the revenue collected from our entire population. We shall total our military and courier service obligations,[40] and the new tax receipts will be allocated to these accounts. In this way the burden falls equally on all, with no exceptions. Everybody will pay and flogging will be superfluous.[41] Presently the taxes collected for the maintenance of musketeers and the communications and transport system are collected unevenly. Some are burdened by these taxes while others escape too lightly. Others pay substantially less, and only after a public beating, while some pay nothing at all because their names are omitted from both the tax rolls and the cadasters. Also foreigners who enjoy our pay and receive subsistence payments, this includes foreign merchants, will pay their just share along with our own townsmen. Merchants will carry salt to all of our cities and provinces free of duty or taxes, to be sold anywhere they wish. They will market it at a fair price, without adding unnecessary costs or creating monopolies. In this fashion many hardships and financial losses can be eliminated."

It is interesting to note in this admission by the government that it lacked a mechanism to correct the problem of unregistered persons, in other words those whose names were omitted from the tax rolls and cadasters. The government's desire to introduce a tax that would make public beatings unnecessary is also noteworthy. Finally, what is most interesting are the efforts of the crown to cheer the Russian people themselves through the promise of making foreigners fiscally responsible under the new system, on an equal basis with everyone else. The absence of partiality towards foreigners could not win over the adherents of the old ways, especially after they learned from the decree that the use of tobacco, that noxious weed brought in by foreigners, for the possession of which noses were cut off during Tsar Michael's reign, would henceforth be tolerated by the administration. The only stipulation was a state monopoly on its sale. At the beginning of 1648 the salt tax was repealed, but the tax on tobacco remained. Morozov also cut the expenses of the tsar's court by dismissing a certain number of servants, and reducing the salaries of those remaining. Needless to say such tactics won him few adherents.

IV

CHANGES IN THE RUSSIAN STATE

THE TSAR'S WEDDING

Early in 1647 the tsar decided to marry. From a pool of two hundred young women he selected six of the most beautiful, then narrowed the choice down to one, the daughter of Raf or Fedor Vsevolozhsky. At the news of her good fortune, however, the young woman was so overcome with emotion that she fainted, leading to speculations that she was prone to epilepsy. The upshot of this was that the hapless woman and her family were dispatched to Siberia. From there in 1653 they were transferred to a remote village which they owned in the Kasimov district.[1] Thus one foreign source relates it. A Russian version suggests that while residing in the palace Vsevolozhskaia somehow was corrupted by the mothers and sisters of the noble girls whom the tsar had rejected. Yet another source implicates Morozov in this affair. It seems that for reasons of his own Morozov did not approve of the Vsevolozhsky family, preferring instead the two Miloslavsky sisters. His plan called for the tsar to marry one of them, while he would wed the other, thereby guarding himself against any possibility of rivalry between him and the tsar's relatives.[2]

Only one excerpt from the official records of the case has survived (it testifies to the use of sorcery). According to the document Mishka Ivanov, a peasant belonging to the boyar Nikita Ivanovich Romanov (the tsar's cousin), was accused in Vsevolozhsky's legal complaint of sorcery, of alienation of affection and casting spells. Clearly no basis existed for proceeding against Morozov on the strength of a single piece of foreign information.[3] In all likelihood suspicion fell on him because within a year, on January 16, 1648, the tsar married Maria, daughter of Ilia Danilovich Miloslavsky, and ten days later Morozov married the tsaritsa's sister Anna. Moreover his predilection for foreigners was well known. For his part, the tsar already had agreed to a change in one old custom, by extending the period of mourning for his late father from forty days to one year. In view of this, there was much talk of widespread apprehension about the undesirable changes likely to follow the introduction of foreign customs at court after the tsar's marriage. In point of fact the fears proved groundless, for no such changes materialized, but the tsar's marriage did cause his subjects much unease.

Ilia Danilovich Miloslavsky's origins were rather insignificant. He was raised by an uncle, the famous crown secretary Gramotin,[4] and used his new position to enrich himself. What is more, the avarice of his relatives, lords-in-waiting such as Leonty Pleshcheev who was in charge of the Chancellery of Crown Revenues, and Trakhaniotov, head of the Chancellery of Artillery,[5] was limitless. Grumblings could be heard everywhere. The people assembled in the churches and determined to press their complaints against Pleshcheev to the tsar, but the individuals close to the tsar who received these petitions consistently misrepresented them. The petitioners' grievances went unheeded, so they resolved to bring them to the tsar in person.

On May 25, 1648 as he was returning from the Trinity monastery a mob seized the tsar's horse by the bridle, demanding that the sovereign dismiss Pleshcheev and replace him with a good man. Securing his promise to comply, the pacified crowd began to disperse. Suddenly several of Pleshcheev's friends from the court hurled curses at them. Adding injury to insult, they charged the crowd on their horses, striking some of the rebellious subjects with their whips. The crowd went wild and stones flew at Pleshcheev's defenders, forcing them to seek cover in the palace. The mob hurried after them. To appease them Pleshcheev was taken away for execution, then seized from the executioner and killed on the spot. Morozov came out to the palace porch to plead with the mutinous mob in the name of the tsar. In response a roar went up from the crowd, and the enraged rabble threatened Morozov with Pleshcheev's fate. The regent only saved himself by darting back inside the palace. Meanwhile the rioters proceeded to loot Morozov's home, killing one of the serfs who tried to protect his master's property. They told Morozov's wife that were it not for the fact that she was the tsar's relative they would have chopped her to bits, then they tore off her valuable adornments and tossed them into the street. They killed the conciliar secretary Chistoy, and threatened with a similar fate the wealthy leading merchant Shorin,[6] whom they blamed for the steep increase in salt prices, but he managed to escape. His home was looted, along with those of Prince Nikita Odoevsky,[7] Prince Alexis Mikhailovich Lvov[8] and other nobles.

The next afternoon a terrible fire broke out and raged until midnight. Petrovka, Dmitrovka, Tverskaia, Nikitskaia, Arbat, Chertolie [districts of Moscow], and the entire artisan quarter went up in flames. After the blaze was extinguished a new revolt broke out, and a detachment of foreign soldiers attempted to defend the palace. They marched to the rhythm of drumbeats with banners unfurled while the Muscovites made way for them, bowing low and swearing that there was no enmity between them. Indeed they assured the foreigners that the Muscovites knew them to be honorable men who disapproved of the way the boyars deceived and oppressed the populace. When the foreign troops positioned themselves to guard the palace, knowing the love that his subjects bore for him, the tsar sent his cousin Nikita Ivanovich Romanov to face the rebels. Nikita Ivanovich went out hat in hand and conveyed to the crowd the tsar's pledge to meet the people's demands. He urged them all to disperse so that the sovereign might proceed with the business of fulfilling his promise. The crowd assured him that they bore no ill will toward their tsar, that their grievance was against those who robbed in his name. They refused to disband until Morozov and Trakhaniotov were handed over to them. Nikita Ivanovich replied that both were in hiding but would be hunted down and put to death, whereupon the mob finally dispersed. Trakhaniotov was seized near the Trinity monastery and executed.

MOROZOV'S FATE

Morozov was exiled to the distant St. Cyril monastery in Beloozero while the court considered how best to placate the crowd in its anger against Morozov. Tsar Alexis ordered that the musketeers be treated to wine and mead, and his father-in-law invited a number of Muscovites to dine with him. He selected some of the hundredmen[9] and entertained them for several days running. The places of those killed quickly were filled by others, all reputedly more honorable men. Finally, taking advantage of a religious procession the tsar turned to the people with a speech. "It saddened me greatly," he said, "to learn of Pleshcheev's and Trakhaniotov's excesses, committed in my name but against my will. Their places have been filled by more worthy individuals, sympathetic to the needs of the people. They shall issue their judgments without resorting to bribes, and everyone is to be treated equally. I personally will see to it."

The tsar also promised to lower the price of salt and eliminate all monopolies, which the populace acknowledged with low bows as the tsar continued. "I promised to turn Morozov over to you, yet even as I admit that I cannot vindicate him altogether, I also cannot bring myself to condemn him. This man is very dear to me. He is the husband of my tsaritsa's sister, and it would pain me to turn him over for execution."

Tears rolled down the tsar's cheeks as he spoke these words . The people shouted "Long live the tsar! Let the will of the Lord and the sovereign be done!" Other sources suggest that things were manipulated so cleverly that in the end the people themselves sought Morozov's pardon.

The precise beginning of Morozov's troubles is difficult to establish. One thing is certain, namely that in August he was still at the St. Cyril monastery because on August 6 the tsar sent this letter to the monastery abbot. It proved how deeply he was attached to Morozov, not to mention how much he feared the public wrath against the boyar. "We are informed," he wrote, "that on the feast of the Dormition [August 15] various people from many towns will assemble in a large gathering at the St. Cyril monastery. According to this same information our boyar Boris Ivanovich Morozov is presently there with you. When you receive our letter you must safeguard Boris Ivanovich from all evil, and together with him consider seriously what best to do. Is it better for him to remain with you in the monastery during the fair or go elsewhere? Most prudent for him would be to leave before the fair begins. When it is over he can return to your monastery, to reside as before. It is imperative that you protect our boyar Boris Ivanovich. Should any evil befall him, you shall find yourselves in our great disfavor."

Even this failed to satisfy the tsar. On the margins at the top, down the sides of the letter and in the spaces between the upper lines, he added in his own hand "You must take this letter and follow its instructions, guarding him from all evil. Once you have discussed its contents with him, should he determine to go elsewhere, you must keep his plans from being discovered. If anyone gets wind of them, be assured that so shall I, and I will see to it that you suffer. You would do well to shield him. It is as if you did it for me, and I shall reward you in a matter unprecedented since the beginning of time. Show this note to him who is my friend."

Upon his return home Morozov no longer filled the post of regent although he remained in the sovereign's inner circle, using his influence to promote the general well-being, helping everyone who turned to him. It is written that in spite of Morozov's sick body, wasted by serious illness, gout and dropsy, he still possessed a strong mind and a great capacity for counsel, which the tsar frequently sought in all important matters at the home of the invalid. In May 1648 Morozov, at least on the face of it, moved well away from the center of activity. Soon a new person, a cleric, stepped into the spotlight. His name was Nikon.

NIKON

In that terrible year of 1605, just as the Time of Troubles was beginning for the Muscovite realm, a son was born to the peasant Mina in the village of Velmanov, or Veldemanov, in the Kniaginin region ninety versts from Nizhny Novgorod. He was called Nikita. We have no way of gauging the extent to which the appalling events which transpired during Nikita's minority were etched in his memory, nor do we know whether the insurrection in the name of faith and the realm which broke out in his native region left an impression on the little boy. We can state with confidence that the events which occurred in his immediate family must have played a role in shaping the child's character. Sorrow haunted his family. Those whose natures are easily tempered are those whom sorrows temper most. Nikita lost his mother when he was very young, and his father brought home a stepmother. We all know too well what it meant to have a stepmother in the Russian family of old. Nikita's was no exception. She so persecuted the child that his very life was often endangered, yet somehow Nikita learned to read. At the time this was the only reliable way for a man of humble origins to make a name for himself.

A wealth of spiritual richness and natural energy made it impossible for Nikita to remain trapped for long in the environment into which fate had cast him. The young man's imagination was inflamed by prophesies of an extraordinary future. Both Christian monks and Mordvinian sorcerers predicted for him either a kingdom or a patriarchate. His ability to read inclined the inquisitive youth towards books, all religious, leading him to join the monastery of St. Makary at Zheltye Vody. Soon the secular world summoned him once more, when Nikita's relatives prevailed upon him to marry. Meanwhile his literacy and talent enabled him to secure a benefice when he was a mere twenty years old. The young priest stood out prominently among his colleagues. It was not too long before the merchants of Moscow led him to the capital.

The priest Nikita Minich had three children and buried them all. Eventually the parish and a childless family became so oppressive to him that he and his wife agreed to separate. She entered the St. Alexis convent, while he proceeded to the White Sea, to the secluded little Anzersk hermitage, where he changed his name from Nikita to Nikon. His passionate nature and lack of self-control, along with a predilection for exposing hypocrisy, made it impossible to get along with the brethren for long. He left the Anzersk hermitage and settled in the Kozheozersk monastery (in the eparchy of Novgorod, district of Kargopol). In this fraternity more discerning judges of his abilities were found. In 1643 he was elected to the office of abbot. Just as the priest Nikita had done earlier, the new abbot Nikon quickly attracted attention. His fame spread and soon reached Moscow.

When Nikon appeared in the capital on monastery business in 1646 the young Tsar Alexis Mikhailovich was particularly attentive to him. Because he was impressionable the pious Alexis soon fell under the influence of this remarkable ascetic. As a result Nikon remained in Moscow, where he became archimandrite of the New Savior monastery. Every Friday he was required to attend matins in the court chapel so that afterward he might converse with the tsar. Not content with confining himself to edifying conversations, Nikon soon expressed his concern about the oppressed, the widows and the orphans. Tsar Alexis appointed him to hear their grievances. Some petitioners were granted audiences with Nikon in the monastery, others met him along the way to the court, and presented their petitions there. In the troubled year of 1648 Nikon was elevated to the office of metropolitan of Novgorod.

PROBLEMS OF TAXATION

When the revolt was over the young tsar was kept busy in Moscow carrying out his promise to the people by removing the source of their complaints. On July 16, 1648 the sovereign conferred with Patriarch Joseph[10] and the entire consecrated assembly. He spoke with the boyars, the lords-in-waiting and members of the boyar council. Alexis inquired about articles written into the rules of the Apostles and the Holy Fathers and into the municipal statutes of the Greek rulers. He asked if any were relevant to Russian governmental and national matters. If so, they needed to be copied. The tsar further instructed that the decrees of earlier great sovereigns and verdicts of the boyars on all governmental and national affairs be assembled and compared with the old law code. The articles of the code against which no decrees of the tsars or decisions of the boyar council were entered in the law code in former times, were to be rewritten and copied by members of a general council. This was to ensure that people of all ranks in the Muscovite realm, from the meanest to the most exalted, received equal justice in their suits and claims. The sovereign ordered all relevant materials collected and recorded. The boyars were to send copies to Prince Nikita Ivanovich Odoevsky,[11] Prince Semeon Vasilievich Prozorovsky,[12] to the nobleman Prince Fedor Fedorovich

Volkonsky,[13] also to the crown secretaries Gavriil Leontiev[14] and Fedor Griboedov.[15] The tsar conferred with the patriarch on this matter which was so vital to both governmental and national issues.

Upon receiving approval from the boyar council the sovereign issued the following instruction. "From amongst the table attendants and crown agents, the Muscovite gentry, inhabitants of Moscow and the officials, two men are to be elected. Also from amongst the gentry and junior boyars two men from each of the largest towns, with the exception of Novgorod, are to be appointed. One man shall represent each of the five boroughs of Novgorod, one shall be selected from every one of the smaller towns, three from within the merchantry, two men each shall represent the leading merchants and Cloth Merchants' Hundreds, and one shall be appointed by each of the tax-paying free settlements, as well as the inner cities and town quarters.[16] We require good and sensible men, that these elected officials assist us in acting on governmental and national affairs, that henceforth all such weighty issues are inviolable, in accordance with the tsar's latest decree and the Law Code of 1649."[17]

The elected officials presented to the tsar a petition in which they stated, among other things, "In Moscow and its environs, and in the towns, patriarchs, monasteries, boyars and other ranking people have converted pastures into personal holdings and arable land, and benefit from their tax exemptions and privileges. This is taking place on territory which traditionally belonged to the sovereign in perpetuity, and has been used as common land from time immemorial. Mortgagers and lien-holders, together with their servants, now inhabit these settlements. They have either purchased or seized homesteads, shops and stone cellars, when payments on them fell into arrears. They trade in a variety of goods. Using their influence and the protection of those indebted to them, they purchase customs houses, taverns and various mortgaged property from their original owners, then use these facilities to impoverish servicemen and taxpayers, causing many to go into debt and abandon their trades. Under our previous sovereigns nothing like this ever occurred, either in Moscow or in any other town of the Muscovite realm. The tsar's officials were always visible everywhere. The sovereign must issue decrees and instructions that all is to be returned to its former condition, that everything once again must belong to the tsar."

Alexis approved the petition and decreed the following. "In Moscow and its environs, in towns and their laboring quarters, and in the various tax-exempt towns and settlements, all artisan and trading quarters shall be subject to fiscal, service and labor obligations to us, and serve us on the same terms as do our other taxpayers. To prevent evasion of fiscal responsibilities no artisan, tradesman or merchant may serve a patriarch, a monastery, boyars or individuals of any rank whatsoever, either in the town quarters and their immediate vicinity, or the tax-exempt settlements." Growing and selling tobacco were prohibited that same year of 1648. The following year the tsar's injunction addressed the earlier requests of merchants. "You English, together with your possessions, shall put out to sea. You will trade with Muscovite merchants in all kinds of goods in Archangel during brief return visits there. Nevertheless you are prohibited from travelling to Moscow and other Muscovite towns, either with or without your wares. The reason why you English are forbidden to sojourn there is because in the past you traded by permission of the tsar's charters, issued in a gesture of love and friendship at the request of your English king Charles. Now it has come to the attention of the sovereign that the English have brought much harm to their land by murdering Charles, their rightful king. Such evil actions preclude your continued stay in the Muscovite realm."[18]

REVOLT IN SOLVYCHEGODSK

At the same time as the government, in response to numerous requests, hastened to eliminate the causes of unrest, a revolt flared up in the Far North. As we have observed, there were insurrections against military governors in the preceding reign. Now, in the summer of 1648, Fedor Priklonsky was sent to Solvychegodsk to collect five hundred and thirty-five rubles from the town quarter and the district for payment of military salaries. As its residents subsequently testified, he resorted to indiscriminate beatings to raise the money. Even prior to this the townsmen and villagers tried to reduce the number of such beatings by pooling their resources and bringing money to the official in return for his agreement not to demand further payments, as well as his promise to return to Moscow. Thus too did the residents of Solvychegodsk deal with Priklonsky. Complying with a popular decision they collected twenty rubles from the entire district, then offered the money on condition that Priklonsky make no further demands, either on the town or the district. Just then some people arrived from Moscow and recounted how they exacted revenge upon those even more powerful than Priklonsky. For his part Priklonsky collected money for Morozov, even after that traitor was no longer present, causing the inhabitants of Solvychegodsk to regret their action.

Why had they paid Priklonsky twenty rubles? The community's money must be recovered. Accordingly on June 21 the district elder Bogdan Shulepov and the public scribe David Khaminov[19] went to Priklonsky and demanded that the money be returned. The matter did not end there. The obnoxious lout Khaminov took advantage of the situation. Pushing himself forward, he shouted at Priklonsky "The same fate that the governors Fedor Golovachev and Alexis Bolshov met awaits you at our hands.[20] Like them you shall be killed." As he left Priklonsky's courtyard Khaminov called out a signal, in response to which the mob besieged the houses of both the governor and Priklonsky, and kept vigil there all night. The following day Priklonsky set out for the assembly hall but the mob, one hundred or more strong, followed him, led by the same Khaminov and Shulepov. The people shouted at Priklonsky "You steal money for a traitor!" From the throng rang out the voices of those who had come from Moscow "He is collecting money for a traitor!" To the people these words immediately spelled a legitimate piece of evidence. The mob rushed the chancellery, seized Priklonsky's credentials [the tsar's decree], the public funds and the documents, tearing many of them to shreds. The people threw themselves at Priklonsky, beat him, dragged him into the street and led him to his lodging, where they confiscated his possessions. Recovering his senses, Priklonsky first went to the court of Prince Shakhovskoy, then to the cathedral, where he locked himself in the rectory. The enraged mob appeared there too, calling for Priklonsky's death, but fortunately for him Fedor Stroganov's mother, the widow Matriona, interceded in his behalf. Inasmuch as the Stroganovs had built the church, Matrena convinced her servants not to surrender Priklonsky to the mob. When night fell he escaped in a boat on the Vychegda river.

On July 17 Priklonsky notified Moscow about the events in Solvychegodsk, and on August 4 word came of a revolt in Ustiug. Mikhail Vasilievich Miloslavsky was the governor of Ustiug at the time. The crown clerks Onisim Mikhailov and Grigory Pokhabov handled all of his affairs. The residents of Ustiug, both from the town and the nearby district, presented Mikhailov with two hundred and sixty rubles from the territorial tax as a mark of respect. According to the news from Moscow, soon they regretted having paid the money and considered how to retrieve it. For several days the peasant Onisim Roshkin, together with his friends, appealed to Mikhailov to return the money, but he refused to part with it. They also requested the governor's intervention in the matter, all to no avail.

As July 8 dawned a huge crowd from nearby areas gathered in Ustiug for the Feast of St. Procopius, the miracle-worker and patron saint of that town. The townsmen and district peasants could talk about nothing but the two hundred and sixty rubles. The next day, July 9, a crowd of peasants filled the chancellery, the courtroom and the chambers of the local magistrate, having decided to recover the money from Onisim Mikhailov without fail. Just then the blacksmith Moisey Chagin arrived in the courtroom and shouted to the local judges "Do you have some sort of a plan for retrieving the money from Onisim?" "It would be a good thing if we could get it away from him, but how," the people wondered, "when the crown clerk refuses to return it?" "If he persists we shall kill him!" cried out Chagin. It appears that the local magistrate Volkov voiced some sort of objection because Chagin threw himself at him, grabbed him by the hands and chest and dragged him out of the chancellery, while his comrades Vaska Shamshurnitsyn and Shurka Babin slammed their fists against his throat and beat him. They carried Volkov out into the town square, and paraded him from one end to the other and back. They also grabbed the local judge Ignatiev, who broke free and with his friend the church treasurer Motokhov burst into the governor's home. He told Miloslavsky everything that was transpiring in the chancellery and town square.

At that precise moment the governor was enjoying a lavish meal with his crown clerk Onisim Mikhailov. Hearing the bad news he hastened to the market square to quash the revolt, viewing it as little more than a peevish quarrel. The agitators abandoned Volkov and went after the governor. They seized him and took him to his court. Chagin and his friends were already there. They broke down the gates, destroyed everything in the court itself—the vestibule, the storerooms, the larders—and looted the governor's possessions. Then they seized the crown clerk Mikhailov, killed him and threw him into the river. Potentially the same fate awaited the governor, the rebels demanding that he hand over his other crown clerk Pokhabov, but Miloslavsky swore that he had no knowledge of his whereabouts. The mob would have dragged the governor to the river when for some inexplicable reason it had a change of heart. The crowd contented themselves with forcing him, his wife and mother-in-law to kiss the icon, and swear that they were not concealing Pokhabov. Meanwhile the tocsin sounded in the town, and five homes were plundered, those of the townsmen Merkury Obukhov, Dmitry Kotelnikov, Vasily Bubnov, Grigory Gubin and the crown clerk Pokhabov, who only saved himself by flight. The parish clerk Ignashka Yakhlakov carried around a folded document, repeating to all and sundry in the town that the tsar's charter authorizing the looting of seventeen houses in Ustiug had arrived from Moscow.

It was not until August 4 that word of these disturbances in Ustiug reached Moscow. The table attendant Prince Ivan Grigorievich Romoda-novsky, with two hundred musketeers, was dispatched to investigate the matter. Romodanovsky arrived in Ustiug on September 7. Chagin, along with his two comrades Ignashka Yakhlakov and Ivashka Bely, decided not to wait for his arrival and vanished. The investigation and interrogations commenced. The peasant Fedka Nogin, who confessed to prodding Chagin into leading the revolt and murdering Mikhailov, was hanged. They also hanged the butcher Tereshko and Ivashko, nicknamed Soldier. Both confessed to the murder of Mikhailov, but only after a confession was elicited from Soldier under torture. He was attached to a strappado and the supporting stone removed from under his heel. Soldier confessed that in prison the robber Buben had taught him sorcery, instructing him on the way to survive interrogation under torture by pouring molten wax into cold water,[21] and pronouncing an incantation "The sky is of bast and the earth is of bast, and just as the dead in the ground hear nothing, so I shall feel nothing, neither the cruelty nor the torture." Ivashka Shamshurnitsyn also was hanged.

Romodanovsky overstayed his welcome in Ustiug. On December 23 the local judge Senka Mylnik appealed to the tsar on behalf of the local community, charging that Romodanovsky tortured innocent people, and townsmen fled from him in all directions. The community gave Romoda-novsky six hundred rubles, and one hundred to his official Kuzma, to no avail. As a consequence of this petition another investigator, the table attendant Nikita Alekseevich Ziuzin, arrived in Ustiug in January 1649 and asked Romodanovsky why he had neglected to submit a report to the tsar. "On January 10," Romodanovsky responded, "I dispatched reports of the investigation and interrogations, together with the instruments of torture and the chancellery list. I sent nothing earlier because I was waiting for many district peasants to be interrogated. It turned out that the tsar's order for the procedure was not a sufficiently compelling reason for many of the townsmen and district peasants to submit to an interrogation. They had become powerful enough to risk refusing to make the journey to Ustiug from the outlying districts. The less powerful among the peasants who could not avoid such interrogations routinely lied to the tsar in their statements and testimonies."

Ziuzin asked the inhabitants of Ustiug for their version of the story. According to their calculations, in addition to the six hundred rubles which Romodanovsky and his underlings had received, one hundred and eleven rubles, twenty-two altyns and two dengas were expended for preparing and serving the food, brewing and serving the beer and distributing monetary gifts at the welcoming procession, banquets and meals for other special occasions. That money, which was a community expense, was borrowed from several sources. Six hundred and fifty rubles from the collector Semeon Skriabin of the Siberian reserve, another six hundred from the Archangel monastery, and a promissory note issued for the remaining two hundred rubles. The community elders then divided the entire sum into portions to be collected from each plowland.

During his interrogation by Ziuzin the crown clerk Kuzemka Lvov testified. "The local judges frequently brought me sacks of money which I refused, reminding them that they had given Onisim two hundred rubles, then killed him for it. I feared the same fate. They insisted that I accept it not as a payment for services, but as a token of respect and wishes for a long life for the sovereign. They also reminded me that in Moscow my own estate had been looted and burned. I agreed to accept the money. It was in a packet bearing their seal. I have no idea how much it contained. When I took it, I made it plain that in Moscow I would turn it over to the tsar's treasury in the Chancellery for Foreign Affairs."

Romodanovsky's people declared that their master had indeed accepted the money, which he vowed to declare when he reached Moscow. They testified that the prince attempted to refuse it several times over, then accepted it only after the people offered it to him on the day after Tsarevich Dmitry Alekseevich's nameday, and begged him to "take it for the sake of the tsarevich." Romodanovsky gave the same testimony, but the magistrates pointed to a discrepancy in his peoples' statements. They showed that initially, on September 22, the people had offered one hundred rubles, then added another five hundred and fifty on October 19, not the twenty-seventh as the prince indicated. What was more, countless depositions proved that he had taken bribes from prisoners.

COMPLAINTS AGAINST MOROZOV

Meanwhile Morozov's name remained on the lips of the disaffected. We noted already that widespread protests evoked reprisals against moneylenders. Deprived of their privileged position, they vented their rage on Morozov. On January 17, 1649 Savinka Korepin, the old moneylender who held the boyar Nikita Ivanovich's mortgage, came to the town house of Ivan Pestsov from Kolomna and complained. "I prospered when I

served the boyar Nikita Ivanovich, but now that I serve the sovereign I
am in a bad way. The boyars Boris Ivanovich Morozov and Ilia Danilovich Miloslavsky are responsible. This enterprise of theirs will cause us
to wade in blood, whereas the boyars Morozov, Miloslavsky and their
friends are certain to be stoned." To this Pestsov replied "Why make such
indecent accusation, you old peasant clod. We would not hesitate to kill
you all if the sovereign so willed it." "We will kill you from our peasant huts," Korepin replied, "and your own peasants will be on our side."
    The same Savinka was at Pestsov's on January 18 and remarked "Our
sovereign is young and relies on the advice of the boyars Morozov and
Miloslavsky. They rule everything and the sovereign is well aware of this,
yet says nothing. Morozov behaves cautiously, with deliberation, pretend-
ing to be powerless and claiming that he has relinquished all of his administrative duties. They wanted to send Prince Yakov Kudenetovich
Cherkassky into exile,[22] and had the wagons all set for his journey. In the
end, fearing us because the village communes were in such a state of
ferment, they decided not to banish him. If they attempt to do it now, and
the boyar Nikita Ivanovich chooses to proceed to the executioner's
block[23] to address the community, we will all support him, and beat
Morozov and Miloslavsky. Those who favored this plan [the plea for
Morozov's return is probably meant] also will suffer our revenge. We will
not personally do all the beating. There is no shortage of strong men
among us, and they will take the initiative. In this matter they shall all be
with us, even the musketeers who had no hand in this business. The
boyars Nikita Ivanovich Romanov, Prince Yakov Kudenetovich Cherkassky, Prince Dmitry Mamstriukovich Cherkassky[24] and Prince Ivan Andreevich Golitsyn shall ride out to the executioner's block. They will be joined
by musketeers and various other people, who will beat and rob Morozov,
Miloslavsky and others."
    The tsar ordered all the boyars to the torture chamber, where Korepin
was tortured mercilessly in an attempt to arrive at the truth of what really had occurred. In his agony Savinka revealed that he was drunk and
acted alone. He added that in the winter, during the St. Nicholas holidays
[following December 6], he was in the stable at Nikita Ivanovich Romanov's court, in the company of some criminals convicted of crimes
against the boyars. They included Afonka "Dog's Snout,"[25] together with
about ten men from the town of Unzha. He discussed these matters with
them, and was told that rebellions, bloodshed and pillage were likely.
Savinka was executed. Under questioning the musketeer Andriushka

Kalinin recounted "About an hour and a half before dark, on January 4, I heard the following from Andriushka Larionov. He was at the house of the boyar Yakov Kudenetovich Cherkassky, and learned from Prince Yakov and his nephew Prince Peter that four musketeers had come to them to say "There will be trouble on Epiphany [January 6] when the tsar goes out to the blessing of the water." At the interrogation Larionov admitted that he had fabricated the entire story without the prince's knowledge, so they cut out his tongue and banished him.

KIEV'S LEARNED MONKS

Other accusations against Morozov began to circulate. We have seen that at the time Moscow needed a system of education, for which the Muscovites naturally had to turn to the Little Russians, because they alone had a well developed pedagogical system. The tsar's chamberlain Fedor Mikhailovich Rtishchev[26] was well known in Moscow for his great love of learning. Not far from Moscow, along the Kiev road on the banks of the [Moscow] river, he erected the St. Andrew monastery, to which he summoned thirty monks from Little Russian monasteries, to teach those who wished to study Church Slavonic and Greek grammar, rhetoric and philosophy and to translate books. Obliged to spend his days at court, Rtishchev spent long nights at St. Andrew's with the learned monks.

There were those who objected to this novel approach. In the spring of 1650 Ivan Vasilievich Zasetsky, Luchka Timofeev Golosov, and the sexton at the Annunciation cathedral, Kostka Ivanov, met at the cell of the monk Saul and whispered amongst themselves. "Fedor Rtishchev is learning to read and write from the Kievans, but there is heresy in these texts." Turning to the sexton, Golosov said "Inform the archpriest (the tsar's confessor) from the Annunciation cathedral that I have no wish to study with the monks from Kiev. Those elders are not good. I have not witnessed a particle of goodness in any of them. For the present I defer to Fedor Rtishchev because I fear him, but I have no desire to pursue learning. Those who study Latin stray from the true path. Advise the archpriest that Perfilka Zerkalnikov and Ivan Ozerov went to study in Kiev. Fedor Rtishchev obtained an entry permit for them, and together they went to study more Latin with the Kievan monks. When they are finished with their studies and return to us, they shall bring us much grief. Somehow we must find a way to recall them to Moscow. Even now they humiliate us all, and demean the pious archpriests Ivan, Stepan and others." The sexton Kostka responded to this with "Foma the priest said to

me 'Please tell me what to do. My spiritual children Ivan Ozerov and Per-
fily Zerkalnikov are requesting permission to study in Kiev.' 'For the love
of God,' I counselled him 'do not let them go, for He will place the guilt
upon your soul.' 'I would gladly refuse permission,' Foma declared, 'but
they persist in their tearful entreaties, and take no account of what I say.'"
Then the three adherents of the true path whispered amongst themselves. They spread rumors about Morozov, charging that "Boris
Ivanovich keeps a spiritual father only for show, while in fact he has
begun to support the Kievans. It is now widely known that he himself
inclines towards these heretics." In Moscow such attempts by malcon-
tents to fan the flames of revolt against Morozov and Miloslavsky, in the
names of Romanov and Cherkassky, were extinguished immediately.

PSKOV AND NOVGOROD IN REVOLT

Although to all appearances peace reigned once more the vexatious name
of Morozov spread anew through the crowds, this time along the northwestern border. A huge rebellion flared in Pskov and Novgorod. According to the Stolbovo treaty[27] both sides [Russian and Swedish] agreed to
surrender each other's fugitives. Nonetheless, over the course of several
decades a great number of inhabitants from the regions which Tsar
Michael had ceded to Sweden fled to the Muscovite side of the border.
The Swedish government demanded their return. In the eyes of the Muscovite government to defer to such demands was tantamount to a con-
scious surrender of Orthodox Christians to the Lutheran faith.[28] The pious
tsar simply could not bring himself to place such a burden of sin on his
soul, so he determined to spare the fugitives instead. A portion of the
required ransom, that is to say twenty thousand rubles, was transferred
to [Login] Nummens, the Swedish agent in Moscow, who took the money
by way of Pskov to the Swedish border. At the same time eleven hundred
chetverts[29] of grain were scheduled for transfer from the tsar's granary in
Pskov to Sweden, also in partial payment of the ransom.

We have remarked already how badly foreigners were received
throughout the Muscovite realm, especially in Pskov. During Michael's
reign the residents of Pskov confined themselves to complaints, which
were dutifully recorded in the chronicles. Since the events of 1648 in
Moscow rumor had it that the young tsar was surrounded by individuals
harboring malevolent designs towards him, that Morozov favored foreigners over Russians.

In February of 1650 the news reached Pskov that a Swede was on his way from Moscow, carrying a large sum in government funds, and that an order was issued for the residents of Pskov to turn over their grain to the Swedes. On February 24, at Shrovetide, a letter from the tsar regarding the transfer of grain arrived for the governor Sobakin. Once the people learned about this they grew extremely agitated. On the twenty-seventh of the same month about thirty of the lower ranking men came to Archbishop Makary, petitioning him to prevail upon the governor not to release the grain, pending their own petition to the tsar.

Makary sent for Sobakin, who hastened to present himself before the archbishop. Upon learning what had transpired, he insisted that it was his duty to obey the tsar's decree to the letter, and to waste no time in turning over the grain, after which they could present petitions to the tsar over his head. Meanwhile the governor felt duty bound to reprimand the people of Pskov, warning them not to meddle in matters which did not concern them. He addressed the crowd angrily, asking the people why they had swarmed the archbishop's court like rabble. The crowd stormed the archbishop's court and called the priests bawlers, not a very nice term to use around Pskov, especially in view of the events surrounding the Time of Troubles.[30] Then one of Pskov's citizens reproached Sobakin with "You, Nikifor Sergeevich, admitted foreigners to the town (into the fortress which no foreigner is permitted to enter), to Fedor Emelianovich's banquet." "What of it?" Sobakin shot back. "I am no recluse. The reason I allowed them to see Emelianov [a Pskov townsman] was because he was ill, and unable to leave the court. Besides, he negotiated a lucrative trade deal for the tsar." A furious quarrel broke out. The governor called for the town clerk and ordered him to compile a list of all the citizens of Pskov who were involved. All rushed out of the [archbishop's] cell where the crowd had assembled, and were met with an uproar. Those on the archbishop's side yelled out at the crowd "It is you who forced us to submit our petition during such a commotion, now the governor will write to the sovereign that we started it, and we will suffer the disgrace!" The din subsided and the crowd dispersed, vowing to reassemble the next day to pursue the quarrel.

On February 28 people of many ranks gathered in the town meeting house square. They exclaimed that grain must not be carried out of the Pskov kremlin. The most prosperous of the traders and musketeers from the old regiment declared authoritatively that such willfulness could not guide action, that the tsar's decree could not be opposed. If grain is scarce the tsar must be petitioned. Tempers cooled, and men of the better sort dispersed to their homes. Suddenly the musketeers came running from the Petrovsky gates shouting "The foreigner is coming. He is carrying money from the Moscow treasury!" At that very moment Nummens, with a bailiff named Timashev, was indeed riding along the outer perimeter of the town wall, following the path of the Velikaia river to the foreign merchants' hostel in Zavelichie [the region beyond the Velikaia]. As he approached the Vlasiev gates a throng of people came out and surrounded him. Some wanted to kill him on the spot with rods, others to drag him to a hole in the ice on the frozen river, and still others wanted to know how he had come by the money from Moscow's coffers. Nummens explained how it all transpired, and requested a meeting with Fedor Emelianov. The fateful name of that despised man, the friend of foreigners, poured oil on the flames. Cries rang out of "Torture the foreigner! Torture Fedor!" They seized the treasure and carried it to the chancellery, whence they took it to the church of the Snetogorsk monastery, placing it under lock and key. Nummens was escorted to the town meeting house where the entire assemblage interrogated him, confiscated his official papers, then moved him to the church of the Snetogorsk monastery, placing him under the guard of five priests, five townsmen and twenty musketeers.

Next they proceeded to Emelianov. He hid from them but his wife turned over the letter which the tsar had sent to her husband. The letter was read out to the entire assemblage. It concluded with the injunction "Nobody in your parts must know about this decree of ours." These words produced even more agitation and the people shouted "The letter was sent to Fedor in secret. The tsar knows nothing of it!" Hearing the noise and the tocsin, and witnessing the people running through the streets with weapons, Governor Sobakin galloped up to the square. He tried to convince the citizens of Pskov that the government's treasury was none of their concern. "The tsar's will is supreme," they replied. "If the money was carried from Moscow with his knowledge it should have been carried through the town openly, not furtively along the outer wall.' Sobakin went to the archbishop. About an hour later Makary appeared in person in the square, together with priests and an icon of the Holy Trinity. He tried to reason with the people, who merely kept repeating "In the end the sovereign's will shall be done, but we refuse to release grain from our kremlin without his decree."

The agitators assembled in the square on March 1 and elected leaders from amongst their numbers. They included the public scribe Tomilka

Vasiliev Slepoy, and the musketeers Proshka Koza and Sorokoum Kopy-to, who immediately issued commands. Nummens was ordered brought before them, they placed two huge vats in the square, and stood on them along with Nummens, so that everyone might see them. The hapless Swede was interrogated yet again. Executioners with knouts were stationed beneath him to loosen his tongue. Documents seized from Nummens were read out to the people assembled below, then in the presence of all they were placed in boxes, sealed and deposited in the church of the Snetogorsk monastery. Papers not needed were returned to Nummens. After March 3 public unrest subsided. It was agreed that petitioners would be sent to the tsar in Moscow.

Traders and various other individuals from Pskov travelled constantly to Novgorod for one thing and another, and conversations with them revealed many troubling matters. Rumors proliferated in Novgorod, especially after the tsar's decree arrived ordering that grain be purchased for him. Criers in the marketplace urged people to buy grain only for their personal use, not in large quantities like chetveriki.[31] A Novgorod resident, Nikita Teterin, returned from abroad, reported that foreigners were assembling to await the arrival of government funds from Moscow. When the money arrived they planned to advance on Novgorod. Rumors circulated to the effect that "the sovereign knows nothing of this. It is the boyars who are releasing the funds."

Five days later, on the evening of March 15, the Danish envoy Grab arrived in Novgorod, and the people said "The foreigner is here with the cash box." In a discussion with the Russian interpreter Nechay Driabin, who was travelling with the envoy, the townsman Trofim Volk learned that substantial government funds indeed were on their way from Moscow to the foreigners, who had arrived from Moscow. He scarcely could be expected to keep such news to himself. Another townsman, Yelisey Lisitsa, appeared in the square in front of the town hall, shouting for all to hear that the wealthy merchant Semeon Stoianov was transporting meat and grain out of the country, while foreigners were taking out large sums of money from Moscow. A huge mob gathered in response to Lisitsa's outcry, and proceeded to deal with the foreigners.

Instead of calming the people the district elder Andrei Gavrilov incited a rebellion. No sooner did the Danish envoy leave Novgorod than he was apprehended and beaten. Volk outdid himself for the benefit of the crowd. He punched Grab on the cheeks, broke his nose, threatened him with a knife and finally stabbed him. The envoy's belongings, among which were found the government funds, were left intact and taken to the armory. The mob then proceeded to loot the homes of its own wealthy citizens, the brothers Stoianov, Vasily Nikiforov, Vasily Proezzhalov, Mikhail Viazma and Andrei Zemsky. From the Liubsky Court they brought the foreign traders to the town hall. In the Stone quarter the rebels overpowered the men guarding the town gates, and sounded the tocsin. The warning bell pealed and pealed. Metropolitan Nikon, the governor and a lord-in-waiting Prince Fedor Andreevich Khilkov, instructed the captains of the musketeers and the junior boyars to subdue the rebels, but they were so few that they accomplished nothing. One, a musketeer commander called Mark Basenkov, nearly was thrown from the tower.

The revolt did not stop here. Next day, on March 16, the warning bell pealed once more. "The tsar does not provide for our needs," the people shouted, "he sends money to foreign lands, feeding their people with our bread." But the rebels had no leader. Fearing the consequences of this dangerous event, the district elder Andrei Gavrilov went into hiding, and the people looked around for another leader. They found their man in an official named Ivan Zheglov, who managed the metropolitan's estates, as well as two junior boyars, Makar and Fedor Negodiaev, who were spending time in the prison. Nikon warned the tsar they were not good men, that they boasted of knowing everything that transpired in the palaces of both the tsar and the king. Criminal records containing accounts of their felonious deeds were confiscated and sent on to Moscow. The same day March 16, a tumultuous mob made its way to the Holy Wisdom cathedral, where the metropolitan and the governor were found. From there the rabble proceeded to liberate Zheglov and his friends.

A new town council was formed in the town hall under Zheglov. It comprised the artisan Yelisey Lisitsa, Ignaty Molodozhnik, Nikifor Khamov, Stepan Tregub, Pankraty Shmara, Ivan Olovianichnik, a sergeant of the musketeers named Kirsha Diavolov and the crown clerk Grishka Akhantov. The governor lacked sufficient means to oppose these new officials, whereas the metropolitan resorted to spiritual weapons. On March 17, the tsar's nameday, a huge throng assembled at the Holy Wisdom to honor the tsar. Both at matins and at mass Nikon cursed the new councillors by name. A murmur rippled through the crowd. "Whereas the tsar distributes rewards on his nameday, and releases criminals from prison, the metropolitan curses people on such a day. Neither does he confine himself to cursing Molodozhnik and Lisitsa, he curses all of Novgorod's citizens as if they are all of one mind." Thus did certain individuals arouse the people's anger against Nikon, in an attempt to turn everyone against him. Hitherto there was no reason to take this disturbance to the Holy Wisdom. A pretext was found on March 19 when the bailiff from the chancellery, a public scribe Gavrila Nesterov, nicknamed Kolcha, came running from the direction of the Holy Wisdom to the chancellery on the Market Side [of Novgorod]. He shouted "Metropolitan Nikon and the lord-in-waiting Prince Fedor are traitors!" The metropolitan and the governor ordered Kolcha be taken into custody. He was brought to the parish quarters of the Holy Wisdom, beaten with rods and imprisoned. Suddenly his father and his wife came running into the town hall, shouting "Citizens, help! The metropolitan and a nobleman are torturing my son. They are beating and burning him." The inflamed crowd made its way to the courtyard of the Holy Wisdom cathedral. A frightened Khilkov hid at the residence of the metropolitan, who ordered the cathedral courtyard barred. The crowd approached the gate, shouting "Release Gavriil Nesterov from prison." The metropolitan and the governor replied "We are not determined to keep him. Do with him what you will." Once freed, Nesterov removed his shirt and showed the crowd his back. Again the people proceeded to the metropolitan's residence, this time breaking down the door. The rebels found Prince Khilkov in the sacristy. "Why do you run from us?" they asked. "We have no business with you now, when we do there will be no escaping us."

That was how the metropolitan's servant Ivan Kuzmin related it. According to other accounts Nesterov was taken to the metropolitan on a matter which fell under the jurisdiction of the ecclesiastical court. It appeared that he did not get along with his wife. Here is the way in which Prince Khilkov related the affair in his report to Moscow. "The jailer Gavrilka and his father," he wrote, "were both flogged with the knout, and beaten with rods for numerous felonies. On March 19 Gavrilka appeared before the metropolitan with flattering words, as if to beg forgiveness. The metropolitan issued instructions that Gavrilka be held in his chambers until the truth of what he said could be ascertained. That same day, at four in the afternoon, the felons came to the Holy Wisdom in riotous disorder, shouting obscenities, and took Gavrilka with them."

There is also Nikon's version of the affair which he recounted in a letter to the tsar's family. "I was in the cathedral at matins on March 18," he explained, "and after the midnight service, as was my custom, I personally said the hexapsalm.[32] Then I whispered to myself the canon to sweet Jesus in the first kathisma.[33] After going through the first article in the second kathisma, I offered up a prayer to Jesus. I gazed upon the icon of the Savior located here in our church, the one entitled the 'Golden Chasuble' which Tsar Ivan Vasilievich caused to be removed to the cathedral in Moscow. It had worked a miracle for the Greek ruler Manuel. Suddenly a gold crown appeared in the air above the Savior's head. Slowly the crown began to move towards me. It frightened me so that I lost my senses. As I beheld the crown and the candle burning before the Savior's icon, the crown hovered over my own sinful head. With both hands I reached out to touch it, and suddenly it vanished. I waited in vain for another visitation.[34]

"On March 19 Gavriil Nesterov came to the courtyard of the Holy Wisdom cathedral, affecting to seek forgiveness for his sins. I sent orders for his detention until mass was over because I wanted to absolve him and pronounce his penitential prayers. Learning of this, Zheglov ordered the tocsin sounded on the Market Side, and the people attempted to force their way into my antechamber. I went out to reason with them but they seized me shamelessly, beating me on the chest with rods and opening up a wound. Using their fists and stones in their hands they struck me on both sides of my body. The treasurer of Holy Wisdom, Brother Nikandr, and the junior boyars who accompanied me, all were beaten. Afterwards I was led to the town hall. As we approached the church I wanted to go in, which they prevented, ordering me to proceed directly to the town hall instead. By the time they escorted me to the golden doors I was feeling faint from my beating, and was permitted to sit near them, on a bench in front of the church. I asked to be allowed to take the crosses to the banner of the Blessed Virgin, because I had been preparing to celebrate the liturgy. Reluctantly they agreed. Then I ordered the church bells rung and, joining the priests attached to the cathedral, as well as a few others, with a mighty effort made my way to the banner, where I alternately stood and sat for a time. I heard the holy liturgy with difficulty and served quickly, then in acute pain I scarcely made it into the sleigh. Now I lay almost lifeless, with a swollen belly and coughing up blood. Feeling my life ebbing away, I anointed myself with oil. Should I fail to recover, have pity on me, your priest, forgive me and let me live out my life as a cloistered monk."

The attack on Nikon was the last spark of the rebellion. People began to cool, come to their senses and think about the consequences of their actions. Dealing with an unarmed governor and metropolitan was easy, now they faced the prospect of settling accounts with the large armies of the mighty sovereign. They began to consider how to influence the nobility and the junior boyars of the five Novgorod boroughs, how to induce them to vow loyalty to the people of Novgorod. All decided to swear an oath, to close ranks and not betray a single soul should the sovereign order investigations and impose the death penalty in Novgorod. Together they would either die or enjoy clemency. They contemplated sending some leading citizens to Pskov to reach an agreement that both towns act as one. To forestall looting, guards were placed on every street. The people regretted having joined in this when it first began because it was the rabble, the riffraff that hung about the taverns and the musketeers, also penniless, who had done the actual looting. "Today's troubles might result in the same sort of misfortune that marked the days of Tsar Ivan," tearfully the better sort of men agonized. Zheglov himself sensed that disaster might follow the looting, but there was nothing to be done about it now. Armed musketeers had control of the streets, and the townsmen were helpless before them.

On Wednesday evening, March 20, Zheglov invited the nobles and junior boyars to a meeting in the town hall, instructing them to sign a pledge stating that they would stand as one with the citizenry to prevent the tsar from transferring cash and grain reserves abroad. The nobles and junior boyars alike promised to sign the petition requesting that the sovereign not authorize removal of any money or grain from the country, but they refused to sign a pledge of solidarity. Having stated their position they proceeded to the Stone quarter. In a state of heightened agitation a mob of musketeers, cossacks and poor townsmen ran to the Stone quarter, crying "We will intercept the nobles, reach the Stone quarter before they do, close the barrier on the bridge and keep them out. We will drive them from the town!" When this crowd approached the fish market near the bridge they were turned back by other musketeers and citizens, all of whom declared "Instead of starting new criminal actions, end the trouble that you began."

To ease the unrest Novgorod chose three townsmen, two musketeers and one cossack, sending them to the sovereign in Moscow with gifts and a petition. "Your sovereign's servants, the nobles, junior boyars, elders from Novgorod's five boroughs, townsmen, cossack commanders and the rank-and-file, cossacks and all categories of regular military servitors, as well as your sovereign's clergy, priests, archpriests and deacons, in addition to

various service men of lower rank, make obeisance. In this year of
[7]158[35] on March 15, two hours from sunrise, some foreigners came
from Moscow and stopped on Nikitin street. At dead of night, at two in
the morning, these same foreigners rode out of Novgorod, and the townsmen who stood night watch in the streets asked them 'Why do you go out
at night without an official escort or a Muscovite interpreter?'
"Overwhelming the street sentries[36] the foreigners rode out of Novgorod. At Miracles crossroads, people of various ranks in a high state of
agitation tried to stop them, asking the foreigners 'Why do you ride out
at night instead of the day? Only thieves ride around at night. Have you
no official escort or interpreter with you?' Whereupon the foreigners
pierced us with their rapiers, which led to a fight. We returned them to
the town hall for interrogation. Here is what they said. 'I am Ivert Grab,
envoy of the Danish king. I was sent here with six men, and some Swedish subjects joined me'. They were in Moscow purchasing grain. The
Danish envoy Ivert Grab entreats you, O sovereign, to forgive him for
riding out at night from Novgorod without an official escort or interpreter,
and for turning his sword on you. He has issued an official statement
concerning his role in all of this, to the effect that he will petition neither
you, nor the Danish king in his own land, against us. He also noted that
the Swedes await your money and grain in Novgorod. It is rumored that
whenever they take your money and grain your Swedish enemies use the
funds to hire other foreign hordes[37] to march on Great Novgorod and
Pskov. Should this come to pass gladly would we lay down our lives for
you, O sovereign, and for the Orthodox faith. O merciful sovereign! Grant
us this favor. Do not permit your money or grain reserves or other staples
be taken from the Muscovite realm, across our borders to the Swedes. Do
not give credence to false reports from the metropolitan and the lord-in-
waiting Prince Khilkov. They vilify us out of anger because we complain
to you about them."

The petition against Khilkov stemmed from his refusal to obey the
tsar's decree, collusion with the traders to remove grain and meat to
Sweden secretly at night, and profiting from such practices without honest exertion. He issued orders that the goods in the wagons crossing city
borders be exempt from inspection at customs points [city entrances].
Customs supervisors or musketeers who conducted such searches were
to be beaten without mercy. It was also Khilkov who entered the homes
of people of all ranks and officially sealed off their stoves, preventing
them from heating their houses on cold days, which caused some small

children to freeze to death. He cajoled Metropolitan Nikon into formally cursing the people of Novgorod on the tsar's nameday, without benefit of any decree from tsar or patriarch. The metropolitan banned all priestly activity among the laity, allowing none of the clergy to sign petitions or official documents for the illiterate. In Novgorod this metropolitan's curse created serious unrest in all quarters of the town. Khilkov and the metropolitan tortured the crown clerk Nesterko with rods and cudgels. The residents of Novgorod petitioned the metropolitan on behalf of the innocent man, so that finally he returned Nesterko to them after beating him half to death. For such savagery and damnation the power of Almighty God Himself has condemned Metropolitan Nikon.

"As he stood next to the crosses and icons in the church and spoke the words 'The light of Christ illuminates everyone,' a light did indeed strike him, refracting his image. In memory of the sovereign's mother and father, Nikon flogged to death various laity and monks for unpaid taxes. When news arrived of the birth of Tsarevna Evdokia Alekseevna the metropolitan released no one from prison to commemorate this joyous occasion. He wanted to demolish the Holy Wisdom cathedral, but because it was constructed after an angel's annunciation we successfully appealed to him and saved the church. Angered by our stand, he denounced us to the sovereign. The metropolitan kept the former director of his chancery, Ivan Zheglov, under guard in chains and fetters for a long time, then drove him around on a sledge for several days, flogging and torturing him half to death with rods for his debts. Thus did he extort three hundred rubles from him. The metropolitan commits many brutal acts, creating grave problems for the community, from which serious problems flow.

"According to the agreement between the sovereign's emissaries and the Swedish queen's councillors, crown funds in batches of twenty and forty thousand rubles have been transferred by different routes from the Muscovite realm to the Swedish lands. During the Great Carnival[38] of the same year, 1650, a Muscovite trader called Moisey Oblezov arrived in Novgorod. In that city and its district he bought up wheat and rye for the Swedish towns but prevented us from purchasing any, impoverishing and forcing us to go hungry. Meanwhile the Swedes violated the peace treaty in many ways. They have deprived Russians abroad of their Orthodox faith, desecrated God's churches, prohibited the installation of priests in annexed Russian territories, and employed their own clergy to baptize children into their Protestant churches. The lord-in-waiting Prince Khilkov sent three hundred musketeers and cossacks to the customs crossing at the city border, yet provided no gunpowder or lead for its protection. From this it is obvious that he favors the Swedes and is ruining the sovereign's people deliberately. Following Khilkov's advice the merchant Semeon Stoianov has travelled to Sweden for many years. He transports rye, meat and various other provisions. They feed foreigners and fraternize with them, while starving and utterly ruining Orthodox Christians. Semeon Stoianov himself eats and drinks, and consorts many nights with the Swedes and other hordes who ride to Novgorod."

News of these events in Novgorod preceded the supplicants' arrival in Moscow. The sovereign immediately ordered a letter written to instruct the people of Novgorod to recall their vow, seize the perpetrators of sedition, and turn them over to the appropriate authorities. The lord-in-waiting Solovtsev carried the letter to Novgorod, where everyone assembled in the town hall to wait for him. The governor Prince Khilkov entered but was denied a seat. Solovtsev summarized the sovereign's message for the assembly, then read the letter. Upon learning that it contained the same message the emissary had just conveyed in his own words, those present cried out to Solovtsev "Were you aware beforehand of what was in the sovereign's letter? It was about a felon, but there are no felons among us! All are good people here. We support each other and the tsar. Letters like this are fabrications, not epistles from the tsar. We could produce a hundred such scrolls in a single night." "If you cannot believe the tsar's letters," Khilkov declared, "what can you believe?" Then he left for the cathedral.

Nikon summoned the elders and various others to the cathedral, directing them to comply with the tsar's orders. "There are no felons among us," they declared as before, "we owe the tsar nothing and are not guilty before him." Rumors started to circulate to the effect that "the letter is a fake. Solovtsev is no nobleman, he is the boyar Morozov's man. We must detain him here until our petitioners have left Moscow safely. Accordingly Solovtsev was detained. "We lack strength!" the leading people despaired. In the town hall the townsmen drew up an agreement stating that they were united in their opposition to the tsar's decree. Then they forced the people to sign it, although Nikon and Khilkov prevented the clergy and many of the laity from doing so. Some of the priests and leading people left town, others agreed that imprisonment would be better than signing such a document. New denunciations of Khilkov followed. "He is a traitor. At Morozov's orders he would not hesitate to hand Novgorod over to the foreigners. Khilkov accepted a bribe from the

Swedish emissary, a barrel full of gold pieces, and gave all the gunpowder in the storage depot to the foreigners. We must take the Novgorod seal and keys to the treasury away from him, inspect the regional treasury and deploy cannon all over the Stone quarter in preparation for the Swedes' arrival."

On March 27 a crowd assembled and proceeded to the Moscow highway. They returned with thirty barrels of ashes. The people claimed that this was the potassium nitrate which Morozov gave to the foreigners but when the barrels were opened, only ashes were found. On March 29 Nikon tried, again unsuccessfully, to lead the inhabitants of Novgorod to abide by the sovereign's will, then on April 3 he convinced them to release Solovtsev. Upon his arrival in Moscow Solovtsev reported his conversations with Zheglov. "Why do you commit such heinous deeds?" he asked Zheglov. "I did not initiate this business," he retorted, "I am here against my will. The entire community freed me from my chains. Had not the ordinary people freed me, it would have been much worse. Their intervention enabled me to prevent further murders and looting, and to save the Danish emissary from mortal blows."

Meanwhile the boyar Prince Ivan Nikitich Khovansky was on his way to Novgorod with a small detachment of soldiers. Zheglov sent him a letter assuring Khovansky that he had started out to meet him, but ice prevented his crossing the Volkhov river. "They await you in Great Novgorod," Zheglov wrote, "and plan to greet you outside the town gates with bread and salt.[39] I do not reproach you, my sovereign, I beg your grace, O my lord, and offer you my obeisance when I write the following. Take only a few men, make haste to Great Novgorod, and show us some kindness. The people of this community eagerly await you and your good will. Henceforth, O sovereign, be so kind as to send only men from Novgorod, not people from other towns who cannot possibly know anything. They are not familiar with our customs and ways. The Novgorod metropolitan Nikon and the lord-in-waiting Prince Khilkov have spread rumors about the community, filled with alarming things. They claim that in response to their requests you, my lord, are on your way to Great Novgorod to hang or cut to ribbons Orthodox Christians, without any investigation or questioning. With such speeches they spread great sorrow and agitation."

For the present Zheglov limited himself to writing to Khovansky, unlike his friend Fedor Negodiaev, who took more decisive action. He went to meet Khovansky and was sent on to Moscow. There the tsar's decree was issued on April 15 directing Khovansky not to proceed to Novgorod but to remain at the Savior monastery on the Khutyn, gather soldiers, erect barriers around the town, not let anyone cross them, and seek to convince the people of Novgorod to surrender. Khovansky carried out these orders, and received a reply from Novgorod's musketeers advising him that when his letter was read out in the town hall the crown clerk, the cobbler Yeliseika Grigoriev, nicknamed Lisitsa, spoke out. "We will not allow the boyar Khovansky to enter our town," he declared, "if he indulges in any excesses we will pick up our standards and drums and together march to Pskov." "If Khovansky arrives with only a few men," the same Yeliseika said, "we shall let him pass, but the way will be barred if he tries to enter with many." Everyone in Novgorod wrote similar letters to Khovansky.

On April 17 the tsar responded. "You submitted petitions in the name of members of the nobility and junior boyars, yet not one of them contains a signature. This makes you frauds. Even without such fabricated letters and your attempts to justify your deeds we, the great sovereign, are well aware that in Great Novgorod you attacked the Danish emissary and other foreigners, that you disgraced and thrashed the metropolitan, that you reviled and humiliated our lord-in-waiting, confiscated his keys to the city, and honor none of our decrees. You petition us to refrain from sending monetary and grain reserves to Sweden, but with God's help we the great sovereign know how to protect and govern our realm. In accordance with the treaty concluded between us and the Swedish king we are bound to extradite our fugitives. Otherwise, this means relinquishing approximately fifty thousand Orthodox souls to the Lutheran faith. Instead we agreed to pay one hundred and ninety thousand rubles for them, only part of that sum, twenty thousand rubles, was turned over to Login Nummens. Had a shortage of grain developed, all that was required of you was to petition us, the great sovereign, and we would have ordered immediate grain deliveries for you. You write that no grain or other food reserves shall be sold to foreign countries, but that is impossible. How are we to function without trading with other countries? If we prohibit the export of any goods the Swedes will refuse to sell us their products and we will experience shortages.

"You complain that the metropolitan has cursed you, yet he acted in an official capacity. If in the future he is ever guilty of acts which exceed his authority we will conduct a formal investigation. As for the Swedish foreigners marching on Novgorod or Pskov, that too is impossible because a treaty of eternal peace exists between us and their queen. In the matter of your request that the lord-in-waiting Prince Khilkov be replaced, we have issued an order for this, and have appointed our boyar Yury Petrovich Buinosov-Rostovsky to govern in Great Novgorod. What is more, your petitioners Sidor Isakov and his colleagues were told to appear before us, then were dismissed without harm even though your own wicked deeds ought to have precluded this. The musketeer Kirilko and the townsman Yevko Krasilnikov have been commanded to remain in Moscow until an official investigation is conducted because they were found in the company of felons, gave conflicting testimony in Moscow and spoke falsely. You should have admitted your guilt and given all agitators to our boyar Prince Khovansky. Instead you sent unwelcome gifts because in your petition you refused to lay your guilt at our feet, and send us the felons."

On the same day yet another letter was dispatched with the threat that if Prince Khovansky was not welcomed in Novgorod, and its people declined to obey him by turning over for questioning the felons and instigators of the rebellion, the tsar would send boyars and military commanders from Moscow with orders to publish the people severely.

In the meantime, while residing in Moscow, Fedka Negodiaev curried favor with tsar and boyars alike. He met with the sovereign and, establishing a cordial relationship, received a pardon. Fedka revealed that even before the present difficulties Nikon caused much disorder in the city. The metropolitan sought to make alterations to the cathedral. In 1649, during St. Peter's fast,[40] large numbers of laity approached him noisily. "We have had many leaders," they charged, "but none has violated ancient custom. We will not tolerate a single alteration to any of the cathedral's ancient features." From the metropolitan's residence the crowd proceeded to the Holy Wisdom, threw down the scaffolding, and prepared to thrash the craftsmen who had erected them in preparation for breaking up the columns, but the workers escaped.

Negodiaev was dispatched from Moscow to Novgorod to talk the population into obedience, to persuade Zheglov to desist from his criminal activity, and to promise the sovereign's forgiveness. Soon thereafter, on April 20, a letter from Khovansky arrived stating that the people of Novgorod submitted. The impression on Moscow of Negodaev's accounts was evident the following day, April 21, when the tsar wrote to Nikon "You should not have ordered the destruction of the cathedral, or the demolition of its columns." Highly offended, Nikon wrote a long letter to the tsar. He described his actions during the rebellion, then continued "Wealthy and responsible merchants spent time in my court, and I offered them food and drink. Many of the nefarious deeds that Ivashko and Ignashko (Zheglov and Molodozhnikov) had planned were thwarted thanks to my perseverance. Had I not stood firm there would have been much more destruction than we witnessed in Pskov. Ceaselessly I prayed for you, my sovereign, and frequently wrote to you, using all available means to hire shadowy individuals to deliver the letters to you. For this and because of Ivashka Zheglov's calumny I am disgraced and broken. It is Ivashka and his friends who falsely petitioned you, accusing me of cursing the populace of Novgorod. I, however, cursed only the felons, not the upstanding citizens. This appears to have led to the troubles, although I did not begin to pronounce my curses until three days after the disturbances began. In a petition they accused me of wanting to demolish the cathedral. The charge is patently false. How could I have contemplated such demolition without your decree? Indeed the Holy Wisdom treasury itself lacks the funds to pay for as much as the renovations, let alone to rebuild what allegedly was about to be demolished.

"Fedka Negodiaev benefited from your sovereign generosity by cunning. Not only is he unworthy of the tsar's benevolence, he does not deserve to live. My sovereign, he told you and your boyars a pack of lies about me. His lying words have turned you against me, so that my numerous letters to you go unanswered. This saddens me deeply. Henceforth I see no point in writing to you about your affairs, or discussing them in this missive. Today in Great Novgorod all is calm, but bitter tears are shed over the sins the people recently committed against you. Gracious sovereign and grand prince Alexis Mikhailovich! Emulate our gracious and benevolent Lord God! Display mercy when they petition you to forgive their sins. As I tried to persuade them to desist, I assured them of your kindness. Had I not done so, they would have despaired over their treacherous deeds, and succumbed to even greater evil. Almost the entire city has come to me on numerous occasions to beg forgiveness for having beaten and dishonored me, and for sending false petitions against me."

"So you, my pious friend," the tsar replied, "have obeyed and followed God's commandments, as told to us by the holy apostles and holy fathers, yearning for the true faith of Christ, emulating the former prelates and the new and praiseworthy confessor of the faith, Patriarch Hermogen.[41] We the great sovereign do graciously praise you for your zeal, your steadfastness and your suffering. Henceforth you must continue to fulfill your pledges to the Almighty God and fervently espouse good deeds. As you have begun, so should you finish."

On April 24 Khovansky began his investigation in Novgorod. In the first instance the Danish emissaries appeared with a complaint against Volk, who admitted under questioning that he had beaten and dishonored the emissary. Everyone pointed him out. Together with Ivashka Zheglov and Yeliseika Lisitsa, Volk incited the rebellion, the felonious actions and violence. To appease the emissary, and avert a rupture between his sovereign majesty the tsar and his royal highness, Volk was taken to the square and beheaded. The executioner who appeared drunk before the emissary and humiliated him, was flogged with the knout. From April 24 to May 7 these agitators and insurgents were interrogated: the elders Andriushka Gavrilov, Yeliseika Lisitsa, Ivashka Zheglov, Ignashka Molodozhnikov, Nikiforka Khamov, Stepka Tregubov, Pankrashka Shmara, the public scribe Nesterko Mikulin with his son Gavrilka, and another public scribe, Akhanatov. In all two hundred and twelve people were charged.

At first Khovansky wanted to build a prison to hold everyone arrested. On May 13 musketeers came with their wives and children to the cathedral to see Nikon, and petitioned the tsar for mercy, begging him not to imprison the accused, their friends the musketeers, for whom they were prepared to answer. Instead each should receive the punishment he deserved, and then be released. Nikon sent for Khovansky. "The tsar has asked," he stated, "that you and I conduct the proceedings together. I am of the opinion that we should grant the musketeers' request for this reason. If everyone charged with a crime is imprisoned, all will anticipate a death sentence. When the citizens of Pskov learn of this, they will conclude that the accused have been sent to prison to await execution, at which point the tsar's affair will end in a fiasco." Khovansky agreed, and most of the prisoners were released to the custody of other citizens.

A verdict arrived from Moscow. Zheglov, the district elder Andriushka Gavrilov, Yeliseika Lisitsa, Molodozhnikov and Shmara were to be executed. Khamov and Tregub were to be flogged with the knout without mercy, then sent to Astrakhan for life. Others were to be flogged and sent to the shores of the Terek river in the Caucasus. Still others were exiled to Karpov or Korotiak. Some were to be flogged with the knout and exiled, while yet another group were to be beaten with rods and released into someone's custody. Nonetheless execution of the sentences was postponed until the arrival of a new edict ordering that the townsman

Yakushka and three musketeers be mercilessly flogged with the knout, three townsmen be beaten with rods, and one hundred and sixty-two townsmen, musketeers and cossacks flogged with the knout and released on bail. The decree was carried out but one of the three musketeers sentenced to merciless flogging, Kuzemka Merkuriev, was nowhere to be found. It finally came to light that he was in Moscow, where he had been sent by the governor with some letters. On June 16 Merkuriev returned from Moscow. Instead of submitting to the punishment he produced a charter from the tsar with instructions that he be promoted to sergeant. He also received five rubles as a reward because together with his brother Fomka he rescued Nikon and Prince Khilkov from the felons during the rebellion, thus saving them from assassination.

Moscow was not happy with Khovansky's dilatoriness. Learning of this, Nikon wrote to the sovereign "I have been apprised that your majesty sent a letter to your boyar Prince Ivan Nikitich Khovansky in which you complain of his delay in conducting your affairs. Your boyar, however, is not without skill in managing and discharging these affairs. I myself have cautioned him not to rush these proceedings, rather to examine the situation carefully to allow matters to be thoroughly investigated. This, not the boyar's negligence, accounts for the apparently unhurried nature of his activity. Such an important investigation cannot be rushed but I assure you, O sovereign, that thanks to the efforts of Prince Ivan Nikitich Khovansky this affair is moving toward a successful conclusion. The boyar has performed his duties toward you not in haste, but in a careful and deliberate manner, to avoid resentment among the people. The slow pace will not weaken the sovereign's interests. Evil persons of various ranks are presently under investigation, and the inquiry has been slowed with Pskov in mind.

NEW UNREST IN PSKOV

In mid-March the social unrest in Pskov once again showed signs of intensifying. The leading people viewed with horror the formerly imprisoned criminals who now walked around unguarded. Criminal activity escalated, and instances of murder multiplied. Bogdan Artsybashev, a citizen of Novgorod, was sent from Moscow to Novgorod and Pskov with an order prohibiting all future purchases of grain destined for the tsar's granaries. Having carried out this commission in Novgorod, Artsybashev arrived in Pskov on March 17. He was taken to the town hall, from which Menshikov, an elder of one of the town's five boroughs, emerged to inquire who he was, whence he had come, and so forth. They confiscated Artsybashev's letters, including one from Archbishop Makary to Khilkov, the governor of Novgorod, thereby precipitating a new wave of unrest. The tocsin sounded, and people surrounded the archbishop at the Rybnitskie gates as he was returning from mass at the Nadolbin monastery. "Why do you exchange letters with the governor of Novgorod," the agitators shouted at Makary. "Your letter has caused him to send our petitioners to Moscow in fetters, and to place one of them under militia supervision!" The archbishop replied that he wrote to inquire after Khilkov's health, not about the petitioners. Next the people demanded that the bishop surrender the junior boyar Turov, who had taken Fedor Emelianov out of town. Makary replied that Turov had run away from him. They seized the archbishop and paraded him about the square, then fettered him in the almshouse, where he sat in chains for about an hour. He was released only after giving his word that Turov would be questioned before March 19. This did not end the unrest. The tocsin sounded every day, circles were formed and councils were held. On May 21 they led the Swede Nummens to Pskov's square once again, where they stripped and questioned him for half an hour. Meanwhile Artsybashev sat chained in prison. He was interrogated to determine whose slave he might be, Morozov's or Khilkov's.

On March 25 another governor, the nobleman Prince Vasily Petrovich Lvov, arrived from Moscow to replace Sobakin. Upon turning the town over to the new governor Sobakin attempted to leave, but the people of Pskov barred his way. "We shall release you after our petitioners return unharmed," they declared. Nor did they leave the new governor in peace for long. On March 28 people of all ranks came to his court, demanding gunpowder and lead. "What do you want with gunpowder and lead?" asked Lvov. "Is it because there is news from abroad? If you have news, we will send investigators to look into it, but we are not at war with any foreigners." "We have had no news from abroad," the musketeer Koza replied. "Our concern is the border between Moscow and ourselves. We have heard that many military servitors from Moscow are marching on Pskov. Though we might not be at war with foreigners, we regard as foreigners any men from Moscow who would have our heads." "Are you seeking a quarrel with the tsar?" Lvov countered. "The only way you will get powder and lead from me is by strangling me and seizing the seal and keys to the storage depot." At this the multitude cried out in unison "To arms! To arms!" They sounded the tocsin, raised a tremendous din, cursed Lvov and screamed "Traitor! Traitor!" Surrounding Lvov's court, they trained muskets on the window. The musketeer Ivashka Kolchin brandished an axe and threatened to cut down the governor. Lvov removed the icon of the Savior from the wall and appealed to the mob. "Orthodox Christians, what kind of traitor to the tsar do you see in me? As this icon of the Savior is my witness, I have never betrayed him. You can take the gunpowder and lead by force, but never will I relinquish it voluntarily." So they seized the powder and lead. Then they took Lvov to the municipal meeting house, demanding his keys to the city.

That was not all. They then proceeded to the homes of Lvov and Sobakin, shouting "If you refuse to send your children to Moscow with our petitioners we will take them from you, not honorably, only after we have given you a good beating. If your children expose our petitioners anywhere along the way, and reveal that they and not your children are carrying petitions, or if the tsar decrees any punishment for our petitioners, we will kill you." The governor's sons were removed by force.

One of the tsar's noblemen, Prince Fedor Fedorovich Volkonsky, arrived in Pskov from Moscow on March 30 to investigate matters. The elders escorted him to Fedor Emelianov's empty house. As soon as the community learned that Volkonsky had settled there, shouts rang out of "Traitor! You have settled in a traitor's home!" Upon his arrival Volkonsky went to the Trinity cathedral as was the custom, but at the Daumantas wall the throng surrounded him with threats. "Here is the traitor! Stone him to death!" Hearing this, Volkonsky rushed into the cathedral. As he entered the church he began kissing the icons. The mob surged into the cathedral after him, seized him by the beard and dragged him outside. The musketeer Senka Zhegara struck him with a flagstone, and the priest's son Zapleva gave him a powerful blow with the butt of an axe. The injured Volkonsky was brought to the square, placed on a vat and questioned. "What have you brought to Pskov?" "I shall proceed presently with the business for which I was sent," Volkonsky retorted. They confiscated from him the tsar's letter of instruction and commenced reading it aloud to the entire assembly. When it came to the passage about criminals being executed, others punished, and the fomenters of the rebellion were listed by name, the instigators cried out "The tsar has sent a man to execute us, but we would sooner execute him who was sent to put us to death." They then flung themselves on Volkonsky with axes and muskets. The elected officials[42] prevented the murder, and the felons only succeeded in wounding him in the head with an axe. Then the instigators sent for Sobakin, placed him on the vat and threatened to kill him, shouting "You wrote to the sovereign that bread is cheap in Pskov. Now we will hold you. Try living among us for a while on this cheap bread!" The cossacks from Pskov returned from Novgorod where they were sent to gather information. According to them, along the road Volkonsky had burned certain letters, while in Great Novgorod there was tumult, and a rebellion raged. This news fanned the flames of local unrest and produced extreme agitation among the rebels, who shouted "We are not alone. Novgorod acts in the same manner. Now two cities are involved in all this." The tocsin sounded, and once more Volkonsky was led into the square for interrogation. He was asked about the letters he burned along the way. Volkonsky replied that he wrote to the tsar concerning events in Novgorod and burned the rough draft of the letter when they stopped to rest because it was of no further use to him. He then told the people of Pskov to look to their own affairs. Such uncompromising talk was ineffective in quelling the disturbance, and the governor had no more strength left. None of the nobility came to Pskov to give assistance while those who happened to be in the city at the time fled the rioting populace. The musketeers stopped obeying their superiors, and the entire regiment began pummeling their commander Boris Bukhvostov, shouting "The tsar does not reward us, and recruits soldiers[43] to take our place!" They took Volkonsky's nephew and sent him to Moscow, warning the uncle "If you try to stop him we will hang you on Rigina Hill."

PSKOV'S PETITIONERS

Meanwhile petitioners from Pskov arrived in Moscow, and on May 12 the tsar summoned them for questioning. The landholder Grigory Vorontsov-Veliaminov said "My brothers, the landowners and the lesser gentry sent me to plead mercy for our miserable sins, and to explain that we signed the petition under duress because the populace caught us, only a few of us, one at a time. The real criminals are the instigators, the public scribe Tomilka Slepoy, the musketeers Proshka Koza, Ivashka Kopytov, Nikita Sorokoumov, Andriushka Savostianov with his brother Vasko, Ivashka Kolchin, Senka Zhegara, the townsmen Dobrynka Branshchik, Prokhora Miasnik, Pashka Shaposhnik, and the two priests Yevsevy and Yakov Zapleva. Now in the town hall of Pskov they have installed the elders Gavrilka Demidov and Mikhalka Mishnitsyn, the musketeer sergeants Nevolka Sidorov, Paramoshka Lukianov, Fedka Snyrka, the cossacks Ivashka Sakharny and Ivashka Khvory, the archpriest of the Trinity cathedral, Afanasy nicknamed Drugan, and the sacristan Dionisy. The sacristan and the archpriest alone are there against their will. With them too is the priest Yakov, from St. George's in the Marshes, who is sympathetic to all of their criminal enterprises and intentions, and shares their convictions. Many townsmen sit with them in the town hall but are silent and do not participate in any of the criminal activities." A petition the people of Pskov carried to the tsar contained the following. "When they begged the governor not to surrender any grain to foreigners, until the tsar's decree Sobakin threatened them with deportation and execution. Under questioning Nummens threatened war. Accompanied by the tsar's deputies, Colonel Crawford examined the fortifications in Pskov. In no way did the signatories dishonor the governor or the archbishop. Foreigners came to Emelianov's house, yet it was he who was punished for past criminal acts. Together with the public scribe Filka Shemashkov, Emelianov doubled, tripled and even quintupled the salt tax, imposing the highest possible fines on everybody. He shares every idea with Troian Stoianov, and they aspire to emulate the foreigners. Indeed, Emelianov praises the foreign faith and sends the foreigners all the news. The tsar would do well to summon Emelianov to Pskov to account for his actions.

"The Swedes will be on the outskirts of Novgorod on Easter Sunday, and at the edge of Pskov either on St. Nicholas Day [May 9] or on Trinity Sunday. That is why the people of Pskov took the keys to the city from the governor. If the queen of Sweden wages war over grain, money and fugitives the people of Pskov would gladly fight the Swedes. No foreigners ever served under previous rulers such as Tsar Ivan Vasilievich [the Terrible], for example.[44] During the reign of Tsar Michael the military received compensation without any reductions, whereas now the wages of military servitors are halved, and some receive nothing at all. Others in the military receive compensation in the form of promissory notes but governors and crown secretaries fail to pay the face value of such paper. Moreover even from such reduced salaries yearly bribes are extorted, totalling approximately five hundred rubles, in addition to payments for the servicemen's suburban settlements in the bytowns. What is more, pandering to the tavern keepers, they release no salaries on the days prescribed by decree. Instead they pay out the money on the eve of holidays, so that all of it winds up in the pockets of tavern owners.[45]

"Muscovy's crown servitors and people of various ranks, innocent of any crime, have been exiled to Siberia. Many were tortured, caned or drowned, others were settled in the mountainous wastelands of Siberia. Ecclesiastical emoluments have been reduced to half their former amount, churches and church buildings are neglected by the archbishops and are falling into disrepair. The governor Sobakin helped himself to various merchandise from the shops and stalls in the market without paying, and forced artisans to perform various services for him without compensation. His sons and their servants abducted numerous widows, matrons and maidens in the wash houses along the rivers, and raped them. Scribes recorded the tax burden. Tradesmen were entered before the peasants. They were assessed seven parts with peasants responsible for the eighth.

"Artemka, a peasant from the Shelonskaia [one of Novgorod's five boroughs], repeated in Pskov a piece of testimony given by a foreigner in Novgorod (in the text of his interrogation). In effect he said that when the foreigners reach the outskirts of Pskov the boyar Morozov is to arrive from Moscow and surrender Pskov without a struggle. When they petitioned the tsar the people of Pskov asked him to send them Nikita Ivanovich Romanov, who is devoted to the tsar and cares for their land, to conduct an official interrogation. Openly demanding that Romanov be sent, the people of Pskov secretly dispatched the cossack Mikhail Karpov to Moscow. He arrived by back roads and delivered to the boyar Nikita Romanov a petition. It was a plea from the people of Pskov that henceforth in their city the governors and crown secretaries, together with elected officials and territorial elders, conduct fair trials, without graft or bribes. They further requested that people of Pskov not be summoned to Moscow. Romanov took the cossack with the petition to the tsar."

The tsar summoned the supplicants, then sent the people of Pskov a letter in which he addressed every item in their petition. With respect to their numerous complaints of abuse of office, the tsar gave one reply. "Our serfs and peasants," he declared, "never gave us, the great sovereigns, orders. You would have done well to petition us before the current rebellion erupted instead of trying to manage things on your own." Concerning Crawford, the tsar's answer was "Crawford is our serf in perpetuity. He provided the plans for fortifying Pskov." On the question of foreigners, "Kings and princes, King Magnus[46] and various other foreigners served Tsar Ivan Vasilievich and my father." On Romanov, "you have written this in a criminal manner. This boyar is our servant, and together with his fraternity of boyars, of whom not a single one is malevolent, serves only us. In the days of our forefathers peasants never joined, nor shall they now join, the boyars, lords-in-waiting and governors in dispensing justice." The tsar finished his letter with a warning that if the people of Pskov refused to submit the boyar Prince Alexis Nikitich Trubetskoy and Prince Mikhaila Petrovich Pronsky would march against the town with formidable military detachments and artillery. In his letter to Archbishop Makary the tsar described as exemplary the conduct of Nikon in Novgorod. Moreover it was because of the metropolitan's care and Khovansky's service that the people of Pskov finally understood their duties.

MARCH ON PSKOV

That same Khovansky was now marching on Pskov, asking the landowners he met along the way for advice on the best site for setting up camp outside the town. They suggested Snetnaia hill. On May 28 as he approached Pskov he was greeted by shots fired from a large cannon. Simultaneously large numbers of foot soldiers and cavalrymen came out of the town firing small arms. The fire was not returned since Khovansky forbade his men to engage the people of Pskov in battle. With no intention of rewarding such civility in kind, the citizens of Pskov attacked the wagon train, capturing six wagons loaded with Khovansky's possessions. Only the supply wagon was recaptured. Khovansky encamped on Snetnaia hill and from there informed the tsar that he had too few men, that their numbers fell far short of what he needed to besiege the town and secure the gates. His entire army consisted of two thousand men, of which he had already stationed seven hundred at the Liubiatin monastery. The distance between the monastery and Snetnaia hill was about ten versts. Supplies were totally depleted and the people in the district, along with the citizens of Pskov, indulged in an orgy of criminal acts. They lay in wait along the roads, seized passers-by and took them to Pskov. They concealed all kinds of grain in the forest. "If military detachments from Pskov attacked us, we would be quite defenseless. As it is, we cannot hold out for more than five days because we lack fodder for our horses."

In the end they were forced to remain longer than five days. With no intention of giving up, the people of Pskov declared "We shall not surrender even if a larger force attacks us. The town cannot easily be penetrated and taken. We are capable of withstanding a long siege. There is enough grain and foodstuffs to last us for ten years." They wrote to Gdov, and the people of that town joined them. The petitioners returned from Moscow and relayed the tsar's response to the community. "You speak," the crowd roared, "as if instructed by traitors." They led one of the petitioners, Fedka Konovalov, away for torture, questioning his motive in

bringing a letter written by someone other than the tsar. In their decision
not to surrender the agitators were sustained by some old wives' tales
from abroad. One of the men related that while he was in Neuhausen on
business he saw a sheet of paper posted on the town gate with a lifelike
portrait of the queen holding aloft a sword. Beneath her appeared the
righteous sovereign Alexis Mikhailovich bowing deeply. Another related
how he had found Lithuanians on the border who told him that Tsar
Alexis Mikhailovich was at that very moment in Poland, having left Moscow with five companions some thirty weeks earlier. With their own eyes
the Lithuanians had seen the sovereign. The Polish king regarded him
with favor. "Indeed everyone looks upon him as they would behold the
beautiful sun." The people of Pskov must continue to oppose Khovansky
because the tsar is expected soon to appear on the outskirts of Pskov, with
the Don and Zaporozhian cossacks to help him protect the town. A third
said that the sovereign was in fact absent from Moscow. Gunpowder was
placed beneath the palace, but Morozov's wife secretly saved the tsar.

Khovansky sent the nobleman Savva Bestuzhev with seven companions to persuade the people of Pskov to surrender. One by one the envoys
were taken to the municipal meeting house for interrogation, where they
were robbed, beaten and accused of treason. "You may have your foreigners," the town dwellers declared, "but whenever there is any trouble
we the citizens of Pskov can rely on the Poles to rescue us." They called
the boyars and council members traitors, and shouted about Khovansky
that "he took Great Novgorod by ruse. We will boil him a cauldron and
eat him!" From the tops of vats in the town square Khovansky's document was read aloud to the entire community, and the boyars were locked
up. After midday the tocsin sounded. A crowd of people assembled and
considered whether to kill Khovansky's noblemen or let them go. The upshot was that Bestuzhev was killed, two men returned to Khovansky and
nine were locked up in prison. The elder Gavrila Demidov was in charge
of the entire proceeding. At one point the insurgents wrote a letter to the
Lithuanian king requesting soldiers to help them, which plan the community rejected, and the letter was never sent.

Khovansky ordered a bridge built below Snetnaia hill, over the Velikaia river, for his men to cut off access to the roads beyond the Velikaia
and prevent ambushes by the men of Pskov. Having learned about the
bridge men from Pskov appeared every day to shoot at the camp site,
stalling completion of the project. On May 31 they organized a sortie and
burned the stockade constructed beyond the Velikaia river to fortify

Snetnaia hill. They also attacked the smaller stockade located between Snetnaia hill and the Liubiatin monastery, but this time were repulsed. Khovanksy reported that the people of Pskov cursed and swore over the corpses of his warriors, behaving worse than wild beasts. The governor continued to write letters of complaint. "Daily there are sorties and battles, O sovereign, meanwhile the supplies of our noblemen and junior boyars are limited. The junior boyars, cossacks and musketeers are forced to eat meat even on fast days. June 18 saw a major sortie out of Pskov, and once more it was repulsed. The people of Pskov were pushed back to the town gates and about three hundred lives were lost.

The inhabitants of Pskov refused to surrender, but it was not Prince Khovansky and his fighting men who then set out against them. On July 4 Bishop Raphael of Kolomna, Archimandrite Sylvester of the St. Andrew monastery, Archpriest Mikhail from Chernigov and elected officials from amongst the table attendants, crown agents, nobles, wealthy merchants and various servitors in the tsar's court journeyed from Moscow to Pskov. The emissaries were charged with convincing the people of Pskov that in return for a pardon they admit Prince Khovansky to the town and surrender the troublemakers Gavrilka Demidov, Mishka Moshnitsyn, Druzhinka Borodin, Proksha Koza and Vaska Kopyto. Ortherwise the sovereign himself would lead a campaign against them, and order their total destruction.

To Khovansky was sent the command "You must write in secret to the elder Gavrila Demidov telling him to reconsider, to admit his guilt and leave the town to join your host. For this he shall receive the sovereign's mercy. You must also send a secret letter to the musketeers, commanding them to open the gates and admit you!" Instead, Khovansky continued to send mournful letters to Moscow. "Soldiers from the Sumerskaia district have turned traitor. They have joined soldiers from Gdov, and the people of Pskov have allowed them until a week before the holiday of St. Elias to come to their town. Should such a large body of infantry arrive, we can expect all kinds of misfortune. There are simply too few men on our side. The inhabitants of Izborsk also have betrayed us and joined Pskov."

On July 26 the tsar summoned a council to consider Pskov's treasonous actions. He insisted on the presence of the boyars, lords-in-waiting and so forth, as well as the noblemen and junior boyars from other towns. Muscovite merchants, traders, clothiers, members of the lower class settlements and musketeers from the towns also were obliged to attend.

Merchants and clothier guilds were required to send five men each, and every lower class settlement of artisans, shopkeepers and day laborers was to provide one representative. At the council the participants were apprised in detail of the conduct of Pskov's inhabitants. Members of the council heard how the rebels rode out of the city to destroy the homes of nobles and lesser gentry, to beat or kill their wives and children, to commit against the nobility atrocities that ran to ripping open chests, slitting throats and tearing out tongues. In the district they killed the landowner Avdey Beshentsov, together with his wife and children, then they burned out and killed Nekliudov, Nogin and the Pskov merchant Nikula Khovin. They also converged on the Shelonskaia borough [of Novgorod] and beat the landowners. On the heels of this revelation a question was put to the council. "How shall we proceed if the people refuse to obey Bishop Raphael and the elected representatives?" The response of the council members has not survived, but we do know that an order was sent to Bishop Raphael instructing him not to demand the surrender of the fomenters of rebellion, rather to persuade the people of Pskov to admit their guilt and to promise that if they repented and swore an oath to the tsar, Khovansky immediately would quit Pskov for Novgorod. It was Nikon who counselled against demands that the instigators of the rebellion be delivered up. As far back as early May he had sent Bogdan Snazin, the episcopal agent at the residence of the Holy Wisdom, to persuade the Pskov citizenry to admit their guilt to the tsar. Guards seized Snazin at the town gates and brought him to the municipal meeting house before the elected representatives, the trader Gavrilka Demidov, the nobleman Ivan Chirkin and his friends. They confiscated the letters, broke their seals and read them, then ordered the warning bell rung. The populace assembled at the meeting house where the metropolitan's letters were read aloud. After learning their contents the people of Pskov rudely cursed the metropolitan in the vilest of terms. "We refuse to pay any attention to his letters. It is enough that he has deceived Novgorod. We are not so gullible as the men of Novgorod. We refuse to send any admission of guilt, nor do we acknowledge any." At first they put Snazin in chains, then released him with the demand that henceforth the metropolitan not write or send anyone to them because they would give no quarter to such people. Nikon, convinced that the ringleaders of the rebellion in Pskov were too powerful, and realizing that the lack of aggressive measures from Moscow merely prolonged the war and its destruction, wrote to the tsar.

"I who pray for you have learned that the inhabitants of Pskov are now much stronger, and have sworn not to betray one another. Those four men whose return you demand are in charge in Pskov, where the people obey them in all things. If the felons in Pskov are forced to shield these four men your patrimony around Pskov and the district of Novgorod, in the Shelonskaia and Vodskaia boroughs, in the regions of [Velikie] Luki and Pustaia Rzheva shall all be ravaged. Many good people, nobles and junior boyars, along with their wives and children, will be hacked to pieces, and their goods and chattels plundered. Villages and towns will burn, people of diverse ranks will be killed near Pskov or on the open road while I, together with my archimandrites, abbots, Novgorod townsmen and peasants, after great expense to hire carts for transporting troops and supplies, simply will perish in the end. Your patrimony will become a wasteland, with townsmen and peasants aimlessly wandering about.

"Command, O sovereign, that those four men, monstrous criminals though they are, not be condemned to death but be granted life so that Great Novgorod and its districts shall not be destroyed completely. Pskov can never be taken by such deaths. We stand to lose even those fighting men who are now on the outskirts of Pskov, and Novgorod will be ravaged by endless demands for wagons and men. In an effort to persuade the people of Novgorod to keep the peace I gave them my word that I would beg your forgiveness for their transgressions. That is why Novgorod and your treasury were spared, the people were not hurt and it remains possible to discuss your affairs with the citizens of Novgorod without interruptions. When the boyar Prince Ivan Nikitich Khovansky came to that city he swore that he would not cause its inhabitants to suffer for their guilt in any way, yet now the people of Pskov, hearing that some criminals have been imprisoned in Novgorod, fear for their own fate. They believe none of our assurances, and point to the felons in Novgorod, those in prison, saying 'This is what is in store for us.'"

How can we explain such reluctance to adopt strong measures? Why was the threat to send a large army under Trubetskoy not enforced? We offer no personal conjectures. Instead, we will voice one misgiving, which the sources clearly indicate. Immediately after the council [in Moscow] the heads of the urban hundreds were summoned to the Chancellery for Foreign Affairs. They were instructed to provide the tsar with information about individuals who expressed treasonous ideas and disseminated them among the people.

Meanwhile the military actions around Pskov continued unabated, the men of Pskov staging a major sortie on July 12. Their goal was to capture the stockade on the other side of the Velikaia river. Khovansky came from Snetnaia hill to defend the stockade, and a mighty battle ensued. The Pskov troops were repulsed, losing in excess of three hundred fighting men, together with artillery and banners. Leaders of the rebellion were furious with Archbishop Makary because he refused to support their cause. One day an armed mob stormed the cathedral, shouted at Makary and threatened his life, demanding to know why he failed to order his subordinates and the junior boyars to stand guard or engage in sorties. They shouted "the Trinity cathedral parish has no business with the people, horses, grain or money. The city needs them all!"

On July 30 elected representatives came to Makary to announce the arrival of the feast day of August 1 [Epiphany].[47] Taking advantage of this, the archbishop urged them to submit to the tsar. He found an article in the Pskov Chronicle where it was written and supported by impassioned vows that the people would never close the town gates to the tsar, nor rise up against him. Returning to the town meeting house the elected representatives put the archbishop's statements in writing, then sounded the tocsin and read the statements aloud to the people. As a consequence, during the liturgy Makary was taken from the church to the almshouse and fettered with a heavy chain. He was released in mid-month when news arrived of the impending approach of Raphael, together with the elected representatives. On August 17 they staged a triumphal entry into Pskov. Makary, his clergy and the people greeted them about half a verst from the city. Service was sung in the Trinity cathedral, after which the tsar's letter was read aloud. When it reached the place stating that Pskov planned to write to the king of Lithuania everyone shouted that they had neither written nor read any such a letter, never ever had such a thought crossed their minds.

NEGOTIATIONS TO END REBELLION

Next day the people of Pskov informed Raphael of their resolve to confess their guilt and swear an oath of allegiance to the tsar, on condition of no mention of a letter to Lithuania. Otherwise they would refuse to take the oath. Raphael deleted the passage.

On the morning of July 20 the elders and the better citizens swore their allegiance. In the afternoon a disturbance broke out, and some people cried out "There are statements in the confirmation of the oath about the foreigner Nummens and the merchant Emelianov, charges that we, the citizens of Pskov, battered the landowners' wives and children in their own districts. Let those who struck the foreigner, robbed Emelianov's house and beat up the landowners in their own districts swear the oath. We refuse."

Some individuals even threw themselves upon the elders and elected representatives, intending to murder them. They shouted "Why did you take an oath in the face of such articles?" The leaders of the rebellion seized upon this, saying appalling things about the tsar, the priest Yevsey,[48] the elder Demidov and Tomilka Slepoy, crying out that nobody should so swear. The following day, with the last group scheduled to kiss the cross in the cathedral, a row broke out right in the church and many people prepared to leave. Raphael and his associates convinced them to return and kiss the cross. "How can it be," he said, "that earlier you swore there were no felons or instigators among you, that you are all equally guilty, yet now you deny your guilt and blame only a few?" The din subsided and they all took the oath, except for the priest Yevsey and his fellow clergy, who refused to sign the confession. Petitioners took the confession addressed to the sovereign on to Moscow.

Raphael announced a general amnesty in the name of the tsar but the moment the rebellion subsided the better citizens began to settle scores with the agitators. They placed the elder Gavrila Demidov in chains and held him in the town meeting house. He was charged with releasing imprisoned felons, inciting brigands to the district to batter the nobles, leading a mutiny and provoking riots in Pskov, then getting drunk and ordering cannons be fired. They also seized the priest Firs of St. George's church, who had joined the brigands in destroying the districts. Governor Lvov ordered the elected elders[49] to take into custody the felons released by Demidov, but they managed to disperse. The governor then ordered their guarantors identified. It turned out that they were the instigators of the uprising, Koza, Kopyto and their friends, who shouted their refusal to search for felons. Fearing a new outbreak of violence, the governor left the guarantors in peace.

The better citizens refused to leave the ringleaders alone. They petitioned against the leaders of the rebellion, Proshka Koza, Yev Kopyto, Nikita Sorokoum[ov] and Ivan Klobuchkov, captured them and turned them all over to Prince Lvov. He ordered them incarcerated. A crowd gathered before the prison and deliberated. "The tsar has forgiven us all, yet Prince Lvov locks up people, punishes them and has them flogged.

Because the tsar tolerates this, we must to maintain our vigilance. Were the sovereign so gracious as to come to Pskov in person, we would submit to him in everything. If he sends boyars and fighting men with orders to annihilate us we shall kill our wives and children and blow ourselves up with gunpowder." Meanwhile the official Zakhar Osipov charged that during the rebellion the elder Gavrilka Demidov took him to the town hall to do some writing. Demidov held Zakhar against his will and ordered him to write a letter to the Lithuanian king requesting the assistance of five thousand soldiers. Osipov declared that only four men conspired in this betrayal.

When the petitioners sent to the tsar with the confession returned from Moscow Prince Lvov summoned all Pskov and informed them of the tsar's mercy. He charged them to oppose the agitators who, even after swearing the oath of allegiance, intended to resume their nefarious deeds. In the cathedral Gavrilka Demidov assaulted a musketeer for revealing his criminal activity. Tomilka Slepoy approached the musketeer Ignashka Mukha with the notion that he incite a new rebellion. The best men surrendered Demidov and Slepoy to the authorities. On November 21 Demidov, Slepoy, Koza, Kopyto, Sorokoumov, Klobuchkov, Shaposhnikov and Semiakov were taken from Pskov to Novgorod and chained in irons. As they were led away, many of the men of Pskov gathered with their wives and children to accompany them out of the city. They complained bitterly that "the tsar had no desire to punish them in Pskov, so he sent them to Novgorod instead. If he orders them punished there, all of us should be arrested and deported together."

On November 23 the district elders petitioned against Druzhinka Borodin, charging him with attempts to resume his past felonies and foment unrest. Borodin was arrested and flogged mercilessly, then placed under guard until he was deported to Moscow. At this time the tsar's decree arrived ordering the transfer of half the musketeers in Pskov for service in Moscow. The wagons to transport them were to be requisitioned in Pskov. Elders, tradesmen, lay brothers from the local monasteries and coachmen assembled in the town hall to complete the arrangements. Borodin sought to exploit the occasion. He sent his wife with an indignant letter to the town hall, but his plan burst back on him. The district elders took his letter to the governor at his court. As to the further fate of the conspirators, in a letter to the Swedish queen Kristina the tsar invited her to send a delegation to Novgorod to witness the execution of the rebels who assaulted Nummens. She did not respond.

Thus were attempts to revive the rebellion resolved. In Moscow the tsar summoned all those present at the council of July 26, informing them "The people of Pskov have admitted their guilt. They have sworn an oath of allegiance and we have forgiven them."

NIKON GOES TO SOLOVKI

In 1651, when life had settled in Novgorod and Pskov, Nikon arrived in Moscow and once again exerted a powerful influence over the young tsar. His former sway waned during his prolonged absence from Moscow. Nikon convinced the tsar to return [to Moscow] the coffin of Patriarch Hermogen[50] from the Miracles monastery to the Dormition cathedral, that of Patriarch Job[51] from Staritsa, and the remains of Metropolitan Philip[52] from Solovki. Together with the boyar Prince Ivan Nikitich Khovansky and Vasily Otiaev, Nikon personally undertook to bring back Philip's remains. This celebration held more than one religious significance. Philip's death was the result of conflict between lay and ecclesiastical authority. He was expelled by Tsar Ivan [IV] for his daring admonitions and was murdered by the crown servitor Maliuta Skuratov. God glorified the martyr by sainthood, whereas the secular government had yet to issue a formal confession of its guilt. Its failure to do so left open the possibility of similar indignities in the future.

Taking advantage of the piety and gentleness of the young tsar, Nikon compelled the authorties to issue at long last its formal confession. He found its model in the Byzantine story about Emperor Theodosius [II] who, when he sent for the remains of St. John Chrysostom, wrote a prayer in the form of a letter to the saint, asking forgiveness for the insults hurled at him by the emperor's mother.[53] Nikon took Tsar Alexis's letter, addressed to St. Philip, to Solovki. "I beg you to come here," the tsar wrote to the saint, "to judge the sin which our great-grandfather Tsar Ivan senselessly committed against you because of his irrational envy and unrestrained rage. Although I am not personally guilty of that grave injustice against you, the tomb of my great-grandfather is a constant reminder of it, and drives me to despair. As a consequence of your exile the reigning city remains today without your holy pastorship. Hence, on behalf of my great-grandfather who was guilty before you, I bow low my crowned head. May you forgive his sin by coming to us. May the shame of your exile, which now lies heavily upon him, vanish. May we all be convinced that you have made your peace with him at last. He repented his sin in his own time. Because of his repentance and our plea to you, we beseech you, holy father, to come to us! The evangelical word for which you suffered has been justified. No kingdom divided against itself shall stand.[54] There is no longer anything here to repudiate your word. Your flock enjoys God's grace in abundance, and is no longer divided. We pray to you in this spirit of unity. Give yourself to those who desire you, come home in peace and your own shall receive you in peace."

Bearing the repentance of one tsar over another tsar's refusal long ago to obey a prelate's admonitions, Nikon felt fully justified in demanding that his noble escorts enforce without demur his own instructions on ecclesiastical discipline. Petitions opposing the unreasonable demands of the metropolitan of Novgorod multiplied. Harsh by nature, and lacking genteel upbringing, Nikon had never learned the social codes which promoted gentle manners. Indeed, society in his day did not require gentleness. Complaints reached the tsar at court. Allow the sovereign himself to relate what transpired in Moscow in the year 1652, during Nikon's absence. Let him tell us about his relations with the dignitaries, the patriarch [Joseph] and especially Nikon. Let him, with his customary frankness, take us back to that age and that society.

ALEXIS-NIKON CORRESPONDENCE

"From the tsar and grand prince of all Russia, Alexis Mikhailovich, to the great shining sun, the illustrious and pious right reverend Nikon, metropolitan of Novgorod and Velikie Luki, from us the temporal tsar, a greeting. Rejoice, O great prelate, in your virtuous acts! How does God favor you, O mighty prelate? Thanks to your prayers the Lord has granted me, a sinner, good health. For God's sake do not fret about my not writing to you over the Savin business. I did send the results of the investigation in writing to the cellarer. Then I simply forgot. Here everyone decided to take his holiday at the same time, and I am weary. Forgive me, holy father. I harbored no ulterior motive in neglecting to write. I beseech you, great prelate, pray to the Lord to multiply my daughter's years. She feels great affection for you. Pray for my wife too, so that your prayers might help the Good Lord to grant her a child. Her time is ripe, and should misfortune strike I might perish from grief. For the love of God pray for her. You should know, O great prelate, that here we sing 'Many Years'[55] without reference to one specific patriarch. We ask the Lord to bless all ecumenical patriarchs, metropolitans, archbishops, all Christians. God bless them all. Write and tell us, great prelate, is that the way it should be sung, or is there some other form? How does the hierarchy sing it where you are?"

It is noteworthy that the tsar begs Nikon's forgiveness because he failed to write about some Savin affair, and swears that there was no concealed motive for this omission. This right to know confirms the fact that the sovereign recognized the metropolitan of Novgorod's spiritual authority over him.

A second letter, even more interesting than the first, began this way.

"To the chosen and uncompromising pastor and mentor to our bodies and souls, gracious, humble, generous, kind, well-wishing, but most of all lover and confidant of Christ and enthusiast of His flock. O powerful warrior and martyr of God in Heaven, my beloved favorite and companion, holy father pray for me, a sinner, and your prayers shall rescue me from the depths of my sinning. With faith in your most pure, benevolent and holy life, I wrote to you who are the most radiant light among the hierarchs, as I would write to the sun which illuminates the universe. So I write to you, who by your presence illuminate our realm, to you with your gracious demeanor and merciful deeds, our great and pious master, the right reverend and glorious Nikon, metropolitan of Novgorod and Velikie Luki, our very special spiritual and corporeal friend. We ask about your holy salvation, how God is protecting you, O light of our soul. You are so kind as to inquire about us. Although I, by the grace of God and your holy blessing, am called the truly anointed tsar, my evil and loathesome deeds render me unfit to dwell among dogs, much less to be tsar. I too am a sinner, although I call myself the servant of Him who has created me. Thanks to your holy prayers, the tsaritsa and I, our sisters and daughter, and everyone in our realm are well.

"Know this, O great prelate. For the sins of Orthodox Christians, and especially for my own accursed transgressions, our Maker, Creator and God chose to take from this illusory and hypocritical world our father and pastor, the great master Lord Joseph, patriarch of Moscow and All Russia. God had him carried to the bosom of Abraham, Isaac and Jacob.[56] You, our father, should know this. Our mother, the ecumenical apostolic church is widowed now. She tearfully laments the loss of her bridegroom. When we enter the church, we behold how this mourning dove abides deserted, without her husband, how she grieves without her betrothed.[57] Everything has changed, not only in the churches but throughout our realm. There is no one to counsel us on spiritual matters. It is not good for children to live without a pastor.

"When the singing started on Holy Thursday, instead of the hymn to the cherubim we started to sing the first verse of the hymn to the Last Supper.[58] As we concluded the first verse the cellarer from the Savior monastery rushed up and said to me 'O sovereign, the patriarch is no more!' At that moment the tsar's bell tolled three times, and we were consumed with such fear and sorrow that we could scarcely continue singing, managing it only through tears. In the cathedral the singers and the hierarchy were weak at the knees in fear and horror because they realized who had departed on this solemn day. Now we are lost like lambs without a shepherd. We sinners know not where to turn, where to lay our heads, for we have lost our father and our shepherd, and are without another. After mass I went to the illustrious one, but our master had already passed on. He lay lifelike, with his beard combed just as it had been when he lived, looking incredibly handsome. Saying my farewell I kissed his hand and went to the washing of the feet.[59]

"On Friday his illustriousness was taken to the church of the Deposition of the Robe.[60] In the evening I went there alone. As I approached the north entrance I noticed that no one was sitting with the body. It seems that all those whom he had anointed abbot had gone, so I ordered the metropolitan to reprimand them. What a sin, holy father, that those whom he had rewarded in life were happy he was dead. The highest among them, the abbot of the New Savior monastery, was the first to leave for home. I reprimanded the junior boyars as much as the Good Lord would allow. One priest read the Psalter over him. Indeed he did not so much read it as bellow it at the top of his lungs, and to make matters worse he had flung open all the doors. 'Why,' I inquired, 'do you not speak in a seemly manner?' 'Forgive me, my sovereign,' was his response, 'A great fear has overtaken me. There was an uncontrollable growling in the prelate's belly, and I became frightened. His belly rose up and his face began to swell at the same time. I was even more frightened. Thinking that he had come back to life I opened the door with the intention of running away.'

"Forgive me, father, but his words caused me such fear. His speech so terrified me that I nearly fainted. Then before my eyes a lump began to move around in his stomach very rapidly, as though he were alive. A wicked thought passed through my mind, that surely it must have come from the Devil himself. Run! At any moment now he will leap up and strangle you! Crossing myself, I took his eminence by the hand, and kissing it thought to myself 'Dust thou art, and unto dust shalt thou return.'[61]

So what was there to fear? At that very moment, I tell you, something crackled in his mouth, and once again I was scared out of my wits. As I continued to stand there my fear vanished, and I recovered completely by taking his hand and saying a prayer.

"He was buried on Holy Saturday and we literally strained ourselves with weeping. As for me, what torment can an abominable sinner such as I now not anticipate? Oh yes, all torments await me for my unspeakably foul deeds, and I, accursed that I am, deserve them all for the sins that I have committed. The boyars and lords, conversing with one another, said similar things about themselves. There was not a man there who was not in tears after viewing him. Just yesterday he was among us, and now he lay silent. This came to pass on the eve of such a great day! My closest companions who accompanied me strained themselves with weeping, most of all Trubetskoy and Mikhaila Odoevsky, Mikhaila Rtishchev and Vasily Buturlin. They all shed their tears for him, our lord, whom God had taken so suddenly,[62] and they recalled their own sins.

"Vasily Buturlin told me, and the patriarchal secretary told him, that the overall opinion of the patriarch was poor. This is why he is known to have complained 'They want to remove me, they wish to see someone else in my place, and if they fail in this my shame shall compel me to petition for my own dismissal.' He even set aside money that he intended to take with him when this occurred. He thought and spoke of nothing else, and who knows why? As the Creator is my witness, neither I nor my spiritual father ever entertained such a thought! It is too terrible even to contemplate. Forgive me, holy father, but even if the patriarch were a confirmed heretic, how could I have removed him by myself, without seeking your counsel? I hope, holy prelate, that even though you are far away from us sinners, you can testify that this is impossible, that this shining light never could have been removed or unseated with dishonor.

"The patriarch's private treasury contains just a little over 13,400 rubles. There are also many exquisite silver vessels, platters, pans, goblets, wine bowls and plates. I myself compiled an inventory of his private treasures. Had I not gone there personally I believe that half his possessions would have disappeared, inasmuch as there was no written record of them. Indeed, there would be nothing left, because it all would have been stolen! Such inventories are extremely rare, and the great majority of items are never recorded because the owner knows everything by memory. Not one of the shopkeepers had ever seen these vessels. The way that he took care of them, holy father, is incredible. There was not a single vessel in the collection without at least five layers of paper or felt wrapped around it. Forgive me, holy father, for I often coveted some of them for myself, but by the grace of God and your holy prayers I restrained myself. Oh no, I took nothing. I could have sold the valuables four times over but I did not want to sin in God's eyes or disgrace myself in the eyes of the people. What sort of steward would I be to take his things, and profit by them? Now I am immeasurably glad that I touched nothing.

"With my own hands I distributed ten rubles apiece to the various petitioners who came before the patriarch. I gathered them together in the sacristy, tearfully begged them to remember this in their prayers, and stop complaining. They wept and thanked me. I advised them to say the appropriate prayers each day, as many as they could manage. Then I asked who among them had never chastised a serf without cause. It is one thing to punish them deservedly, and quite another to get drunk and chastise or even beat them for no good reason. Even if our holy father did discipline someone without cause on occasion, his punishment should be borne and overlooked. Whatever might have happened in the past, it is time to cast off malice, to pray as fervently as possible and accept his radiant light with joy. At the same time, if we did not give them something, if we did not cheer them up with some money, there would be grumbling because, when all was said and done, they were destitute. He, the generous one, had always supplemented their meager resources.

"You our great holy man are aware that I have installed Vasily Buturlin in the palace. Prince Alexis [Trubetskoy] petitioned for retirement and I complied. Now my word is feared at the palace and my orders are executed without delay. I have been informed that Prince Ivan Khovansky wrote in his letters that he is ruined. He described his abyss as one forced to live daily by the rules of the church. They gossiped about me as well, saying that until now they had never been subjected to the disgrace of a sovereign turning them over to the jurisdiction of metropolitans. I beseech you, holy father, have mercy and do not force him and yourself to conform to ecclesiastical rules. It is beneficial, O master, to teach those who are already wise because they will become wiser, whereas all instruction is wasted on the foolish. If you decide to broach the subject with him, make it come from you directly, and make it sound as if someone else, not I, wrote to you regarding this.

"As for me, I am writing my confession to you. Vasily Otiaev writes to his friends that it would be better for them all to disappear somewhere in Novaia Zemlia beyond Siberia with Prince Ivan Ivanovich Lobanov than to be with the metropolitan of Novgorod, who forces them to fast but cannot compel anyone to believe in God. I urge you, holy father, to save this letter, and keep it a secret. I also ask, O great master, that you read it for yourself, that you not disdain us, a poor sinner, and our foolish and confused writing."

Better than anything this letter explains the phenomenon of Nikon, whose character alone cannot clarify the metropolitan's relationship with the sovereign and the realm. The emotions expressed by Tsar Alexis Mikhailovich in that letter transport us to the time of consolidation of papal authority in the West, an authority rooted in the character of Western leaders themselves. Such a tradition of sovereignty and its customs were unknown to Byzantium. The religiosity of the Eastern rulers notwithstanding, their traditions and customs never allowed them to forget their own elevation in relation to that of the ecclesiastical hierarchy. On the other hand, leaders of young nations, similar to our Tsar Alexis Mikhailovich, with their effusion of Christian religious sentiments full of submission and humility, never knew how to subordinate them to their precedence as sovereign. For them the sovereign was eclipsed by the human being. Naturally this raised the stature of the church pastor, the unifier and decision-maker, the highest judge and interpreter of God's law. It was especially true when such a prelate inspired feelings of submission and humility in others, when he also knew how to use his boundless influence and position to elicit the sovereign's good will.

Thus Tsar Alexis Mikhailovich strained himself weeping for Patriarch Joseph, even though as a virtuous man himself he could not avoid being saddened by the unworthiness, pettiness and unspiritual behavior of this prelate. He tried to banish all such sinful thoughts of Joseph's blameworthiness from his mind, as an affectionate and respectful son would of an unworthy father. Hence, so much greater was the force with which that pious young man directed his love toward the worthy pastor Nikon. Here he did not stint on words to demonstrate his love, to elevate the beloved subject while humbling himself before him, for the means of all kinds of love are the same. Thus did Alexis himself, by the very nature of his character, place Nikon higher than any patriarch or metropolitan ever had been raised by a tsar or grand prince.

Scattered throughout this remarkable epistle is evidence of other kinds of relationships as well in that era. Liturgical services played a vital role in everyone's life, and the tsar remarked in his letter how difficult it was for him to deal with the fact that the patriarch passed away during such a great religious holiday, that he would not officiate at the Easter service. The holiday celebration would not be the same! "The church exists like a lone dove, without a friend." Russians of that time were reared on curious ideas. At the viewing of the remains the tsar had a sudden thought, "Run! Any moment now the deceased will leap up and strangle you." Also curious is the patriarchal realm itself, with its simplicity of relationships that takes us back to the beginning of the Middle Ages. The tsar personally was in charge of everything, with his own hands catalogued the property left by the deceased, and at the same time good-naturedly pronounced such a dreadful indictment of his own contemporary society. "If I did not take the inventory personally, all of his property would have been stolen." This reveals how deeply embedded were ideas of the Household Manager[63] in the Russian soul. It was with great astonishment and respect that Alexis Mikhailovich reacted to Joseph's meticulous ways. "I cannot even imagine the sort of person he was. He did not possess a single vessel that was not protected by five layers of wrapping."

Finally we gain some insight into the young tsar's attitude towards his courtiers. The old head of the tsar's palace[64] had retired, and a new one appointed. The tsar was very pleased with the change because now his instructions to the court were feared and handled expeditiously.

The boyars were less satisfied with the young tsar's devotion to the metropolitan of Novgorod, for the prelate sought to bring them under his authority. "Never have we experienced such humiliation," they whispered, "after the tsar subjected us to the metropolitan's authority." Alexis found himself in a precarious situation. He was deeply attached to Nikon, fervently wishing his elevation to the patriarchal see, but Nikon, with his devious ways, alienated the boyars. Alexis Mikhailovich wrote to him suggesting that he be more flexible, that he not coerce Khovansky into living according to ecclesiastical rules. At the same time the tsar enjoined Nikon not to reveal his own role in the matter when discussing the problem with Khovansky. Alexis did not want the boyars to learn of his devotion to Nikon, or that he sided with the metropolitan against them. The goodness of such people as Alexis Mikhailovich renders them dependent on those around them. They cannot bear dissatisfaction at close range, even though further away there might be many who are unhappy, but distance makes them invisible. To be sure, in a moment of rage Tsar Alexis might fiercely berate and strike someone close to him, inflicting punishment with his own hand, yet the idea that those around him might be dissatisfied, or angry, was intolerable to him.

Twice in his letters to Nikon the tsar mentioned the election of a successor to Joseph. "For the love of God," he wrote at one juncture "return as quickly as you can to elevate Theognostos to the patriarchate, for without you we cannot begin." In another letter he wrote "Pray, holy prelate, for the Good Lord to send us a pastor and a father who is fit for this holy office, namely the already named Theognostos. We await your arrival for the elevation, O great prelate. Three men know this individual, I, the metropolitan of Kazan, and my spiritual pastor. He has the reputation of a holy man." Naturally Nikon understood the tsar's hints only too well, being aware of the true identity of this Theognostos (the name means 'known to God"). Nikon arrived in Moscow in July of 1652 and was elected patriarch. He declined the honor in order to force an election on his own terms, to assure himself that Khovansky's friends would not obstruct him. Shedding copious tears, the tsar and those around him lay on the ground in the Dormition cathedral, near the remains of St. Philip, begging Nikon not to reject the office. Addressing the boyars and the people, Nikon asked if they would respect him as their archpastor and father, and allow him to set the church in order. After everybody swore to respect his wishes, Nikon agreed. This was July 22. On July 25 he was duly elevated.

NOTES

Additional information on personalities and topics found in the text and notes is available in Joseph L. Wieczynski, et al., eds., *The Modern Encyclopedia of Russian, Soviet and Eurasian History* (MERSH, formerly *The Modern Encyclopedia of Russian and Soviet History*); Harry B. Weber, et al., eds., *The Modern Encyclopedia of East Slavic, Baltic and Eurasian Literatures* (MESBEL, formerly *The Modern Encyclopedia of Russian and Soviet Literatures, Including Non-Russian and Emigré Literatures*); Paul D. Steeves, ed., *The Modern Encyclopedia of Religions in Russia and Eurasia* (MERRE, formerly *The Modern Encyclopedia of Religions in Russia and the Soviet Union*); and David R. Jones, ed., *The Military Encyclopedia of Russia and Eurasia* (MERE, formerly *The Military-Naval Encyclopedia of Russia and the Soviet Union*) all published by Academic International Press.

INTRODUCTION

1. "First Letter. On the Need for a True History of France and the Chief Defect of Existing Histories," *The Varieties of History. From Voltaire to the Present.* Edited, Selected and Introduced by Fritz Stern (New York, 1973), pp. 67-70.

2. Books written in the Belarusian language and published abroad, then smuggled into Belarus for distribution.

3. During the course of the Time of Troubles, Muscovy made serious overtures to Sigismund III to put forward a Polish candidate, preferably his son Prince Władysław, for the Muscovite throne. See Volume 15 of this series.

4. Jaroslaw Pelenski, in his "The Contest for the 'Kievan Inheritance' in Russian-Ukrainian Relations. The Origins and Early Ramifications," *Ukraine and Russia in their Historical Encounter*, ed. Peter Potichny et al. (Canadian Institute of Ukrainian Studies, University of Alberta, Edmonton, 1992), discusses the three major theories or schools of historical interpretation of the Kievan legacy. Among them is the monolineal and exclusivist school mentioned above, in which he places Soloviev. It rests primarily on "historical-ideological claims and political-juridical theories" based upon the transfer of the Kievan metropolitan see from Kiev to Vladimir and subsequently to Moscow, as well as the uninterrupted dynastic continuity of the heirs of the house of Riurik.

5. The Zaporozhian Cossack Host was Ukrainian, and the earlier blend of Ukrainian and Belarusian to convey a Rus identity no longer applies.

6. It was in the eyes of many a political nation, or at least a proto-nation.

7. Soloviev's own Orthodoxy doubtless rendered him unsympathetic to a Russian churchman such as Nikon, and made it possible for the author to convey the patriarch's excesses in ways that spared other important church leaders. Nikon became a key figure in the great schism, which produced a permanent cleavage in the Russian Orthodox church. As head of the church he not only attempted to assert his authority over the tsar, he introduced the issue of reforming religious texts which had become corrupted through copying and recopying over time. This caused some of the leaders of a simultaneous moral and religious revival in the church to turn against him. Attempts to extend his reforms to the correction of rituals strained relations to the breaking point, not only between him and the reformers, but with the tsar himself, who severed his connection to his former protégé in 1658. Notwithstanding the support which Nikon received from Constantinople and the expertise of the learned monks in Kiev, who were summoned to assist the Greeks from Mount Athos and the Orthodox East in correcting the works, in 1666-1667 a church council defrocked and deposed the "great sovereign" as Tsar Alexis had styled Nikon. The prelate ended his days in exile at a distant monastery. See Volume 21 of this series.

CHAPTER I

1. The origin of the Muscovite state begins with the development of the Vladimir-Suzdal and Moscow principalities by the Russian people. They share certain ties, such as the Eastern Orthodox religion and a ruling dynasty—a princeling of the Riurik dynasty founded Muscovy—with the Rus ancestors of the Ukrainians. The Rus fell under Polish control as early as the fourteenth century. In the mid-seventeenth century eastern Ukraine was joined to Muscovy (see Note 3, below), while the western provinces remained in what had become by then the Polish-Lithuanian Commonwealth. In 1918 Ukraine was united and independent for a brief period, then in the 1920s it broke up again. Its component parts came under the control of a number of foreign states, the largest being the USSR and Poland. During World War II Western Ukraine passed to the jurisdiction of the Russian-dominated Soviet Union, resulting in a political connection of Western Ukraine and Russia for the first time in history. For an excellent treatment of Ukrainian history, see Paul Robert Magosci, *A History of Ukraine* (Seattle, Wash., 1996), especially pp. 12-24.

2. Known as smutnoe vremia, it lasted from 1598 to 1613, although Soloviev favors the date 1604 as the real beginning of Muscovy's troubles. In the absence of a legitimate successor Michael Romanov was elected to the Muscovite throne and founded the Romanov dynasty. The fifteen years preceding his accession were filled with social strife, some of it the result of natural and human disasters such as famine and a proliferation of pretenders to the Muscovite throne which Ivan IV (the Terrible) effectively left vacant. Much of the unrest

can be traced back to the social disruption caused by his oprichnina, the complex of crown estates created in 1564 by Ivan which was exempted from the jurisdiction of the general administration. The oprichnina, which came to stand for a separate jurisdiction, functioned like a powerful security police. Originally it consisted of about twenty towns and their hinterlands, several special sections of the country, and a part of Moscow where Ivan built a new palace. Its members came to constitute a parallel governing structure, virtually "a state within a state" answerable directly to the tsar. Ivan used it to conduct a reign of terror in Muscovy aimed, it is said, against the landed nobility which Ivan mistrusted, and wished to destroy as a rival focus of power. Concerning the oprichnina, consult Nicholas V. Riasanovsky, *A History of Russia,* 3rd ed., (Oxford, 1977), pp. 151-152, 159; also David MacKenzie and Michael W. Curran, *A History of Russia and the Soviet Union,* 3rd ed., Homewood, Ill., 1977), pp. 179-184. For a fresh interpretation of the Time of Troubles see Chester S.L. Dunning, *Russia's First Civil War. The Time of Troubles and the Founding of the Romanov Dynasty* (University Park, Penn., 2001).

3. In his text the author uses the term "Western Russians" to signify what were then collectively known as Rus (Rusyns), or Ukrainians and Belarusians, creating the impression that all were a single people which shared a common identity, the interests of which were embodied in the person of Tsar Michael. Notwithstanding that the Ukrainians lost the towns of Chernigov and Starodub to Muscovy in 1522, the country was not tied to Russia until a large part of its territory (central and eastern) was annexed to Muscovy following the Pereiaslav Agreement of 1654. Ukrainians and Belarusians were part of the grand principality of Lithuania until 1569, when Poland and Lithuania united to become a Commonwealth. Although the Orthodox Ukrainians passed to Catholic control, while the Belarusians remained connected to Lithuania, it is difficult to separate the cultural history of the two peoples. For their part, as Paul Bushkovich attests in his article "The Formation of a National Consciousness in Early Modern Russia," *Harvard Ukrainian Studies,* No. 3/4 (December, 1986), pp. 355-376, sixteenth-century Muscovites never identified with any other East Slavs as one people.

4. See Volumes 16 and 17 of this series.

5. The name Lithuania is first mentioned in the sources in 1009, but the early feudal state was not formed until the thirteenth and fourteenth centuries, at which time it became the bi-national Lithuanian-Ruthenian grand principality of Lithuania. Numerous princes of the Gediminas dynasty embraced Orthodoxy, and Ruthenian became the official (chancery) language of the government, spoken by the vast majority of the Lithuanian population as well. It is very difficult to create a strong distinction between Ukrainians and Belarusians in this early modern period of their development, when they were known collectively as Rus. There is a good discussion of this and other Lithuanian history in Orest Subtelny, *Ukraine. A History.* 2nd ed., (Toronto, 1994), pp. 70-72. In the late fourteenth century Poland and Lithuania were

threatened both by the Teutonic Order which controlled the Baltic coast, and a Muscovy that was growing rapidly in power and prestige. For these and other political reasons the rulers of the two countries concluded the Union of Krewo in 1385. In return for the hand of the Polish queen Jadwiga and the title of king of Poland, Jogaila agreed to embrace Catholic Christianity, and to attach his Rus and Lithuanian lands to the Polish crown.

6. During the fifteenth century, with Rus under Lithuanian domination, whenever the latter became too aggressive in its dealings with the Rus they turned to Muscovy. Chernigov, which today is a Ukrainian city (Chernihiv), at that time was on the border between Muscovy and Lithuania and therefore was particularly vulnerable. Beginning in the 1470s, owing to increased Lithuanian pressure against the Rusyns, the princes of northern Chernigov slowly began to transfer their allegiance to Moscow. The process was concluded around 1500. After a brief respite religious persecution of the Rus resumed in Lithuania. Mykhailo Hrushevsky treats this issue in *A History of Ukraine* (New Haven, Conn., 1941), pp. 140-143. See also Oswald P. Backus III, *Motives of West Russian Nobles in Deserting Lithuania for Moscow, 1377-1514* (Lawrence, Kansas, 1957).

7. Known as oblasti (plural) in both Ukrainian and Russian, they are roughly comparable to provinces.

8. After Stefan Bathory became king of Poland in 1572 he scored repeated victories over Ivan the Terrible of Muscovy, causing the latter to appeal to Pope Gregory XIII for mediation in the conflict, whereupon the Pope dispatched the Jesuit Antonio Possevino (see Note 10, below) to help end the hostilities. Meanwhile the Poles dreamed of converting the Muscovites to Catholicism, an agenda which Rome supported wholeheartedly. A detailed discussion of this is to be found in MacKenzie and Curran, p. 176.

9. The full title of the work is *On the Unity of God's Church under One Shepherd and the Greek Departure from this Unity*. It was first published in 1577 at Wilno. The Greek departure refers to the religious schism in 1054, a consequence of papal claims of primacy over the Eastern church, producing a breach which to date has not been healed notwithstanding numerous efforts to accomplish this. Skarga, a brilliant Jesuit polemicist, persistently argued that the state of Orthodoxy was so hopeless that its only alternative was union with Rome. Piotr Skarga was a committed conservative who favored the Counter-Reformation theory of the divine right of kings and the prerogatives of the church.

10. See Note 8, above. Antonio Possevino (1534-1611), an Italian diplomat, scholar and determined opponent of Protestantism, was charged in 1577 by Pope Gregory XIII with recovering the Swedish court and its people for Roman Catholicism. As an imperial envoy he used very effectively his ties (through marriage) with the Polish royal family. He worked for the cause of Catholicism in Poland, Russia and Ukraine until his recall to Italy in 1586, where he devoted himself to literary work until his death. See the entry with extensive bibliography in the

Modern Encyclopedia of Russian and Soviet History (Academic International Press, 1976-, henceforth MERSH), Volume 29, pp. 109-114, by Hugh F. Graham, who has also translated Possevino's memoir *The Moscovia of Antonio Possevino, S.J.* (Pittsburgh, Penn., 1977).

11. Muscovy was never involved in the Union of Brest. Indeed, when reunification was first proposed in 1439, as the Union of Florence, Muscovy most emphatically rejected it.

12. Many of the problems which beset the Rus Orthodox church at this time had their roots in the so-called "right of domination." It was introduced by Grand Prince Alexander of Lithuania (reigned 1492-1506) when he broke with the tradition of electoral councils determining who would fill the metropolitan see of Kiev, and appointed one Yosif Bolgarinovich (Yosyf Bolharynovych) to the office in 1498. This inaugurated a century of abuse in the Rus church, as a succession of unqualified candidates with questionable morals succeeded to high church offices. Royal appointments routinely were made to discharge state debts, with a fine disregard for the fitness of the candidate. The example of King Stefan Bathory elevating a Catholic layman to head a Rus Orthodox monastery in 1577 illustrates this well. Once in office the newly-appointed hierarchs habitually transformed church wealth into personal property held in perpetuity. For details consult Ivan Wlasowsky, *Outline History of the Ukrainian Orthodox Church* (New York-Bound Brook, N.Y., 1956), pp. 172-175. This work is in two volumes, the first in English and the second in Ukrainian. See Chapter II, Note 95, below.

13. Progenitors respectively, of the Rus and Lithuanian princely families.

14. Governor Vasily Konstantinovich (Vasyl Konstantynovych) Ostrozhsky of Kiev was born in 1526 or 1527 in Volhynia, and died in 1608. He was a Rus nobleman and an extremely wealthy magnate. As leader of the Rus in their negotiations leading up to the Union of Lublin in 1569 he demanded that they be treated as equal partners in the Polish-Lithuanian Commonwealth. Prince Ostrozhsky used his considerable wealth to provide generous financial assistance to the Rus Orthodox church and Rus cultural projects. During the second half of the sixteenth century Prince Ostrozhsky created a famous cultural center in Ostrog. Here the first successful attempt was made to establish a Rus institution of higher learning, a printing press and an educational and cultural circle. The most active ideological activity of this center came during the period immediately preceding the Union of Brest, and continued through the beginning of the seventeenth century. Several excellent polemical works appeared during this intense period of anti-union ferment. For a fuller discussion, see V.M. Nichyk et al., *Humanistychni i reformatsiini idei na Ukraini* (Humanist and Reformation Ideas in Ukraine) (Kiev, 1991), p. 135. It is worth noting that Prince Ostrozhsky was a candidate for the Polish throne following the death of the last Jagiellonian king Sigismund II Augustus in 1572 and in 1598, upon the death of Tsar Fedor Ivanovich, he became a candidate for the Muscovite throne.

15. Prince Andrei Mikhailovich Kurbsky (1528-1583) was born into one of Muscovy's ancient families. He spent his early career in the service of Ivan IV, who appointed him table attendant in 1549. Between 1549 and 1564 Kurbsky was associated chiefly with the armed forces. In 1553 he earned Ivan's trust and gratitude by pledging to support his infant son when Ivan was stricken with what appeared to be a fatal illness. When unexpectedly the tsar recovered he demonstrated his appreciation by promoting Kurbsky to the boyar council. Kurbsky became disaffected during the mounting terror associated with the tsar's oprichnina, and in 1564 deserted at the Livonian front. In so doing he sacrificed his wife, son and mother, all of whom were held hostage by Ivan and ultimately killed. Kurbsky settled in a castle in Volhynia on lands given to him by the Polish king, and accepted a commission in the Polish army. He also assembled a group of scholars and writers and devoted much time to literary pursuits. Kurbsky corresponded with Rus individuals of distinction, appealing to them to remain true to their Orthodox faith. In his correspondence with the Muscovite tsar Kurbsky justified his flight. Additional details are to be found in Norman Davies, *God's Playground. A History of Poland*, Volume I (New York, N.Y., 1984), pp. 361-363. See also Backus, "A.M. Kurbsky in the Polish-Lithuanian State (1564-1583)," *Acta Balto-Slavica*, 6 (1969), pp. 29-50; also the entry by Karl W. Schweitzer, MERSH, Volume 18, pp. 171-174.

16. After the Union of Lublin in 1569 separate chanceries and chancery records, known as Crown Metrica and Lithuanian Metrica, continued to exist. During the fifteenth and sixteenth centuries, for both administrative and judicial functions, Latin was the principal language in the crown chancery. Throughout the lands of the grand principality of Lithuania, Ruthenian, a linguistic predecessor of modern Ukrainian and Belarusian, and distinct from the language of Muscovy, was the main chancery, as well as the judicial and administrative language. Crown chancery documents pertaining to the Western Rus lands, Ruthenia and Bełz, in addition to the palatinate of Podolia (Podillia), established in the mid-fifteenth century, continued to be written in Latin. The 1569 Act of Annexation, which transferred the sovereignty of the remaining Rus lands (Volhynia, Bratslav and Kiev) from the grand principality to Crown Poland, guaranteed the continued use of Ruthenian as the official language for these lands.

17. Although Muscovy had its own fraternal organizations, they differed substantially from the Western Rus variant. For one thing the sphere of their concerns and activities, largely economic and parish affairs, was significantly narrower than that of the democratic lay Rus brotherhoods, nominally affiliated with the local Orthodox church. The latter were organized along the lines of medieval guilds with an emphasis on ritual, especially on feast days and during funeral processions, and regulated not only the daily life of their own members, but also of the entire community, lay and clerical alike. The Rus brotherhoods spearheaded a sixteenth-century cultural "renaissance." Conflict with the Catholic church helped to sharpen their collective self-definition, and caused them to

organize such fraternal associations as a way of combating Catholic proselytizing, which threatened not only their ancestral faith but by extension their ethnicity as well.

18. Although he uses the term Lithuanian Russia Soloviev in fact is referring to Rus territory in the Polish-Lithuanian Commonwealth.

19. Modeled on the administration of the German city of Magdeburg, this statute was introduced into the kingdom of Poland by Casimir III (reigned 1333-1370), who began his conquest of Ukrainian territories in the fourteenth century. It provided for local self-government and facilitated the development of guilds along Western European lines. Although nominally applicable to all inhabitants of Crown Poland, the Magdeburg code discriminated against the Orthodox. As a result they were deprived of burgher rights, barred from artisan guilds, eventually forbidden to own property in some city centers (Lvov is the outstanding example), generally persecuted and treated as second-class citizens. This, coupled with mounting pressure to convert to the Catholic faith, stimulated the founding and proliferation of Orthodox brotherhoods as one avenue of defense.

20. When Rus formed part of the grand principality of Lithuania the primary component of the nobility was the thirty or so princely or magnate families who traced their descent from the Riurikid or Gediminas families. The wealthiest among them was the Ostrozhsky family already mentioned, which owned one hundred towns and more than thirteen hundred villages. The lesser nobility was called szlachta, the Polish term for the gentry or nobility, the privileges of most of which derived from their military service.

21. Sigismund II Augustus (1548-1572) was both king of Poland and grand prince of Lithuania. He was also last of the Jagiellonians to rule.

22. In his day Terletsky was accused of numerous crimes, including murder, manslaughter, rape, robbery and pillage for which, as a minimum, he should have been deprived of office. Eventually he was tried for manslaughter, rape and assault, but won acquittals on all counts.

23. In 1551 Gedeon's merchant father Arseny became the first member of this family to occupy the episcopal see of Galich (Halych) which was transferred to Lvov the same year. Gedeon was elevated to that office in 1569. Antagonism between the Rus in Lvov and the Balaban family went back to the tenure of Gedeon's father who upon his elevation to episcopal office contested the right conferred by King Sigismund I of Poland of the Dormition brotherhood to administer the St. Onufry monastery, and attempted to seize it for himself. The deep-seated conflict escalated when Gedeon became bishop and challenged the same royal privileges, viewing the St. Onufry monastery as a sinecure connected with his new office. Eventually, as parishioners and patrons of the Dormition church, the brethren successfully argued that it was they who should administer both the church property and the monastery.

24. On January 1, 1586 Joachim, patriarch of Antioch, set his seal to the founding charter of the Lvov Dormition Brotherhood. It was written in a mixture of Old Slavonic and Rus. Because Joachim knew only Arabic we can assume that the

charter was drawn up by the Rus prior to his arrival. Although the document gave the laity sweeping powers in the community there remained some confusion as to its ultimate jurisdiction in some cases. Seven articles in the charter provide for episcopal participation in the punishment of violations, and there is some question as to the actual right to administer punishments. When all was said and done, regardless of patriarchal privileges, brotherhood authority could be exercised only to the extent that the members of that community themselves agreed to honor it. Evidence suggests that the brethren did indeed enjoy widespread confidence in the community.

25. One of the original versions of the document, translated almost immediately from Greek into Rus, a fact which Soloviev does not acknowledge, uses the Russian form groshi, in the original form hrishi. In 1622 four of these equalled one thaler, or six copecks. One kopa grosh equalled sixty hroshei, or one Muscovite poltina, which amounted to half a Muscovite ruble. Consult *Arkhiv Iugo-Zapadnoi Rossii* (Archive of Southwestern Russia), Part I, Volume XI (Kiev, 1904), p. 363.

26. In practice this was not always the case. Sometimes a fine of money or more frequently of wax was considered sufficient. In extreme circumstances the patriarchs of Antioch and Constantinople both permitted the brotherhood to demand excommunication of anyone in the community who was in serious violation of its rules.

27. A bezmen was not a unit of measure but a kind of scale upon which a measure of wax was computed.

28. The brotherhood operated its own hospital, evidently a rather modest establishment resembling more a halfway house for invalids and the indigent, rather than a hospital devoted to the care of the sick.

29. In fact business loans were frequently made, but they were not interest-free. The brotherhood grew relatively wealthy from it numerous commercial enterprises, especially the sale of real estate. Proceeds often were used to advance the Rus cause as well as to stimulate its cultural and educational activities. By this time Rus town dwellers were subject to severe discrimination at the hands of the Catholic Poles, and the brethren were tireless in their exertions to secure economic and social justice for Lvov's Rus, and by extension to all of their countrymen. To finance its efforts the brotherhood frequently conducted fund drives. Because the lists of donors, many of them well preserved in *Arkhiv* (see Note 25, above), contain vital data on the donors, such as their place of residence, membership in guilds, amounts pledged, sex and relationship to other community members, they are an invaluable resource for social history of early modern Ukraine.

30. According to Iaroslav Isaievych, "Confraternities in Ukraine and Byelorussia," *Richerche Slavistiche* (Slavistic Researches), Volume 38 (1990), pp. 269-293, various scholars have dated the emergence of the Dormition Brotherhood to the mid-fifteenth century, although there do not appear to be any reliable supporting documents for this. The reader is reminded that even if religious

confraternities, alleged forerunners of the later brotherhoods, were in existence earlier they would have been under the jurisdiction of local bishops, who themselves usually were unfit for clerical office. Hence the legitimacy of these early confraternities is considered highly questionable.

31. The text of the founding charter is found in a number of published collections including *Diplomata Statutaria a Patriarchis Orientalibus Confraternitatis Stauropigianae Leopoliensis a 1586-1592* (Statutary Diplomata if the Stauropigian Confraternity of Lvov, 1586-1592) (Lvov, 1895), pp. 1-13; *Arkhiv*, Volume XI, pp. 2-7. Documents include information on women, who were permitted to be non-voting members of the organization. Although not confirmed by any surviving brotherhood register, it has been suggested in some secondary sources that the sister of Peter Mogila, the future metropolitan of Kiev and founder of the celebrated Mogila Academy, was along with two other women a founding member of the Dormition Brotherhood.

32. Rus was also taught, and a number of books soon were published in that language.

33. They were called zoloti in Ukrainian, and złotys in Poland.

34. Jeremiah (born 1530 or 1535, died 1585) was born in Anchialos, Thrace (today Pomorie, Bulgaria), an ancient city on the Black Sea. This was a Turkish-dominated region without any organized Greek schools, so Jeremiah was educated privately. At an unusually early age he was elected patriarch of Constantinople only to be deposed twice, in 1579 and 1584, owing to the Turkish practice of changing patriarchs. With each reinstatement by popular demand Patriarch Jeremiah contributed further to raising the standard of ecclesiastical and cultural life, both of which he found at an intolerably low level, and advanced education by advising his Orthodox bishops to establish Greek schools. Jeremiah also reformed the clergy and monastic life, even as his visits to the Orthodox churches served to strengthen the authority of the patriarchal office. At the insistence of Tsar Fedor Ivanovich of Muscovy (reigned 1584-1598) the ecumenical patriarch elevated the Muscovite church to the status of a patriarchate, making it the fifth in the pentarchy after Constantinople, Antioch, Alexandria and Jerusalem. Jeremiah refused to accept the new Gregorian calendar, mandated by Pope Gregory XIII. When Orthodox and Lutheran turned to one another for support and assistance against the Roman Catholic church, Jeremiah pointed to serious differences in dogma that precluded cooperation. Although his dialogues with Lutheran theologians on this matter eventually broke down, they began in good faith and a spirit of friendliness and, as such, became the forerunners of today's ecumenical dialogues.

35. The Rus dioceses were under the jurisdiction of the metropolitan see in Kiev, the metropolitan answering directly to the patriarch of Constantinople. In 1589 the patriarch of Constantinople undertook a fund-raising mission to Moscow, planned to coincide with the installation of a new patriarchate in that city. Taking the same route traversed by the patriarch of Antioch three years earlier, patriarch of Constantinople too stopped over in Lvov. At the request of the

Dormition Brotherhood he reviewed the original charter which Joachim approved, and clarified sixteen of its articles. At the same time he placed the organization under his direct jurisdiction. To emphasize its special standing the patriarch of Constantinople conferred stauropigia status upon the brotherhood, according its recipients the right to display the patriarchal cross on their coat of arms. This signified that the fraternal institution was free of all episcopal control. When the metropolitan was made patriarchal exarch shortly thereafter, in that capacity he acquired jurisdiction over the brotherhood, although the lines of authority were never clearly drawn. The final version of the brotherhood's charter was amended by patriarch of Constantinople in 1592. It left the organization with the exclusive right to supervise Rus public education in Lvov, and to operate a printing press for both religious (a serious bone of contention for Bishop Balaban) and instructional materials. It also gave the brethren complete control over the selection of priests for the Dormition church. The organization's role of watchdog of public morals, lay and clerical alike, was expanded to offer the same authority to new brotherhoods which modeled themselves on the Lvov prototype, and agreed to accept the Lvov charter. For further details on the stauropigia status of the brotherhood, consult *Arkhiv*, Volume XI, pp. 15-17. In 1708, when the organization and much of the community finally became Uniate, this status was confirmed by the pope, and the ruling remained in force until 1788, when the Brotherhood became the Stavropigiia Instytut.

36. Onisifor Devochka was metropolitan of Kiev, 1579-1589. He defended the interests of the Orthodox church before the Polish kings Stefan Bathory and Sigismund III. He was consecrated metropolitan in violation of canon law, having been married twice, and personally permitted gross infringements of church law. Owing to complaints from the laity in 1585, on July 21, 1589 Patriarch Jeremiah of Constantinople divested him of his office.

37. The Diet or Sejm is the Polish chamber of deputies. A lesser body is known as a dietine or sejmyk.

38. The Polish word for church is kościół. The Russian homonym is kostël which usually denotes pejoratively a Roman Catholic place of worship, not a proper (Orthodox) church, for which the noun is tserkov.

39. In 1579 Rogoza became archimandrite of the Minsk Dormition monastery. In 1589 the Polish szlachta government appointed him to the metropolitan see in Kiev and the following year, together with several of the Orthodox bishops, he entered into secret negotiations for church union. In 1596 he convoked the Synod of Brest. His szlachta background inclined Rogoza to preserve his privileges. With the help of the Polish szlachta he seized a number of Rus Orthodox churches and monasteries and forcibly converted them to the Uniate confession.

40. Digamy, or serial monogamy, in Russian dvoezhenstvo, was not at all uncommon among clerics at that time. Although prohibited by canon law, some priests remarried after being widowed. The frequency with which stricture against digamy was pronounced suggests that the regulation was rather laxly enforced, and the practice itself widespread.

194   NOTES TO CHAPTER I

41. Originally in the Eastern Orthodox church an exarch was an archbishop or patriarch. Later, in the period under review here, the title came to mean a bishop or other clergyman serving as the patriarch's deputy or legate.

42. Formerly a silver coin of small denomination which circulated in Turkey and Egypt.

43. The abbots in the most important monasteries were called archimandrites, whereas the ones in lesser monasteries were called hegumens. Consult Sergei G. Pushkarev, *Dictionary of Russian Historical Terms from the Eleventh Century to 1917* (New Haven, Conn., 1970), pp. 2, 30 for Russian equivalents.

44. The Rogatin Brotherhood also received the patriarchal privileges, or stauropigia status.

45. Strelets, or streltsy in the plural, means shooter or musketeer. The musketeers were the first permanent regiments, or prikazy, of the armed forces, organized in the mid-sixteenth century during the reign of Ivan the Terrible. In addition to muskets (hence musketeers), their weapons consisted of swords, pikes and battle-axes. Although approximately ten percent of the regiments were mounted, the musketeers were overwhelmingly an army of foot soldiers. About five thousand of these military men were stationed in Moscow, and another seven thousand in various frontier towns. During the seventeenth century the regiments were added as auxiliary forces to the mounted army of lords-in-waiting or petty gentry. In Moscow alone there were some twenty regiments, each commanded by a streletskii golova (musketeer head), which later became known as polkovnik (colonel). Under him came the polugolova (lieutenant colonel) sotniki (centurions), piatidesiatniki (commanders of fifty men) and desiatniki (roughly equivalent to corporal. Although initially the streltsy served by contract, eventually their service became lifelong and hereditary. They lived with their families in suburban settlements, received from the government plots of land, as well as a salary in money and grain, plus armaments and uniforms, and engaged in trade and manufacturing on a small scale without paying taxes. At the end of the seventeenth century the Old Believers, a religious sect which split off from the mainstream Russian Orthodox church over differences in religious texts and icons penetrated their ranks. The resulting religious dissent, political troubles and internal struggles provoked riots among the musketeers in 1682, 1689 and 1698. The final incident was more a show of disobedience to the tsar, but Peter the Great severely punished over one thousand rebels by death. See Pushkarev, *Dictionary*, pp. 149-150.

46. There is a confusion of terms here. Soloviev uses the Russian term paskha, but what in fact is meant is the Ukrainian Easter paska, a rich bread elaborately decorated with symbols of birth and Christianity. The Russian paskha is a pyramid-shaped mixture made largely of pressed cottage cheese.

47. In contrast to the Orthodox, Catholics use unleavened bread for the Eucharist.

48. 1 Corinthians 12:9 "My grace is sufficient for you, for my power is made perfect in weakness."

49. For the exact text in English see Mark 10:27 "With men it is impossible, but not with God; for all things are possible with God."

50. See Notes 8 and 10, above. In response to a complaint about the endangered unity of Christendom from Ivan IV of Muscovy in 1581 the Vatican dispatched the Jesuit diplomat Antonio Possevino as papal legate to Poland and Muscovy to see what could be done. His chief concern was to promote the long-cherished dream of a union between the Orthodox and Catholic churches, but the mission failed to make any progress. For further information see Volume 12, Chapter VI, Note 94.

51. This passage is based on Jeremiah 9:1 "O that my head were waters, and mine eyes a fountain of tears, that I might weep day and night for the slain of the daughters of my people."

52. The original reads "Muscovite" (singular), although it is not clear whether Soloviev is referring to the tsar or the patriarch.

53. John 10:14.

54. The "pagan bondage" is a reference to the jurisdiction of Constantinople.

55. The term hetman means a Ukrainian cossack military commander elected by the cossack council. In the late 1590s he became head of the Ukrainian hetman state. In Poland it also signified one of the "great offices of the Polish crown. Zamoyski was a hetman in the Polish sense.

56. This is a reference to the Julian calendar which Orthodox believers still use. In 1582 Pope Gregory XIII corrected it to compensate for a small loss of time (one day in 400 years). Thereafter the Julian calendar progressively fell behind the Gregorian calendar to the extent that in this century thirteen days separate the two. An attempt by a Catholic king to impose the new calendar on the entire Commonwealth evoked a fierce anti-Catholic reaction on the part of the Orthodox Rus. As a symbol of their ancient faith, the Julian calendar represented not only Orthodox Christianity, but their ethnic identity as well. The Julian calendar enabled the Rus to observe religious holidays at different times from their Catholic counterparts, thereby reinforcing their separate identity in the Polish-Lithuanian Commonwealth. Scholars have pointed out that the calendar issue was a particularly sensitive one for the Rus, who were manifesting early stirrings of a Ukrainian national consciousness.

57. Earlier in Soloviev's text the Roman Catholic was referred to as prince-bishop of Lutsk. Suddenly without warning he becomes prince-bishop of Kiev.

58. Potey uses the expression "fat pirogi" or dumplings stuffed with meat or potatoes, as a symbol of ritual gluttony.

59. Matthew 7:20 "Thus you will know them by their fruits."

60. By "Christian" Rogoza means Orthodox.

61. The Reformation brought new religious currents to the Commonwealth. Calvinism, especially, with its emphasis upon lay participation in religious affairs, made the greatest inroads. Schools and printing presses spread all such new ideas throughout the Commonwealth.

62. As representative of the ecumenical patriarch at the council, he carried the full weight of patriarchal authority.

63. Matthew 26:37 "And taking with him Peter and the two sons of Zebedee, [Jesus] began to be very sorrowful and troubled."

64. Poland was one of the few states in Europe that preached and practised religious toleration in the sixteenth century. Pope Clement VIII (1592-1605), however, pronounced liberty of conscience "the worst thing in the world," and the Vatican continued its vigorous pursuit of religious unification in Poland.

65. Although construction of the new St. Peter's basilica began in 1503, it proceeded slowly. After the sack of Rome in 1527 all building was suspended, not to resume until 1539. Further interruptions followed until 1547, when Michelangelo was appointed to redesign the structure. He produced a new central plan with a great dome over it, conceptualized according to the original model by Bramante, which itself had been altered. By the time of Michelangelo's death in 1564 a rough prototype was ready, prepared while work on the basilica was still in progress. Then the design underwent a further series of modifications. The interior, with Bernini's changes to Michelangelo's design, dates almost entirely to the seventeenth century.

66. "The Rusyns having been received."

67. By the Warsaw Confederation of 1573 the Polish gentry pledged to keep peace among themselves in matters of religion, and to avoid religious oppression in general. This pledge was honored only in part by Poland's kings and most of their subjects. The much-lauded Polish toleration was in fact relative, inasmuch as Poland's Orthodox inhabitants continued to endure oppression and persecution.

68. Rendered voevodstvo in Russian and Ukrainian, this can mean either the office of the voivode, a governor of a province, or a province in Poland.

69. Ivan Vishensky (Ioann Vyshensky) was born some time between 1538 and 1550 in Sudova Vishnia (Vyshnia). He received his early education there before moving to Lutsk and thence to Ostrog. He travelled around Ukraine and then moved to Greece some time in the 1570s or 1580s, and lived for about forty years in a cave on Mount Athos as an ascetic hermit. He left once during this time for an interval of two years, between 1604 and 1606, to visit Ukrainian lands. He paid a visit to the Dormition Brotherhood in Lvov, which adopted him as their teacher and patron. Vishensky died some time in the 1620s on Mount Athos. Soloviev's renditions are free, truncated versions of Vishensky's Middle Ukrainian original. Soloviev does not inform his readers that he is translating from the Ukrainian, thereby conveying the impression that Vishensky wrote in Russian. Neither does he use ellipses, either here or in many other passages, to indicate his numerous internal deletions, a familiar pattern in Soloviev's work.

70. The original reads "holy laws," not "secular laws."

71. Matthew 19:17-19 "And [Jesus] said unto him, 'Why do you ask me about what is good? One there is who is good. If you would enter life, keep the commandments." He said unto him, "Which?" And Jesus said, "You shall not

kill, You shall not commit adultery, You shall not steal, You shall not bear false witness, Honor your father and mother, and, You shall love your neighbor as yourself."

72. An untranslatable play on words. In Ukrainian the term rohozyna is both a pejorative diminutive of Rohoza (Rogoza), and a pun on that name Rohozyna also means a piece of rough cloth. Rohoza derives from the same Ukrainian word for bulrush. Vishensky ignores that derivation.

73. Although the Eastern Orthodox church rejected instrumental music it introduced singing, as opposed to chanting, into the Christian religious service. Apart from the old psalms the Eastern church developed new forms of song, the canon and the kondakion (collect hymn). Collections of such hymns, including the *Oktœchos*, formed part of the liturgical books. According to the chronicles, the Greeks, who were experts in church singing, were brought to Kiev. They came with their families around 1051, during Yaroslav's reign, bringing "eight-part" and "three-part" choral singing. The word *Oktœchos* means eight voices. In 1491, in Cracow, where Ukrainian printing had its beginning, and when the German printer Schweipolt Fiol produced the first printed books in Church Slavonic, *Oktœchos* was published. Wlasowsky, *Outline History*, contains a variety of references to the work.

74. This is what Vishensky calls the royal appointees to clerical office. He objected strenuously to the Polish king's intense interest in the union.

75. The residence of the bishop of Peremyshl.

76. The Rus performed carnivalistic playlets and indulged in other amusements on Christmas Eve. As for the Eve of Epiphany, January 5 (Shchedryi vechir or "generous evening"), Vishensky's meaning is not altogether clear. He might have had in mind ancient carols, doubtless of pre-Christian origin, which have shchedryi vechir as a refrain, and which now are sung by Ukrainians on the Eve of Epiphany, also called shchedryi vechir. They too exhibit a carnivalistic spirit. Vishensky goes on to pun on the folk taboo euphemism for the Devil which is "he who sits in the mud," and the folk belief that the Devil occupies the marshland (wasteland), or the pagan land of the dead. This in turn stems from ancient magical spells and incantations by means of which illnesses, misfortunes and death were banished to the marshlands.

77. A gift in the form of a braided wheaten loaf and a few painted eggs offered on Easter Monday to one's friends and acquaintances as a form of well-wishing. Vishensky is punning again, as volochelnoe and volochyty (to drag) are morphologically related.

78. This ritual of communing with the dead by sharing a meal at the gravesite was commonly observed at Easter and during the so-called "Green Holidays," the equivalent of Memorial Day in the United States. Another such occasion is providna nedilia, or St. Thomas Sunday. Both in the West and Ukraine, Ukrainians ritualistically assemble at gravesites to share a meal with the deceased.

79. The androgynous summer solstice deity, akin to Yarylo. It falls the same time as the holiday of St. John the Baptist (June 24). Among the rituals which celebrate its sexuality is the custom of young people leaping over bonfires.

80. Swings are offered to the rusalki or forest nymphs. The swings are suspended from birch trees throughout the spring months.

81. Szcesny Zebrowski, *The Tares that Stefanek Zyzany is Sowing in the Rus Churches of Wilno* (Wilno, 1595). Note the use of the diminutive in the subject's name, Stefanek (Stefanko in Ukrainian), which is employed as a sign of contempt.

82. Stefan Zizany, *The Sermon of St. Cyril, Patriarch of Jerusalem on the Antichrist and His Signs, Together with the Dissemination of Learning against Various Heresies* (Wilno, 1596). Cyril (315-386) was the bishop of Jerusalem from 350 but because his doctrine was substantially anti-Arian he was repeatedly exiled by Constantius II (357-362) and Valens (367-378), both of whom were Arian emperors. The Copts recognized him as Orthodox. In Coptic history the episode of the cross on Golgotha is especially well known. In Coptic literature, a translation (possibly incomplete) of his *Catecheses* was adopted at an early date. Later a series of homilies was attributed to Cyril, although some scholars later adjudged them to be spurious. See the entry on Cyril of Jerusalem in Aziz S. Atiya, ed., *The Coptic Encyclopedia* (New York, N.Y., 1991), Vol. 3, pp. 681-682, and Donald Atwater, *The Penguin Dictionary of Saints*, 2nd ed. (Harmondsworth, 1983), p. 99.

83. Christopher Filalet, which means Crossbearing Truthlover, was probably a pseudonym of Marcin Broniewski, although we are not absolutely certain of this, which is perhaps why Soloviev merely notes that the name is a pseudonym. Filalet was Prince Ostrozhsky's friend, and it was the prince who commissioned the work, the full title of which is *Apokrisis or a Response to the Works on the Synod of Brest in the Name of the Worshippers of the Ancient Greek Religion Offered by Christopher Filalet in Haste* (Wilno, 1598). Originally written in Polish, it was translated into Ukrainian the following year (1598) either by the Cleric of Ostrog or Gavrilo Dorofeevich (Havrylo Dorofeiovych).

84. Exodus 32:19-28. "And as soon as he came near the camp and saw the calf and the dancing, Moses' anger burned hot, and he threw the tables out of his hands and broke them at the foot of the mountain. And he took the calf which they had made, and burnt it with fire, and ground it into powder, and made the people of Israel drink it. And Moses said to Aaron, 'what did this people do to you that you have brought a great sin upon them?' And Aaron said, 'Let not the anger of my lord burn hot; you know the people, that they are set on evil. For they said to me, 'Make us gods, who shall go before us; as for this Moses, the man who brought us up out of the land of Egypt, we do not know what has become of him.' And I said to them, 'Let any who have gold take it off;' so they gave it to me, and I threw it into the fire, and there came out this calf.' And when Moses saw that the people had broken loose (for Aaron had let

them break loose, to their shame among their enemies), then Moses stood in the gate of the camp, and said, 'Who is on the Lord's side? Come to me.' And all the sons of Levi gathered themselves together to him. And he said unto them, 'Thus says the Lord God of Israel, "Put every man his sword on his side, and go to and fro from gate to gate throughout the camp, and slay every man his brother, and every man his companion, and every man his neighbor."' And the sons of Levi did according to the word of Moses; and there fell of the people that day about three thousand men."

85. 2 Kings 16:10-18. "When King Ahaz went to Damascus to meet Tiglath-pileser, king of Assyria, he saw the altar that was at Damascus. And King Ahaz sent to Uriah the priest a model of the altar, and its pattern, exact in all its details. And Uriah the priest built the altar; in accordance with all that King Ahaz had sent from Damascus, so that Uriah the priest made it, before King Ahaz arrived from Damascus. And when the king came from Damascus, the king viewed the altar. Then the king drew near to the altar, and went up on it, and burned his burnt offering and his cereal offering, and poured his drink offering, and threw the blood of his peace offerings upon the altar. And the bronze altar which was before the Lord he removed from the front of the house, from the place between his altar and the house of the Lord, and put it on the north side of his altar. And King Ahaz commanded Uriah the priest, saying, 'Upon the great altar burn the morning burnt offering, and the evening cereal offering, and the king's burnt offering, and his cereal offering, with the burnt offering of all the people of the land, and their cereal offering, and their drink offering; and throw upon it all the blood of the burnt offering, and all the blood of the sacrifice; but the bronze altar shall be for me to inquire by.' Uriah the priest did all this, as King Ahaz demanded."

86. Auxentius was the bishop of Milan during the second half of the fourth century (died 373 or 374 A.D.) He was Cappodocian by birth and Arian in theology.

87. Archimandrite in Constantinople.

88. Luke 6:39.

89. In 1555 the Peace of Augsburg made permanent the division of Christendom into Catholic and Protestant, and enshrined the territorial sovereignty in religious matters of the princes. In so doing the Peace recognized in law what was established already in practice, that is, *cuius regio, eius religio*, in other words, the ruler of the land determines the faith of his subjects. After more than a century of religious conflict throughout Europe, in 1648 the Treaty of Westphalia reasserted the major features of the earlier religious settlement. It also confirmed the territorial sovereignty of Germany's numerous political entities, thereby perpetuating German political division until the nineteenth century. More specifically, Skarga is referring to the case of Gebhard Truchsess, archbishop-elector of Cologne, who in 1583 converted to Protestantism, married his mistress and tried, unsuccessfully, to retain his archbishopric.

90. This refers to Ukrainian cossacks who fought in the Turkish wars. After being taken prisoner some converted to Islam and became janissaries.

91. Widely known by the first word of its title in the original, *Perestoroha*, and attributed to Yury Rogatinets (circa 1605), who was not a priest, but a renowned saddlemaker.

92. *Antirresis or an Apology against Christopher Filalet* (Wilno, 1600). See also Note 83, above.

93. An Orthodox theologian who studied in the brotherhood school in Lvov. Between 1614 and 1624 he served as archimandrite of the Caves monastery in Kiev.

94. One of the most divisive issues to plague the brotherhood and its bishop was the establishment of a print shop, and the extensive monopolies granted it by the patriarch, especially the exclusive right to publish liturgical materials. Publishing was a long-standing monopoly of the church, as well as a lucrative source of income for the bishop. In the beginning, Balaban supported its establishment. When the shop was set up, and the brotherhood made it clear that the bishop would share neither in its operations nor in its profits, he was not prepared to relinquish his interests without a determined fight. Both the patriarch and the Orthodox council at Brest consistently supported the brotherhood in its conflict with Balaban over this issue, creating even more episcopal resentment. At one point Jeremiah II threatened the bishop with excommunication for his numerous hostile actions toward the brethren "because you obstruct and injure all who strive to do good… we perceive in your person an enemy who destroys all that is fine and good. Your conduct is not that of a churchman, but an enemy of the Lord." A copy of the full text is to be found in *Yubileinoe izdanie v pamiat 300-letnogo osnovaniia L'vovskogo Stavropigiiskogo Bratstva* (Jubilee Edition Commemorating the Tercentenary of the Foundation of the Lvov Stauropigian Brotherhood) (Lvov, 1886), Document LXXXV.

Another bone of contention was the monopoly on education with which the patriarch endowed the brotherhood. Balaban never subscribed to the right of the lower classes to be educated. In his opinion, education and religion alike were best left to those suited to it by birth or calling. See K.V. Kharlampovich, *Zapadno-russkie pravoslavnye shkoly XVI-nachala XVII veka* (Western Rus Orthodox Schools of the Sixteenth and Early Seventeenth Centuries) (Kazan, 1898), p. 294; also W. Milkowicz, ed., *Monumenta Confraternitatis Stauropigianae Leopoliensis* (Monuments of the Lvov Stauropigian Brotherhood) (Lvov, 1895), Document XCIX.

95. Shortly before the bishop's death he reconciled with the brotherhood, although years of wrangling over the control of Ukrainian Orthodox life in Lvov left their mark.

CHAPTER II

1. Krzystof Kosiński (died 1593) came from the Polish gentry. From the king he received lands in Rus and occupied a prominent position among the

elders of the Zaporozhian Cossacks in the 1580s. In 1591 the registered cossacks elected Kosiński hetman. He waged the first Ukrainian peasant war against the Polish and Rus landowners, which spread to regions around Kiev and Bratslav. He took Belaia Tserkov (Bila Tserkva), Boguslav (Bohuslav) and Trepolie (Trypilla), then mounted an attack on Kiev. In 1593, near Piatka, he unsuccessfully fought his final battle against the army of the nobility. Prince Ostrozhsky relieved him of his duties but Kosiński assembled an army of about two thousand and moved on Cherkasy. A resident member of the gentry, Oleksandr Wiśniowiecki, lured him into the city where Kosiński was killed, allegedly in a tavern brawl. See entry (unsigned) in MERSH, Volume 17, pp. 218-219.

2. The city of Cherkasy is not to be confused with the Cherkasian (Ukrainian) people.

3. The nucleus of the cossack host was established in the Dnieper (Dnipro) basin during the late fifteenth century. In 1553-1554 Dmitry Vishnevetsky (Dmytro "Baida" Vyshnevetsky) assembled a group of cossacks into one cohesive unit on the island of Khortitsa (Khortytsia) below the Dnieper rapids, where he built a fortress to obstruct Tatar raids on Ukraine. Thus he laid the foundation for the cossack territory known as the Zaporozhian Sech (Sich) or camp, generally viewed as the cradle of Ukrainian cossackdom. Other cossacks lived in the Ukrainian towns. By the early seventeenth century three major categories of cossacks evolved, the "registered," a relatively small minority, most of whom lived in towns, and the "unregistered' who fell into two categories, the Zaporozhians, residing virtually beyond the pale of the Commonwealth in the territory known as Ukraina, and the vast majority of cossacks on the frontier without any officially recognized status. For a good discussion of the various cossack groups, see Orest Subtelny, *Encyclopedia of Ukraine.* Vol. 1 (Toronto, 1985), pp. 108-113. The somewhat later development of the Don Cossacks belongs to Russian history. Grigory (Hryhory) Loboda commanded a detachment of Ukrainian cossacks when they launched a campaign against Moldavia in the spring of 1594 against Turkish forces. In October of that year he and Severin Nalivaiko (Severyn Nalyvaiko) launched successful campaigns against Moldavia. Because he favored an agreement with the Poles, Loboda was accused of treason by his own cossacks, who executed him as Polish forces were laying siege to the cossack camp in the Solonitsa (Solonytsia) valley near the town of Lubny, in May of 1596. For further information on Loboda see entry (unsigned) MERSH, Volume 20, p. 122.

4. A cossack leader from the Khmelnitsky (Khmelnytsky) region who was orphaned in his teens and found refuge with Ostrozhsky. He led the second cossack rebellion against the Poles. In 1595 Severin (Severyn) Nalivaiko took twenty-five hundred men and made a successful raid on the Ottoman Turks in Moldavia. He then proceeded to the Rus province of Bratslav, where with widespread peasant backing he staged a rebellion against the gentry. Eventually, exhausted by hunger, disease and mounting casualties, the cossack supporters of Loboda, who favored negotiation, turned Nalivaiko over to the Poles. They

executed him, then massacred most of the unarmed rebels after they had laid down their arms in anticipation of negotiations. According to one version, Nalivaiko was cut into four pieces which were hung on poles in the four corners of the city. Another account has it that he was burned inside a copper bull.

5. This was a military tactic peculiar to the Ukrainian cossacks in he sixteenth and seventeenth centuries. Typically the cossack army marched with five or six trains of supply wagons on either side of a marching column. To defend itself against an approaching enemy, the army would stop and arrange its wagons in a rectangle, link them together by chains, and reinforce the arrangement with a stockade surrounded by a trench. The resulting encampment could be used either defensively, or as a base for launching operations such as cannon bombardments, skirmishes and infantry or cavalry attacks. By the end of the seventeenth century advances in artillery rendered such encampments obsolete. See entry by Subtelny, *Encyclopedia of Ukraine*, Vol. 1, p. 591.

6. For further information on Zółkiewski, see Volume 15 of this series, Chapter III, Note 4.

7. On his occasion Loboda used a typical cossack encampment consisting of five wagon trains.

8. This is an allusion to Metropolitan Filaret, Prince Vasily Vasilievich Golitsyn and other members of the Muscovite high embassy (1612-1619) interned in Poland during the war between Muscovy and Poland. For further details see Volume 16, pp. 256, 279-280.

9. Here Potey, Orthodox cleric tuned Uniate, is making a subjective value judgment, especially when he refers to these people pejoratively as peasants. An overwhelming majority of the brethren were artisans, and there is substantial evidence to show that not only were they relatively sophisticated and educated town dwellers, they managed to accomplish what the clergy and nobility were unable or unwilling to do at the time. That is to say, they established an impressive level of scholarship, pedagogy and publishing, and produced some outstanding leaders who made important contributions to the Rus cultural renaissance of the late sixteenth and early seventeenth centuries. They also played a major role in the evolution of a proto-Ukrainian national consciousness in the early modern period of the nation's history. There is no denying that the sweeping powers which the patriarchs accorded these brotherhoods antagonized their bishops, who saw so much customary authority and privilege slipping from their grasp. Doubtless this contributed to their willingness to enter into a church union in the hope, amongst other things, of having their privileges restored. For an introduction to these lay-clerical relations, see Marian J. Rubchak, "From Periphery to Centre. The Development of Ukrainian Identity in Sixteenth-Century Lviv," *Canadian Review of Studies in Nationalism,* 21 (1994), pp. 117-133.

10. Jeremiah 4:22

11. See Chapter I, Note 36.

12. Matthew 21:41

13. Luke 3:9. The remainder of the citation reads "every tree therefore that does not bear good fruit is cut down and thrown into the fire."

14. Based upon Luke 13:6-9. "A man had a fig tree planted in his vineyard; and he came seeking fruit on it and found none. And he said to the vine dresser, 'Lo, these three years I have come seeking fruit on this fig tree, and I find none. Cut it down; why should it use up the ground?' And he answered him, 'Let it alone, sir, this year also, till I dig about it and put on manure. And if it bears fruit next year, well and good; but if not, you can cut it down.'"

15. The term reads papezhniki in the original. This is a derogatory term referring to supporters of the Pope.

16. Not only did the traditional dates of holidays change with the new calendar, Catholic leaders were known to select such customary occasions for the purpose of persecuting and physically attacking Orthodox worshippers.

17. He was a saddlemaker by trade, so skilled that he was exempted from the customary Polish restrictions against Orthodox artisans, who were forbidden to join legitimate guilds and thus forced to pursue their crafts as partachi, or members of semi-legal Ukrainian associations. Yury was one of the founding members of the Dormition Brotherhood.

18. H. Pociej, *Poselstwo do papieża rymskiego Sixta IV od duchowienstwa y od książąt y panów ruskich w roku 1476* (Embassy to the Roman Pope Sixtus IV from the Clergy and from the Rus Princes and Lords in the Year 1476) (Wilno, 1605).

19. The full title is M. Smotrycki, *Threnos, That is, the Lament of the Single Holy Popular Apostolic Eastern Church with an Explication of the Dogmas of Faith* (Wilno, 1610). The pseudonym can be translated roughly as Lover of God, He of the True Word.

20. Piotr Skarga, *Na treny y lament Theophila Ortologa do Rusi Greckiego nabozhenstwa, przestroga* (Cracow, 1610).

21. H.J. Morochowski, *Parehoria albo utolenie uszczypliwego lamentu mniemaney cerkwie swętey wschodniey zmyślonego Theophila Ortologa* (Wilno, 1612).

22. L. Kreus, *Obrona jednośći cerkiewny, abo dowody ktorymi się pokazuie iz Grecka cerkiew z laćinska ma być ziednocaona* (Wilno, 1617).

23. He was known widely for his staunch defense of Orthodoxy.

24. Psalm 43:1, the full text of which reads "Give sentence for me, O God, and defend my cause against an ungodly people; O deliver me from the deceitful and wicked man."

25. In 1596 five of the seven Rus bishops, including the metropolitan, went over to Rome, and Orthodox Rus was left virtually without an ecclesiastical hierarchy until 1620, when the patriarch of Jerusalem restored the metropolitonate in a secret ceremony at the Holy Wisdom cathedral in Kiev. Although still illegal until 1632, it became a rallying point for the Ukrainian Orthodox faithful.

26. "When Andrew was teaching in Sinop and came to Kherson... he observed that the mouth of the Dnieper was near by. Desiring to go to Rome, he journeyed to the mouth of the Dnieper, thence to ascend the river, and by chance he halted beneath the hills on the shore. Upon arising in the morning, he observed

to the disciples who were with him, 'See ye these hills? So shall the favor of God shine upon them that on this spot a great city shall rise, and God shall erect many churches therein.' He drew near the hills, and having blessed them, he set up a cross. After offering his prayer to God, he descended from the hill on which Kiev was subsequently built, and continued his journey up the Dnieper." *The Russian Primary Chronicle. Laurentian Text.* Translated and edited by Samuel Hazard Cross and Olgerd Sherbowitz-Wetzor (Cambridge, Mass., n.d., third printing, 1973), pp. 53-54.

27. Soloviev and his source, *Pamiatniki, izdannye vremennoiu kommissieu dlia razbora drevnikh aktov* (Monuments Published by the Provisional Commission for Investigating Ancient Acts) (Kiev, 1848), Volume 1, Part 1, Document No. XXXII, pp. 224-251, employ the terms Rus and Rossiia interchangeably in the txt of the *Exhortation to Piety*, the content of which is quite truncated in the author's work.

28. The reference is to Terence (Publius Terentius Afer (185-159 B.C.), the Roman writer of comedies. The braggart soldier and frustrated wooer Thraso appears in his comedy *The Eunuch*.

29. The Czech version of the name is Svatopluk. The Moravian king who actually played host to Cyril (then Constantine) and Methodius was called Rostislav. The emergence of a written language for the East Slavs, using the Cyrillic alphabet, is associated with the baptism of Kievan Rus. The writing was devised by St. Cyril and St. Methodius, apostles to the Slavs in the ninth century. The Rus conversion to Christianity firmly established this written language.

30. Algirdas (Olgerd) was the son of Gediminas. The issue of Lithuania's baptism is a complex one. Certain Lithuanian sources name Gediminas, while others argue for his son Jogaila as the baptizer of Lithuania. In fact Algirdas had political motives for establishing ecclesiastical institutions in Lithuania, but no baptism of the Lithuanians was general during his rule. Algirdas sought to wrest the title of metropolitan of all Rus from Muscovy and establish a metropolitanate in Kiev, which was part of Lithuania at that time. He negotiated with Constantinople with the net result of two metropolitans, one in Kiev, the other in Moscow. Algirdas and other Lithuanian grand princes also negotiated with Rome while fighting Poland for Galich (Halych) and Volhynia. As part of a lengthy correspondence between Lithuania and Rome, mediated by Poland in 1373, Pope Gregory XI urged Lithuanian conversion to Christianity. Algirdas did seem favorably disposed towards Catholicism, yet nothing came of this.

31. This new Orthodox metropolitan of Kiev hailed from Galich, where he was known as Ivan Boretsky. When he became metropolitan, Ivan was renamed Job. In 1625 because he foresaw a bleak future for Orthodox Rus in a Catholic country, Job offered to submit to the authority of the Muscovite tsar.

32. The Rus cossack host also comprised Poles, Belarusians, Moldavians and Tatars. Gradually they moved southward along the Dnieper and its tributaries to the unpopulated "wild field" where they formed closely-knit groups and

became a permanent organization. Although the authorities were worried about such an independent force on the periphery of the Commonwealth, the cossacks provided a useful buffer against marauding Turks.

33. The term used is kozlyshche, a derogative form of kozël, or he-goat. See Matthew 25:32-33. "Before him will be gathered all the nations, and he will separate them one from another as a shepherd separates the sheep from the goats, and he will place the sheep at his right hand, but the goats at the left."

34. After the fall of the False Dmitry in May, 1606 a faction of the Muscovite nobility elected Prince Vasily Ivanovich Shuisky as tsar. The cabal opposed to him approached King Sigismund III with a view to adopting the candidacy of the king's adolescent son Prince Władysław. After Shuisky's deposition Władyłsaw was proclaimed in 1610 by the faction of boyars in nominal charge of the Kremlin while it was under Polish occupation. This candidacy had no support from the forces of resistance led by Minin and Pozharsky which led to the convocation of an Assembly of the Land at which Michael Romanov was elected in January, 1613. Władysław in 1616-1618 launched a campaign to reassert his claim to the Muscovite throne, was defeated, and the Truce of Deulino concluded. After becoming king in 1632 Władysław IV tried to renew his Muscovite claims only to relinquish them after the Truce of Polianovka (1634). For further details, consult Volumes 15-16 of this series, also entry by G. Edward Orchard, MERSH, Volume 44, pp. 15-18.

35. Urban VIII (Maffeo Barberini) was from an arisrocratic Florentine family. He was baptized in Florence in 1564 and died in 1644. He succeeded Pope Gregory XV in 1623. His pontificate largely coincided with the Thirty Years War, during which he was determined to strengthen the papacy's defense and resources. Unfortunately his good work did not preclude Urban's pontificate from large-scale nepotism. His massive building program, military campaigns and promotion of the arts, together with the enrichment of his family, drained the papacy's financial resources.

36. Jeremiah 12:13. "They have sown wheat and have reaped thorns, they have tired themselves but profit nothing. They shall be ashamed of their harvests because of the fierce anger of the Lord."

37. Jeremiah 9:11. "I will make Jerusalem a heap of ruins, a lair of jackals; and I will make the cities of Judah a desolation without inhabitants."

38. See Henryk Sienkiewicz's novel *With Fire and Sword* (1893), which follows a similar line of reasoning.

39. Kishka was hetman of the registered cossacks between 1599 and 1602. He participated in sea raids against the Turks, from whose captivity he delivered cossacks. His other accomplishments included helping the Poles protect Moldavia and Wallachia, and fighting on the Polish side against the Swedes in Livonia (now Estonia).

40. Kutska was his *nom de guerre*. His full name was Ivan Kutskovich (Kutskovych).

41. Soloviev uses the tern Niz, in Ukrainian Nyz, an area round the southern part of the Dnieper river. It comprises a somewhat larger geographical territory than the Sech, the actual cossack stronghold. From the term Niz, or Nyz, the adjective nizovyi, or nyzovyi, is formed and is applied to cossacks of this region. They were known in Russian as nizovye kazaki, or in Ukrainian nyzovi kozaky.

42. A cossack hetman who hailed from an Orthodox gentry family in Galich, Sahaidachny was born some time around 1570 in Kilchitsi in the province of Sambor (Sambir). He studied at the Ostrog Academy, after which he went to the cossack Sech where he created a regular military formation out of the crude cossack forces he found there. He led a number of battles against the Turks during which many Christian captives were liberated. In 1618 Sahaidachny joined the anti-Turkish Christian Militia. That same year he led twenty thousand troops in Władysław's offensive against Muscovy, and routed the Muscovite forces several times over. As hetman between 1614 and 1622 Sahaidachny belonged to the conservative faction of the cossack leadership. He fought for the Orthodox religion and the Rus people, but his campaigns never assumed the character of a national liberation struggle. As a show of support for the development of Rus culture he enrolled his entire cossack host in the Kiev Brotherhood and helped to create a major Rus cultural center in Kiev. In 1621 he led a force of forty thousand, Rus and Poles, against the Turks in a battle near Khotin (Khotyn, Chocin) in which he was wounded. He died the following year.

43. A year earlier the Poles were defeated by the Turks at Cecora (Tsetsora), but in 1621 forty thousand cossacks under Hetman Sahaidachny (see preceding Note) saved a Polish force of thirty-five thousand which was trying to hold off the Ottoman Turks.

44. The Russian term dumnyi diak (conciliar secretary) used between the end of the fifteenth and the seventeenth centuries designated the lowest rank in the Boyar Council. In the fifteenth to the seventeenth centuries the diaki were the "mainspring of the Moscow bureaucratic apparatus." In the seventeenth century they assisted the boyars and other heads of prikazy (central government departments), and sometimes served as heads of these departments. The diaki might also be the associates of provincial governers. They played a variety of important roles in the administrative, financial and judicial institutions, and in the diplomatic relations of Muscovy. Further details are found in Pushkarev, *Dictionary*, p. 12.

45. Ivan Tarasievich Gramotin was a large landowner and Russian diplomat. His origins are obscure, but it is known that he was appointed conciliar secretary by False Dmitry I in 1606, and played a prominent part in Dmitry's negotiations with the Poles. In 1608 he transferred his support to False Dmitry II, then in 1610 became a confidential agent to King Sigismund III, for whom he directed the Foreign Chancellery. That same year he made an impassioned plea to Sigismund to become the protector of the Orthodox faith, and urged a union between Poland and Muscovy under Sigismund's son Prince Władysław. In 1612 the boyars who

supported Władysław for the Muscovite throne sent him to the Polish king to hasten the coronation. Meanwhile Moscow fell to the liberation forces, and after this and other reverses Sigismund abandoned his campaign. In captivity along with the members of the Muscovite high embassy, between 1612 and 1617 Gramotin became closely associated with Metropolitan Filaret. In 1618 he returned to a brilliant career in Muscovy but in 1625 apparently fell victim to his own intrigues, which resulted in his exile. In 1634 he regained his influence and returned to court. He died early in 1638. See entry by Orchard, MERSH, Volume 13, pp. 92-95.

46. Cherkasy is a Muscovite name for Ukrainians used especially in the sixteenth and seventeenth centuries. See Pushkarev, *Dictionary*, p. 7, also Note 2, above.

47. Tushino was a village near Moscow where False Dmitry II set up his rival capital between 1608 and 1610. The term Tushinites in this case refers to his supporters. See Volume 15 of this series.

48. During the war between Muscovy and Poland, False Dmitry II lost the support of his Muscovite followers and secretly fled his encampment at Tushino on December 27, 1609. Following his departure the Tushino Muscovites sought an accommodation with Sigismund. It resulted in a treaty, the conditions of which were set down in writing on February 4, 1610. Despite his numerous assurances to the Muscovites, in the mind of Sigismund III the treaty opened the way for extending the boundaries of the Polish-Lithuanian Commonwealth. There is a lengthy treatment of the entire matter in Volume 15.

49. They refer to it as the source of their zipuny, rough peasant coats, although the same word can mean Turkish caftans or sumptuous cloaks. The term is also an idiom for livelihood.

50. The new metropolitan was a native of Bircha, in Galich. In 1604 he became rector of the Dormition Brotherhood school, then moved to Kiev in 1618 to occupy the same post in the Epiphany Brotherhood school. In 1620 Patriarch Theophanes of Jerusalem elevated him to the metropolitan see in Kiev but in 1628-1629, along with the Uniate metropolitan Rutsky, Boretsky threw his support behind the Uniate church. He was unable to win the cossacks over to his cause.

51. To apply the term "Little Russia" at this time is inappropriate, since it was not introduced until the eighteenth century.

52. Patriarch Filaret is meant.

53. Stanisław Koniecpolski was a castellan from Cracow and a crown hetman with vast Rus estates. In 1625 he led the Polish gentry army at Dorovitsa (Dorovytsia) in a battle that resulted in severe losses for the Ukrainian cossacks. Koniecpolski was their avowed enemy, but he also fought against the Turks and Tatars. See *Radianska Entsyklopediia Istoriyi Ukrainy* (Soviet Encyclopedia of the History of Ukraine), Volume 2 (Kiev, 1970), p. 462.

54. Many of the cossacks, some of whom were registered by the Poles, lived in towns on the Rus frontier. The Poles used registration as a mechanism for exercising a measure of control over the chronically rebellious and ungovernable cossacks.

208   NOTES TO CHAPTER II

55. Some sources refer to Izmail as Zhmaylo, claiming that he was the hetman in Zaporozhie who came up to Krylov to join the battle.

56. The terms tsariki and gospodariki are used in Soloviev's text. The terms refer to rulers of small countries, but can also mean warlords. In Soloviev's text they become pejorative forms of address equivalent to "little kings" and "little rulers" (or governors) respectively, suggesting inferiority.

57. Purporting to be the son of the Turkish sultan Mohammed, he appealed to the Muscovites for assistance in regaining his patrimony, which was lost when he was taken out of Turkey by his mother. This created a dilemma for the Muscovites, who were unable to verify his identity, and feared repercussions if they behaved inappropriately.

58. Sotniki, or in Ukrainian sotnyky, or hundredmen, captains.

59. On Tuesday, May 29, 1453 Constantine XI, last heir of Byzantium's first emperor Constantine the Great, was killed in battle with the Ottoman Porte. In 1454 the sultan enthroned Gennadios as patriarch of Constantinople. Because the Sublime Porte sought to concentrate ecclesiastical affairs at Constantinople, the remaining Eastern patriarchates—Alexandria, Antioch and Jerusalem—were relegated to positions of inferiority. Up to 1453 the emperor was the supreme Christian authority in Byzantium, then control shifted to the patriarchal court, itself subject to the jurisdiction of the Turkish sultan. This is presumably the court to which Soloviev refers. For a full account, see Sir Stephen Runciman, *The Great Church in Captivity* (Cambridge, 1968).

60. Soloviev's use of Lithuania as the home of the Zaporozhian Cossacks is puzzling in the light of the fact that earlier he refers to Ukraina as the frontier territory controlled by the Zaporozhian Cossacks. The author appears to have regressed to an earlier period, the fourteenth century, when the Rus lands were part of the grand principality of Lithuania.

61. The forelock, characteristic of the cossack hair style, also was worn by the Poles. It was known as oseledets, or a khokhol, the latter a derogatory name for the Rus.

62. Grigory Cherny (Hryhory or "Hrytsko" Chorny) was elected in 1629. He seemed to be a very good choice for the Commonwealth owing to his allegedly pro-Polish sentiments. But these sentiments and subsequent actions so enraged many of the cossacks that they abducted him to the Sech, there to be tried and executed.

63. His name was Taras Fedorovich (Fedorovych), nicknamed Triasylo, suggesting one who shakes things up. History loses track of him after 1636. The nineteenth-century Ukrainian poet Taras Shevchenko wrote a celebrated poem *Tarasova nich* (The Night of Taras) about the victory at Pereiaslav.

64. The fortress was constructed by the Poles to emphasize their authority in the Ukrainian lands of the Dnieper region. After Sulima and his forces destroyed it, the same year the Poles rebuilt it. In the autumn of 1648 Bogdan Khmelnitsky sent a contingent of cossacks under Nestorenko to take the fortress, which they did, and used it as a stronghold. It was razed in 1711. For further details see entry (unsigned) MERSH, Volume 17, p. 93.

65. Ivan Sulima (Sulyma) was a Ukrainian military commander and member of the Rus nobility who led campaigns against the Turks and Tatars in 1621, 1628 and 1633. He became hetman of the non-registered cossack forces and in 1625 led an attack on the fortress of Kodak (see preceding Note). After the fortress was destroyed the cossack elders feared Polish reprisals and surrendered Sulima to the Poles. On December 12, 1635 he was taken to Warsaw where he was quartered, and his body parts were distributed to all four corners of the city.

66. Kisel was a Rus magnate who participated in suppressing Ukrainian peasant and cossack uprisings. From the Poles he received Rus estates for his role in this and various negotiations he conducted between the cossacks and the Polish government. During one round of negotiations in 1637 he promised the Rus amnesty, but the Poles reneged on this promise and dealt brutally with the rebels. In 1639 Kisel became castellan of Chernigov, in 1641 a senator, in 1646 castellan of Kiev and governor of Bratslav, in 1651 governor of Kiev. That same year he was appointed to conduct talks with Khmelnitsky, but fearing reprisals went to Poland where he died a year later. *Radianska Entsyklopedia*, Volume 2, p. 377.

67. The expression mezhdu dvukh ognei, literally "between two fires," in Russian is tantamount to "between a rock and a hard place" in American popular parlance.

68. In Ukrainian Pavlyk is the diminutive of Pavlo, or Paul. Pavliuha suggests a large terrifying man with an ugly character. Soloviev uses Pavlik throughout (I have found no such usage elsewhere) and thus it will be rendered in this text. He was also known variously as Petro But, Pavliuha, Pavlo Mykhnovych, Baiun, Polorus, Huzdan and Karpo. He was a Turk by birth. During the summer of 1638 he led an anti-Polish rebellion. After the cossacks seized Khorsun and the ecumenical patriarch issued a universal calling Rus to battle, the rebellion assumed massive proportions as it spread to the Left Bank. In December of that year the rebels were routed by the Poles, and Pavlik was surrendered to them, who executed him at Warsaw in April 1639. As for the term Cherkasy, Soloviev's text suggests that he is referring to the registered cossacks, but what actually must be meant in this case is the town of Cherkasy.

69. An ethnic Russian.

70. Pavlo Skidan (Skydan) was a colonel in the non-registered cossack army and Pavlik's field hetman. In 1637 he fought at Pavlik's side. In June 1639 he was wounded at the battle of Zhovnin (Zhovnyn), captured by the Poles and probably executed.

71. Mikołaj Potocki, a Polish magnate and from 1646 crown hetman. During the rout of the Polish gentry army in the battle at Korsun, in 1648, he was captured by Khmelnitsky, and turned over to the Crimean khan. The Poles paid a huge ransom to free him. Potocki came back to lead the Polish gentry army in the battle at Brest in 1651.

72. Iliash Karaimovich (Karaimovych] was a pro-szlachta colonel of the registered cossacks. He fought in Severia against the Muscovites in 1634. On

orders from Potocki, in April of 1648 Karaimovich together with Ivan Barabash and an army of four to five thousand registered cossacks set out in boats to Kodak to join the main Polish gentry army. Their aim was to attack the Zaporozhian Sech, where Khmelnitsky was leading an uprising. But the registered cossacks called a "black council," a popular democratic assembly, and killed Karaimovich, Barabash and their supporters at a place called Kamenny (Kamiany) Zaton. On May 5, 1648 the cossacks joined the insurgents near Zheltye (Zhovti) Vody. *Radianska Entsyklopedia*, Volume 2, p. 311.

73. A cossack sotnyk (officer) who unsuccessfully sought to join Pavliuk's main army in 1637 with four thousand troops. After the cossacks were routed in the battle of Kumeiki the registered cossack surrendered to the Polish szlachta. He was impaled in Kiev.

74. The reader is reminded that Kisel earlier received assurances from the Poles, and gave his word to the cossack leaders that they would be spared.

75. Yakov Ostranin (Yakiv Ostranyn, Ostranitsya—a diminutive) was a colonel in the registered cossack army. In 1634 he took part in the wars against Muscovy in Severia. After the rout of Hetman Pavlik near Kumeiki in 1637 the non-registered cossacks elected him hetman. With his troops and regular cossack forces he defeated the Poles near Goltva (Holtva) in the province of Poltava. Counting upon linking up with Skidan, Ostranin chased the Poles, but on June 3, 1638 was forced to fight them just outside Zhovnin, where he was wounded. Taking part of the Host with him, he left for Slobodska Ukraine (Slobidska Ukraina) and settled near Chernigov. Ostranin was killed in 1641 during an internal cossack rebellion. Slobidska Ukraina was a huge territory located east of Poltava around present-day Kharkov (Kharkiv). Technically it was within Muscovite borders at this time, but because it was virtually unpopulated and vulnerable to Tatar attacks the tsar's government permitted several waves of Rus refugees to settle there in the middle of the seventeenth century, and to establish cossack forms of government. Moscow was, careful not to allow Ukrainian cossacks in its borders to elect a common leader who might become the focus of a united opposition. For additional information, see Subtelny, *Ukraine*, p. 153.

76. In fact, as already indicated, he left for Chernigov, located near the Muscovite border.

77. Yet another hetman who led an anti-Polish rebellion in 1637, following Pavlik's rout near Kumeiki, near Borovitsia, where he liberated the Ukrainian prisoners. In the summer of 1638, after the cossack defeat near Zhovnin, Hetman Gunia fled with some of his comrades towards Slobodska Ukraine. Fending off the Poles, he erected an unassailable encampment near the falls of the Starets river on the way to Sula. This enabled Gunia to save the remainder of the cossacks, and proceed with them to Slobodska Ukraine.

78. Also known as Maslovy Brod (Brid).

79. Her name was really Yelysaveta Hulevych, not Huhulevych (Gugulevich) as Soloviev writes, and she was popularly called Halshka. She was a

wealthy noblewoman who donated a parcel of land in Podol, the old artisan quarter in Kiev, for a monastery and a school. The newly organized Epiphany Brotherhood built the monastery and the school, which became the foundation for the celebrated Mogila Academy established in the eighteenth century. Used by the Soviets as a military academy, it was reclaimed as an institution of higher learning in 1992, and today functions as a university offering instruction in both Ukrainian and English.

80. Notwithstanding certain differences, the school in Kiev was basically modeled after that of the Dormition Brotherhood. In the early stages of its existence it depended heavily on instructors and teaching manuals from the Lvov school. Like the latter, the Kiev school reflected a Graeco-Slavonic orientation, though Latin and Polish were part of its curriculum. In Lvov Latin was added only in 1604. The school charter defined the educational goals of the school which placed much greater emphasis than did the Dormition Brotherhood school on the need to instruct pupils in a "firm possession of faith, and the immutable doctrinal teachings by the seven Holy Councils of the Eastern church." In other words, whereas the objectives of the Lvov school were to develope outstanding citizens and community activists capable of polemicizing with the Catholics during this time of ecclesiastical crisis and arbitrary measures against the Orthodox, the goal of the Kiev school was to train churchmen. For the text, see Pamiatniki, Volume II, No. 4, pp. 66-67. A more detailed discussion of the school is found in Alexander Sydorenko, The Kievan Academy in the Seventeenth Century (Ottawa, 1977), pp. 24-26.

81. According to the Poriadok or the School Regulation of the Dormition Brotherhood, which the Lutsk Brotherhood used virtually in toto as its model, members of the brotherhood organization, not the monks, engaged both the rector and the teachers. This was the brotherhood's school and as such not under clerical jurisdiction owing to the organizations's stauropigia status (freedom of all but patriarchal control). The brethren themselves, virtually all members of the laity, established and implemented the regulations after they were approved by the patriarch of Constantinople. The same right transferred to subsequent brotherhoods which chose to organize themselves according to the Dormition model. By 1620 more than twenty brotherhood schools were in existence on Rus (Ukrainian and Belarusian) territory, though not all enjoyed the same stauropigia status as that accorded the Orthodox brotherhoods and schools in cities like Lvov, Lutsk and Kiev.

82. For reasons that are unclear Soloviev relied on the first School Regulation of the Lutsk Brotherhood school, which appears to be a hastily drafted document consisting of twelve articles (article 11 is used twice) that served only until a permanent Regulation could be put into place. The second version, which quickly superseded the first, consists of twenty articles, and is virtually a copy of the document first adopted by the Dormition Brotherhood more than three decades earlier (in 1586). Unlike the first Regulation of the Lutsk school, it contains no reference to trading or business transactions on school premises, nor

does it mention firearms or artisan tools being brought into classrooms, two articles which were part of the first Regulation. Such references, soon to be deleted, would have been more appropriate to the brotherhood charter, for which the founding document granted to the Dormition Brotherhood by Patriarch Joachim of Antioch provided the prototype. Because the second Regulation was the one that the Lutsk Brotherhood used, it should have been the document upon which Soloviev based his critical examination of the workings of its school. It deals with matters that pertain specifically to the process of education, and illustrates the egalitarian nature of the school itself. It provides for equal treatment of all pupils, their seating arrangements according to academic performance and their extracurricular activities. These include a heavy emphasis on church attendance and observation of religious holidays.

83. In Lvov and in Lutsk all pupils without exception were required to perform various housekeeping duties, including chores such as lighting fires and sweeping floors. They were also responsible for monitoring the school premises, and the behavior of their classmates on their way to and from school. Older pupils helped their younger classmates by reviewing homework and coaching them during the school day. Indigents supported themselves by begging or by amateur performances for the community, the brotherhood defraying the cost of their education.

84. These stipulations were also absent in the second document.

85. Tuition was based upon ability to pay. It was calculated on a sliding scale but provided for indigent pupils to study without charge. The first Regulation does not clarify this.

86. No such stipulation appears in the second Regulation. Payment of the four-grosha fee was mandated for membership in the brotherhood organization, not for tuition.

87. As noted, the Lutsk Regulation like its brotherhood charter was a virtual copy of the Dormition Regulation, which became the model for brotherhoods and their schools as they spread eastward throughout Rus. When they reached Kiev, both the character of the brotherhood and of its Regulation were modified.

88. At this stage the curriculum was based upon the European liberal arts program of study, the trivium and quadrivium. Although the school did offer the quadrivium, the trivium was much better developed, at least in the beginning. There is also some evidence that part of the instruction was given in the Rus language.

89. Isaiah Kopinsky (Kopynsky), from a Ukrainian gentry family, also studied at the Dormition Brotherhood school and at an early age became a monk. Although elevated to the Peremyshl eparchy in 1620, he never took up his office. After Job Boretsky's death in 1631 he was elected to the metropolitan see in Kiev. The following year, when the church was finally legalized, the Polish government considered him unsuitable for the office because of his pro-Moscow orientation and conservative views. Charging that the election was illegal,

the Poles forced him to resign. Mogila had him jailed in 1632, but following his release in 1635 Kopinsky continued to agitate against the union. *Radianska Entsyklopedia*, Volume 2, p. 471.

90. A famous philologist, polemicist and preacher, Melety Smotritsky (Smotrytsky) was born in Smotrich (Smotrych) in Eastern Podolia. He studied at the Wilno Brotherhood school and the Ostrog (Ostrih) Academy. Around 1605 Smotritsky left for Europe to tutor the son of a Belarusian magnate. He took advantage of his situation to study in universities at Leipzig, Nuremburg and Wittenberg. Upon his return to Wilno he taught in the brotherhood school. In 1616, under pressure of citizens who disapproved of his connection to the Uniates, he became a monk in the monastery of the Holy Ghost. Between 1618 and 1620 he served as rector of the brotherhood school in Kiev. In 1623-1625 he journeyed to the patriarch in Constantinople, Cyril Lukaris, and convinced him to limit the privileges of the Lvov stauropigian brotherhoods. Smotritsky secretly harbored Uniate leanings, which eventually were censured at the Council of Orthodox Churchmen in Gorodok (Horodok) in Volhynia in June of 1628. Forced to abjure at the council, he soon openly declared his conversion to the Uniate church, for which he received a monastery at Derman, where he lived out his days.

91. Meletii Smotritskii, *Appoleiia apologii* (Appeal of the Apology) (Lvov, 1628).

92. M. Smotrycki, *Protestatia przesiwo soborowi w Kiiowie obchodzonemu* (Protest Against the Council Held in Kiev) (Lwów, 1628).

93. In the sixteenth and seventeenth centuries the corresponding term narod had several meanings, one of which was natio. There was already an incipient Ukrainian national consciousness, as recent studies have shown, and the Rus people were treated in some contemporary works as one of three nations, Polish, Lithuanian and Ruthenian, in the Polish-Lithuanian Commonwealth. For a discussion of this matter consult David A. Frick, "Meletij Smotryc'kyj and the Ruthenian Question in the Early Seventeenth Century," *Harvard Ukrainian Studies*, Vol. 8, No. 3/4 (1984), pp. 351-375. At one juncture in their numerous pleas for social justice Lvov's town dwellers financed a deputation to King Sigismund III to request certain rights matching those of the Catholic Poles. At a crucial juncture in their petition for equality the Rus from Lvov emphasized their ancestral roots, which they traced to the original inhabitants of the city, whose civil rights and liberties were usurped by the victorious Poles in the fourteenth century.

For its emissaries the Dormition Brotherhood composed a Lament to be read before the Polish Sejm in addition to the formal Instructions, an abbreviated version of the Lament. The Instructions begin with the phrase "We the Rus nation [or people] are burdened by the Polish yoke," then refer to Rus as their native land. The Lament itself reveals their sense of "otherness," of belonging to a separate people. A portion of it bears quoting. "Four nations were founded within these walls...of old Lviv who along with their dwellings constructed the churches, and in the case of the Jews syagogues...of their confession in Lviv. Hence there are Polish, Armenian and Jewish nations. The Polish and Rus nations share a law and [in theory] bear the same burdens, whereas the Armenians and the Jews have their own governments and jurisdictions. We the Rus nation are burdened by the heavy Polish yoke which is especially onerous because it keeps us in Egyptian captivity...." For the full text see S. Golubev, "Materialy dlia istorii zapadno-russkoi tserkvi (Materials for the History of the Western Rus Church)," *Chteniia v istoricheskom obshchestve Nestora Letopistsa* (Readings in the Historical Society of Nestor the Chronicler), Book 5. Ed. by M.F. Vladimirskii-Budanov (Kiev, 1891), Document No. VII, pp. 209-210.

94. *Prawa i priwileie polskich y W.X.L. nadane* (Rights and Privileges Granted by the Polish Kings in the Grand Principality of Lithuania) (Wilno, 1632).

95. Not all historians subscribe to this view of Mogila's conduct. The conflict between him and Kopinsky is presented as a much milder affair by Ivan Wlasovsky, *Narys istorii Ukrain'skoi Pravoslavnoi tserkvy* (Outline History of the Ukrainian Orthodox Church) Vol. 2 (New York-Bound Brook, N.Y., 1956), pp. 102-103.

96. Sylvester Kosov (Kosiv) was a churchman and writer who came from a Belarusian szlachta family in Vitebsk. He studied in Wilno, Lublin and Zamość, then taught in the Dormition Brotherhood school. In 1631 he became a teacher and prefect in the Kiev Mogila Collegium. He also took part in the reforms of Mogila and his group of scholars. In 1635 Kosov became bishop of Mstislav (Mstyslav), Orsha and Mogilev (Mohyliv) and in 1647 was elevated to the metropolitan see in Kiev. In December 1638, with great pomp and ceremony he greeted a victorious Khmelnitsky as the latter made his triumphal entry into Kiev. Antagonistic to the idea of a union of Ukraine and Muscovy in 1654, Kosov favored the independence of the Rus Orthodox church under the jurisdiction of the patriarch of Constantinople.

97. Helicon is the largest mountain in Boeotia. It was the site of the sanctuary of the nine Muses.

CHAPTER III

1. The boyar Boris Ivanovich Morozov was a zealous westernizer. At the accession of Alexis, Morozov became very influential at court. He was responsible for numerous reforms in military organization and weaponry. Among other matters Morozov revived foreign-style military regiments, established new military chancelleries, and an officer corps based upon training and ability, as opposed to the old system of mestnichestvo, or place based on birth, social class and privilege. Initially foreigners were preferred for these posts. Morozov also worked to replenish the tsar's treasury. He introduced the sale of tobacco over the fierce objection of the church, and a new salt tax. These measures, together

with the conduct of many corrupt officials, so enraged the common people of Moscow that they rose in rebellion in 1648. A number of officials were killed in the fray, and some of the more corrupt were executed. Morozov escaped this fate, but was forced from office. For further details see MacKenzie and Curran, pp. 116, 228.

2. See Volume 17 of this series, pp. 18-19. A letter by a Swede from Moscow in 1647 mentions Morozov, Chistoy and a third party, Prince Roman Nikitich Trubetskoy. The latter should read Alexis Nikitich. *Severnyi Arkhiv* (Northern Archive), No. 2 (January, 1822), pp. 152-153.

3. See Volume 17, pp. 141-142, and Chapter V, Note 18 of the same volume.

4. Ivan Dmitrievich Luba was the orphaned son of a Polish nobleman who was killed in Muscovy during the Time of Troubles. Subsequently Luba's life became one prolonged adventure, and on a number of occasions he was passed off (with Polish complicity) as the son of Tsarevich Dmitry, pretender to the Muscovite throne. For a time King Sigismund III of Poland supported him. When things became too uncomfortable for Luba in Muscovy, his story resumes here. There is considerable data on Luba and his adventures in Volume 17, pp. 79-83, and Chapter III, Note 30 of the same volume.

5. Valdemar, the third son of the Danish king (born to his second wife whom King Christian IV married clandestinely), and Irina Mikhailovna, eldest daughter of the Muscovite tsar Michael, were betrothed. Before they could be married, Valdemar was required to convert to Russian Orthodoxy, which he declined to do several times during his stay in Moscow. Ultimately his refusal rendered the proposed union impossible. See Volume 17, pp. 53-74.

6. Peter Marselis was a highly trusted official in the tsar's service who was dispatched to Denmark to negotiate the terms of a marriage between Prince Valdemar and Irina Mikhailovna. Marselis tried hard to succeed where former envoys, Proestev and Patrikeev, failed. Arranging a marriage for one of the ruling family was a protracted and difficult affair under the best of circumstances. In this case the process was complicated by the fact that there were many in Denmark, especially those who favored a match between a Bohemian princess and Prince Valdemar, who had no desire to see him marry a Muscovite. Delegations journeyed back and forward to both courts, the negotiations coming to nothing. Finally Tsar Alexis sent Marselis to mediate and attempt to dispel Danish misgivings. See Volume 17, Chapter III for further details.

7. Such form might have been considered appropriate during the dvoevlastie (joint rule) of Michael Romanov and his father, Patriarch Filaret, who exerted a good deal of influence. There was no diarchy in Alexis's reign, notwithstanding the young tsar's obvious devotion to Nikon, who was elevated to the patriarchal office in 1652. It is quite possible that Polish scribes simply copied old formulas.

8. Igorskoy is a misspelling of Iugorskoy, deliberate or otherwise.

9. Known as the Polianovka Peace, a treaty negotiated between the Polish-Lithuanian Commonwealth and Muscovy in 1634, after the Smolensk campaign.

Even though the Commonwealth was ill-prepared, the Muscovite forces were routed. In exchange for a substantial cash settlement Władysław renounced Polish claims to the Muscovite throne. The adversaries agreed to settle their border disputes, and to establish new title protocols for the sovereigns of both realms. The treaty was conceived as one of "eternal peace," as opposed to a truce. It recognized the Romanovs as the legitimate rulers of Muscovy, and provided for the Commonwealth to keep the lands which it had won in the Smolensk campaign. For further details consult Frank Sysyn, *Between Poland and the Ukraine. The Dilemma of Adam Kysil, 1600-1653* (Cambridge, Mass., 1985), pp. 75-76, also Volumes 15-16 of this series, and the entry by V.I. Buganov, MERSH, Volume 28, p. 182.

10. The suffix -ёnok in Russian is a pejorative diminutive.

11. The Novaia Chetvert, also known as the Novaia Chet, was the chancellery for the collection of the tavern monies, especially in the southern towns. Founded in 1619, in 1680 it was absorbed by the Great Treasury. See entry by V.D. Nazarov, MERSH, Volume 24, p. 181.

12. This is a double-diminutive of Konstantin, proceeding from Kostia to Kostka.

13. Petrushka is a diminutive form of Peter. For some reason the author has placed a question mark after Petrushka, perhaps because of some confusion with Ileika Muromets, the alleged Tsarevich Peter, who took part in the Bolotnikov rebellion of 1606-1607.

14. See Volume 17, pp. 46-49.

15. No longer able to defend their own coasts and sea routes in the seventeenth century, the Ottomans lost their naval supremacy. Sailing down the Dnieper, the Zaporozhian Cossacks also harassed the inhabitants along the Ottoman coast. In 1614 they burned Sinop.

16. In Islamic culture circumcision was equally obligatory for both sexes. A barber performed the ceremony, and healing usually took about a week. The age at which this was done depended upon the specific culture and geographical region. It could occur in infancy or be postponed to later years. The one time it was not postponed was when there was a conversion, because circumcision of the infidel represented the ceremony of reception into the Islamic faith. For a fuller account, see C.E. Bosworth, et al., eds., *The Encyclopedia of Islam* (Leyden, 1986), Vol. 5, pp. 21-22.

17. Soloviev uses the term voevody (plural), which can either mean the provincial governors or military governors. In this volume I have rendered it according to what seemed most appropriate to a given situation.

18. See Note 9, above.

19. The term nemtsy is used in the original. It can mean either Germans, or those who do not speak the Russian language, and are therefore "dumb" (from the Russian word nemoi, meaning dumb). It was generally applied to foreigners of Northern European origin.

20. By 1645 mastery of the seas passed from the Maltese and Tuscan privateers based on Crete to the Venetians, who blocked the flow of Ottoman reinforcements to Crete. In 1649 the Ottomans hired English and Dutch ships and formed a fleet at Istanbul. It too proved powerless against the Venetians, and drove the Ottomans to seek help from the English navy. In return the Ottomans granted new facilities to their allies. The year 1656 was critical for the Ottoman Porte. It tried to reinforce Crete with troops and supplies, then suffered yet another reversal at the hands of the Venetians. Eventually the Porte reversed this situation and drove the Venetians from the Straits. The defense of Crete dragged on for twenty-two years, incurring huge costs in men and money. This drain on the treasury played an important role in the eventual decline of the Ottoman empire.

21. This is a pejorative term for Muslims. See Genesis 16:1-16 and 21:8-21.

22. The Russian term samoderzhets means autocrat, and was one of the titles used by Muscovite monarchs. Ivan III (1462-1505) formally assumed the title after Moscow's emancipation from the tutelage of the Tatar khans. Around 1500 the term indicated a ruler independent of any foreign power. In the sixteenth century Ivan IV (the Terrible) interpreted it as unlimited and arbitrary power of a monarch over his subjects. In 1547 his title became tsar or velikii kniaz vseia Rusi(i) samoderzhets (grand Prince of All Russia and autocrat). In 1721, during the reign of Peter the Great, it evolved into imperator i samoderzhets vserossiiskii (Emperor and All-Russian autocrat), followed by a list of Russian possessions. For a fuller summary, see Pushkarev, *Dictionary*, p. 119, also Note 7, above.

23. Belarusian and Ukrainian linguistic contacts arose in prehistoric times. Although not precisely the same, the two languages have much in common, stemming in part from borrowings, also from periods of common development. There is an excellent entry on the concurrent development of the two languages by G.Y. Shevelov in *Encyclopedia of Ukraine* (Toronto, 1984), p. 200.

24. In the original chaika. This was a unique type of small, narrow boat which was very maneuverable. It was designed by the cossacks for Black Sea raids. See illustration on p. 84.

25. Rasstriga in the original. The word is derived from the verb strich, to tonsure, therefore meaning one who had renounced his tonsure, or monastic vows. More specifically, hence the capitalization, it refers to Grishka Otrepiev, generally believed to be the true identity of the first False Dmitry, who reigned June 1605 to May 1606. Shortly thereafter there emerged another False Dmitry who was acknowledged and married by Marina Mniszech, the Polish wife of the first pretender. Marina gave birth to a son in 1610. At the triumph of the national liberation forces and the enthronement of Tsar Michael the four-year-old Ivan Dmitrievich, known as Vorënok (the Little Brigand) was hanged at the Serpukhov gates in Moscow. As we have seen, this did not prevent the appearance of pretenders to the residual claim of the False Dmitrys. For more information, consult Volumes 14-15.

26. Putivl is located on the Seim river, in the center of Ukraine's Sumy region. It was established in 988 at the crossroads of several trade routes, and is first mentioned in the Hypatian Chronicle in 1146, where it is described as a fortress in Kievan Rus. Between 1356 and 1523 it formed part of the grand principality of Lithuania, then passed to the control of Muscovy. The Ukrainian hetman Sahaidachny recaptured it in 1618 but by this time Settlement Ukraine was becoming colonized, and Putivl lost its strategic importance. During the Time of Troubles Putivl was an organizing center through which supplies and reinforcements were channelled for the Bolotnikov rebels and for the supporters of the second False Dmitry. See Volume 15.

27. In the mid-seventeenth century Polish dominion over the Ukrainians collapsed. The weakness of the Polish-Lithuanian Commonwealth was exposed by a Ukrainian cossack revolt in 1648. It led to a widespread rebellion and emergence of a new polity known as the Ukrainian Hetmanate. It was involved in a general Eastern European struggle with Muscovy. Emerging victorious, it annexed much Ukrainian territory. At that time Adam Kisel was an Orthodox Rus leader of the nobility as well as an official of the Polish government. This development, coupled with his deep concern over the religious strife resulting from the Union of Brest in 1596, as well as the unrest among the Zaporozhian Cossacks, made him an ideal if ultimately unsuccessful mediator between the cossacks and the Polish government.

28. Psalm 133:1.

29. In 1625 Charles I succeeded his father, James I of England and James VI of Scotland, as king of England and Scotland. In 1629 parliament grew more powerful with its several centers of opposition to the monarchy, and the king was stalemated. In 1642 king and parliament came to open warfare, which brought the hitherto relatively unknown Oliver Cromwell, a devout Puritan, to the foreground. Charles was defeated and lost his head on the scaffold in 1649. Cromwell ruled for eleven years as lord protector, after which the monarchy was restored in the person of the late king's eldest son, Charles II (reigned 1660-1685).

30. Among other reasons John Merrick came to Moscow as a representative of James I to negotiate a free trade agreement, as well as an open road to Persia by way of the Volga. A detailed account of his presence in Muscovy appears in Volume 16. See also Geraldine M. Phipps, *Sir John Merrick. English Merchant-Diplomat in Sevententh Century Russia* (Newtonville, Mass., 1983).

31. See Volume 16, p. 192.

32. An efimok was equal to one thaler, one ducat or approximately a Russian ruble.

33. Beginning with the fourteenth century the term designated peasants and the urban poor. In Muscovy when addressing the tsar they referred to themselves as tvoi gosudarevye siroty (your majesty's orphans). The more exalted the addressee, the more demeaning the petitioner's references to himself. See Pushkarev, *Dictionary*, p. 126.

34. When not on active duty musketeers were permitted to engage in trade to supplement their wages without paying taxes, which frequently were in arrears.

35. This category of military servitors, especially the musketeers who engaged in manufacturing and trade, belonged to the sluzhilie liudi po priboru, the lower service class. The upper service class was compensated largely by pomestie landholdings, which were hereditary, and service land grants, whereas the middle service class, also based in the provinces, lived exclusively on their land grants. Like the upper service class the latter possessed the right to use peasant labor, and its members received a small salary. The lower service class lived on an annual salary paid by the treasury, and was forbidden to hire peasant labor. Its ranks were filled by impoverished deti boiarskie (junior boyars, landowning gentry), town dwellers and free peasants, although by the mid-seventeenth century its numbers were sustained by hereditary succession. It was customary for the lower service class to be garrisoned for training outside Moscow and other provincial towns, where they supplemented their incomes by working collective garden plots. Richard Hellie in his *Enserfment and Military Change in Muscovy* (Chicago, 1971) provides additional data.

36. Until the mid-seventeenth century the basic unit of taxation in Muscovy was called a sokha, a measure of plowland. It was a measure comprising either arable land or a number of households. Its size varied widely according to region. It was based on the presumed productivity of the land or the value of the household, and the tax-paying capacities of its inhabitants. Crown lands were taxed at a higher rate than privately owned estates, where landlords imposed their own levies upon the peasants. During the sixteenth and the first half of the seventeenth centuries the customary Muscovite sokha measured five hundred chetverts, one chetvert equalling half a desiatina or 2.7 acres of good land, six hundred chetverts of medium land or seven hundred chetverts of marginal land. The units belonging to private landlords and monasteries respectively were larger. Because these measures were based on a single field in the customary three-field system of agriculture of the time, the numbers were tripled. In the cities various numbers of households, according to their economic status, made up a sokha. The normal range was forty of the most prosperous households, eighty of the medium sort, and one hundred and sixty of the newer or poorer kind, the numbers varying from town to town and from time to time. For a more detailed explanation, see Pushkarev, *Dictionary*, pp. 136-137.

37. The urochnye leta (free years), when the ban on peasant movement did not apply, from the end of the sixteenth century grew increasingly rare, and by this time were virtually nonexistent.

38. To meet their military obligations to the crown the middle service gentry received service holdings and peasants to work them. To keep their peasants from migrating or being forced into other holdings the middle service class pressured the government to repeal the free years when peasants upon discharging certain obligations were free to move. The middle service class also sought an end to the time limit for the recovery of fugitive peasants.

39. The mobility of Russian peasants was not significantly restricted until the reign of Vasily II (1425-1462). Their enserfment may be traced to the second quarter of the fifteenth century. Surviving records indicate that serfdom was initiated by certain crown land grants to monasteries. The first known restriction on peasant movement occurred some time between 1455 and 1462. The other step, that of limiting peasant mobility to only one period during the year, was taken at the request of some monasteries. In return for a fee peasants were permitted to leave in the autumn when the harvest was in, during the weeks before and after St. George's Day in the autumn (November 26). Although this became the general practice for the next century, the peasant came through this phase in the development of serfdom still relatively free. Upon introduction of the service landholding system late in the fifteenth century and developing over the sixteenth century, the crown sought to guarantee the members of the middle service class sufficient labor force to cultivate their estates. The zapovednye gody (forbidden years) were imposed, banning peasant movement even around St. George's Day. In 1597 the "lost decree" of Tsar Fedor Ivanovich made the forbidden years the general rule, though originally it was envisaged as a temporary measure. By this time the free years had ceased to exist. See Part II of Hellie's work cited in Note 35, above, for a description of the entire process of peasant enserfment in general.

40. The duty of local populations, the community of tiaglye liudi, or people who owed fiscal and labor service to the crown, was to help the government in the organization and maintenance of the system of transportation and communication. The people were called upon to build post stations on public roads, hire post drivers and deliver horses together with vehicles for traveling crown agents, as well as to transport goods. In the sixteenth century a monetary tax called iamskie dengi replaced this service duty.

41. In Muscovy the customary penalty for tax delinquency was beating the prisoner across the shins while he was in the stocks.

CHAPTER IV

1. The fate of Vsevolozhskaia constitutes a curious parallel with that of Maria Khlopova, Tsar Michael's original intended bride. See Volume 16, pp. 161-162.

2. Yet another interesting version is that Alexis's first choice was a young woman named Evdokia. For her first appearance in regal attire, the source suggests, the ladies-in-waiting plaited her hair so tightly that she fainted in the tsar's presence, causing the court physicians to pronounce her an epileptic. In those days marriages in the ruling family were known to produce desperate intrigues, which sometimes resulted in the death of the intended bride. Poison was the preferred method of eliminating a rival. The sudden influence at court of the newly-favored relatives of the bride caused enmity between and among families seeking to acquire or hold on to power. When the tsar passed away the currently favored family expected a fall from grace, and fought hard to retain its privileged position.

3. According to a note (29) of the editors of the Russian edition of 1959–1966, the source is a letter of 1647 written by a Swede from Moscow.

4. See Chapter II, Note 45, above.

5. In 1592 the lord-in-waiting Nikita Vasilievich Trakhaniotov was governor of Perm. He also served as treasurer from 1613 to 1618. A close associate of Morozov and an unpopular member of Morozov's government, he was lynched by a mob during the riots of 1648. If the testimony of his contemporaries is to be believed, by 1648 Morozov, Miloslavsky, Pleshcheev and Trakhaniotov were all related by marriage.

6. By the time of his death in 1678 or 1679 Vasily Shorin was described as the most important merchant in Russia. He controlled fisheries, fish processing plants, transport facilities, saltworks and several estates, enabling him to sell grain on a massive scale. Shorin built a major economic empire on his fisheries on the lower reaches of the Volga, near Astrakhan. The close relations between fish and salt extraction caused him also to develop an impressive salt business. He also held interests in the garment industry, military hardware, wax, flour and beads, all of which made him extremely wealthy. Shorin's economic expertise could have been used to draft legal reforms in Muscovy. When he financed three trading expeditions to Persia all ended in disaster, as did the salt tax which he proposed, which resulted in stores of salt dribbling away, his influence dwindled for a time. Although the salt tax was repealed in 1647 it had earned him the undying enmity of the Russian people. But for the fact that he was a customs collector in Archangel at the time he might have come to a bad end, as did Nazar Chistoy, another official blamed for the hated tax. Shorin also failed to find favor with the English merchants who, in 1662, expressed outrage at the unfair way in which he collected the tsar's duties from them in Archangel. Shorin enjoyed tremendous political influence during the reign of Alexis. The tsar appointed him privy boyar, and in 1651 he became governor of Kazan. So great was his influence that he was able to play a major part in bringing down Patriarch Nikon. In 1682 he played a part in the Assembly of the Land which abolished mestnichestvo in Russia. For further details consult Joseph T. Fuhrmann, *Tsar Alexis. His Reign and his Russia* (Academic International Press, 1981), pp. 125-134; Philip Longworth, *Alexis. Tsar of All the Russias* (New York, N.Y., 1984), pp. 42, 152; and Samuel H. Baron, "Vasily Shorin. Seventeenth-Century Russian Merchant Extraordinary," *Canadian-American Slavic Studies,* 6 (1972), pp. 503-548, reprinted in Baron, *Muscovite Russia. Collected Essays* (London, 1980), No. VII.

7. Prince Odoevsky was one of the Tsar Michael's groomsmen and a constant companion. In 1632 he took part in some skirmishes around Moscow, for which he was rewarded with estates and the rank of table attendant. In 1633 Odoevsky became governor of Rzhev. Other honors soon followed. In 1635 he was promoted to the rank of senior table attendant, and in 1640 became a boyar, then served for three years as governor of Astrakhan. In 1643 Odoevsky was placed in charge of the Chancellery for Kazan and Siberia. After Michael's

death Tsar Alexis promoted him to privy boyar. Odoevsky also played a prominent role in the compilation of the 1649 Law Code. His illustrious career continued on into the regency of Tsarevna Sophia, though by this time advanced age made all but ceremonial duties impracticable. See entry by Orchard, MERSH, Volume 51, pp. 34-36.

8. Lvov, a wealthy landowner, was a partisan of Morozov. He served Muscovite rulers with distinction from the time of his first mention in 1607, when he captured Arzamas for Tsar Vasily, to 1627 and his promotion to the rank of lord-in-waiting by Tsar Michael. Between 1627 and 1647 he sat on the council of the Chancellery for the Tsar's Household. In 1634 he was promoted to the rank of boyar and given additional estates in recognition of his service at the peace talks following the Smolensk war. Lvov served at the court of Tsar Alexis until the time of his death in 1654. For further details, see Volume 17, Chapter I, Note 4.

9. Presumably what is being referred to here is the so-called gostinnaia sotnia, or merchants of the second guild, whose support the tsar needed badly in 1648 during Moscow's urban riots.

10. For information on Patriarch Joseph, see Volume 17, Chapter III, Note 17.

11. See Note 6, above.

12. Prince Semeon Vasilievich Prozorovsky, a large landowner and lord-in-waiting, served as one of the commanders in the Smolensk war. Alone of all the commanders he possessed military experience. Because the Muscovites were unable to withstand the Polish-Lithuanian relief of the siege of Smolensk Prozorovsky withdrew to an encampment on the far side of the Dnieper, abandoning several cannon and supplies as he retreated. The Muscovites were forced to surrender. For his part in the failed campaign Prozorovsky was exiled to Siberia, his family dispersed and his possessions confiscated. By 1643 he was back in Moscow as head of the Chancellery of Posts. There is a good account of the war in Volume 16, pp. 215-227. See also Robert O. Crummey, *Aristocrats and Servitors. The Boyar Elite in Russia, 1613-1689* (Princeton, N.J., 1983), pp. 46, 148, 183.

13. Prince Fedor Fedorovich Volkonsky was appointed lord-in-waiting by Tsar Michael in 1634. In 1650 he rose to the rank of boyar. Crummey, *Aristocrats and Servitors*, pp. 47, 60, 86, 184.

14. He was not particularly influential in the events that transpired at this time.

15. Fedor Osakimovich Griboedov (died 1673) was a conciliar secretary in the Chancellery of the Court of Kazan from 1632 to 1664, during which time he became a member of the commission to compile the Law Code of 1649. Between 1664 and 1671 he occupied the post of Secretary of Crown Registers. At the behest of Tsar Alexis, in 1669 Griboedov compiled *Istoriia o tsariakh i velikikh kniaziakh zemli russkoi* (History of the Tsars and Grand Princes of the Russian Land), up to 1667. Its objective was to enhance the tsar's legitimacy by connecting the house of Romanov to the ancient Riurikid dynasty, then trace

the Romanov line back to the Roman empire of Augustus. For all its grand intent the work had very little impact on subsequent Russian historiography. See entry in MERSH, Volume 13, p. 147.

16. The terms gorod and posad are used here. Pushkarev defines gorod as "originally a fortified settlement; later an administrative center and market for the surrounding countryside.... In Muscovy a gorod was pedominantly a military or administrative center, whereas the [lower classes] traders and craftsmen... inhabited the *posad* or settlement surrounding the fortress (the Kreml). They were called *chernye sotni*." Posadskie liudi is the customary term for the urban population as a whole. Pushkarev, *Dictionary*, pp. 22, 139.

17. This code of laws is usually referred to as the Sobornoe Ulozhenie because the Zemskii Sobor (Assembly of the Land) approved the original draft. For a concise but detailed study of the Ulozhenie, see the entry by Hellie, MERSH, Volume 40, pp. 192-198.

18. The tsar and members of his government were ever mindful of the recent Time of Troubles in Muscovy, which they compared to the English protectorate, when the military revolt of 1647-1648 resulted in the purging of both houses of parliament in England. In January 1649 the English monarch, Charles I, was executed and England declared a Commonwealth. The English monarchy was not reinstated until 1660, when Charles II was anointed as the new Stuart king. See also Chapter III, Note 29, above.

19. Known as ploshchadnye posadchie, they were public scribes who worked in the market square in a variety of capacities, which included composing documents for private persons.

20. See Volume 17, p. 166.

21. This was also a popular method of sorcery among the folk. They poured liquid wax into a vessel filled with cold water, while making an incantation over it while it hardened. The resulting shape was examined and through it the future interpreted or revealed for the one who had poured the wax.

22. Yakov Kudenetovich Cherkassky was a Kabardinian prince whose surname was Uruskan-Murza until his baptism in 1624. In 1641 Tsar Michael sent him to the southern Russian frontier to serve as the military governor of Tula. Upon the accession of Alexis in 1645 he became a boyar, and from 1654 to 1657 commander the military forces against Poland. He was one of the wealthiest and most influential officials at the tsar's court. For further details, see Volume 17, Chapter IV, Note 58, and MERSH, Volume 6, pp. 234-235.

23. Called Lobnoe Mesto in Russian, it was an elevated area in Moscow's Red Square, adjacent to the Kremlin wall, where the tsar made official appearances, government statements and proclamations were read, the public assembled on special occasions such as executions of prominent individuals. Pushkarev, *Dictionary*, p. 58. Translated here as "executioner's block."

24. Prince Dmitry Manstriukovich Cherkassky was connected to the ruling house through the marriage of his aunt Maria Temriukovna to Ivan IV. In 1601 he fled his native Kabardia and was taken into Muscovite service, but in 1608 crossed

over to Tushino. After the murder of the second False Dmitry he switched sides once more, swearing allegiance to the Polish prince Władysław. Then, forsaking the Poles, he established a base at the St. Anthony monastery where he turned to clearing out the cossack bands roving about Uglich. At the Assembly of the Land he was briefly considered as a candidate for the throne. Instead the newly-elected Tsar Michael appointed him table attendant, and in 1619 he was raised to the rank of boyar. From 1624 to 1636 he served ably as head of the Chancellery for Kazan. For further details see Volume 16, Chapter I, Note 78.

25. Sobachaia rozha in Russian means "dog's snout."

26. Fedor Mikhailovich Rtishchev, the son of a lord-in-waiting, was a cultural activist who in 1656 himself became a lord-in-waiting. He was a close adviser to Tsar Alexis, headed a number of chancelleries, and promoted cultural exchanges with the Rus, which included bringing a choir from Kiev in order to acquaint the Muscovites with polyphonic music, and founding elementary schools. He also established a system of medicine and social services in Russia. Rtishchev was so distinguished that an anonymous author wrote his biography in his lifetime. *Bolshaia Sovetskaia Entsiklopediia* (The Great Soviet Encyclopedia), 3rd ed. Volume 22 (Moscow, 1975), p. 982.

27. When Michael Romanov was elected to the throne in 1613 he inherited a plethora of problems stemming from the reign of Ivan the Terrible (1533-1584) and the so-called Time of Troubles (1598-1613). His government could claim a measure of success in resolving some of the most pressing, including foreign aggression. During the Time of Troubles Muscovy was at war with both Poland and Sweden. In 1617 Tsar Michael concluded a peace in Stolbovo with Gustav II Adolf. According to the agreement the Swedes evacuated Great Novgorod, Staraia Rusa, Porkhov and their districts, in exchange for the Karelian isthmus. Tsar Michael was obliged to pay the Swedish king twenty thousand rubles. For a comprehensive treatment, see Volume 16, Chapter II.

28. Soloviev employs the term liutorskaia vera, which is a distorted version of liuteranskaia vera, or Lutheran faith. Used in this manner, it has a folksy ring to it, conveying a certain disdain for the confession, and at the same time expressing a fear of it. This was a popular method of denigration.

29. Although there were numerous deviations, in the seventeenth century the oficial chetvert equalled eight puds (the pud being equivalent to 36 American pounds) of rye. Pushkarev, *Dictionary*, p. 7. In a footnote on p. 492 the editor of the 1959–1966 edition notes that according to the archival evidence the correct sum was ten thousand chertverts.

30. See Volume 15, pp. 58-62, 240-243.

31. An old Russian dry measure equalling 26.239 liters.

32. The hexapsalm comprises six entrance psalms recited by a lector at the start of the night-prayer component of Orthros. This is the service on the eve of major feast days, lasting well into the night, and is probably better translated as "vigil." While the hexapsalm is recited the priest prays the twelve morning prayers before the royal doors of the iconostasis.

33. The term kathisma (or cathisma) refers to a portion of the liturgy during which the participants remain seated. More precisely it is one of the twenty groups of psalms into which the psalter is divided in the Greek rite for continuous recitation. The participants sit during the kathisma but stand at the end for the doxology or prayer. These kathismata are sometimes called sessional hymns.

34. The icon of the Redeemer which Tsar Alexis had placed above the Savior gate to the Kremlin, and decreed that every man passing through that gate must remove his hat as a sign of respect to the icon. It was said to possess miraculous properties. According to legend a band of Tatars once attempted to capture the Kremlin, which the icon prevented by blinding them.

35. Muscovite chronology began with the creation of the world in 5508 B.C. The year 1650 corresponded with the year 7158 from the creation. The initial 7, inadvertently or for the sake of brevity, must have been omitted.

36. In Great Novgorod the ulitsa (street) was an administrative subdivision of a sotnia (hundred). Its inhabitants formed an association headed by an elected elder, and enjoyed a degree of self-government. Pushkarev, *Dictionary*, p. 168.

37. Although the reference is simply to other nations, the pejorative Tatar word is used to describe them.

38. Known as velikii miasoed, it was the season which spanned Christmas to Shrovetide, during which eating meat was permitted every day except Wednesdays and Fridays with one exception, the Week of the Publican and Sinner, or the third week before the Great Lent, when meat could be consumed every day.

39. This is a traditional East Slav ritual greeting.

40. The feast of St. Peter and St. Paul (June 29) is preceded by a period of fasting which commences on the Monday eight days after Pentecost. It is also known as the Fast of the Apostles. See Timothy Ware, *The Orthodox Church* (Harmondsworth, 1963), p. 306.

41. Hermogen, formerly metropolitan of Kazan, was installed as patriarch by Tsar Vasily Ivanovich Shuisky in 1606 and was starved to death in Polish captivity in 1612. He was regarded as a martyr for the national and religious causes, although he was not formally canonized until 1913. For further details see the entry by Nickolas Lupinin, MERSH, Volume 14, pp. 11-13.

42. They were known as vybornye liudi who, prior to 1861, were elected peasant representatives, but they might also be auxiliary agents of the state and manorial administration. Pushkarev, *Dictionary*, p. 57.

43. Soldaty (pl.), as a term for soldiers was introduced in Muscovy in the seventeenth century when the government turned to foreign officers to train regiments of soldiers on the Western European model. They were disbanded once Mucovy faced no immediate dangers. Later, when Peter I formed his standing army, he used the term soldat to indicate all military men. Later still, the term was applied to all enlisted men.

44. In the seventeenth century foreigners were invited to enter Muscovite service. They were known as sluzhilye inozemtsy, or foreign servitors. Foreign officers helped to organize trained regiments for the Muscovite army, (the Regiments of the New Formation), along Western European lines. Another

category of foreign servicemen came from the East. Called iurtovskie sluzhilye liudi, they formed auxiliary troops recruited from the yurts (settlements) inhabited by Tatars and various tribes native to the Siberian and Ural regions.

45. One way the Muscovite government managed its liquor revenues was through farming out, or otkup, under which the otkupshchiki (pl.) paid the government in advance for a monopoly on the sale of liquor.

46. Magnus (1540-1583) was the brother of King Frederik II of Denmark. In 1573 Ivan IV's cousin Maria Vladimirovna married Magnus, who was duke of Holstein at the time. In 1570, when Ivan IV's title to Livonia was recognized by the Danes, it was given by the tsar to Magnus, who assumed the title of king of Livonia. Magnus was too simple-minded to cope with his office and too profligate to make a fortune. He switched sides in 1578 and entered the service of Stefan Bathory. Nevertheless he died in obscurity at Pilten, on the Baltic coast, leaving his wife and daughter, Evdokia, in abject poverty. Maria was a potential claimant to the Muscovite throne and was held initially as a bargaining counter by the Poles. Early in the reign of Tsar Fedor Ivanovich (1584-1598) she was urged by the English agent Jerome Horsey, on behalf of the regent Boris Godunov, to return to Muscovy, where allegedly a new husband would be found for her. Eventually she did return, largely because the Poles wanted to be rid of her. Both she and her daughter took religious vows, probably involuntarily. See S.F. Platonov, *Ivan the Terrible*. Ed. and trans. by Joseph L. Wieczynski (Academic International Press, 1974), pp. 89-90; Lloyd E. Berry and Robert O. Crummey, eds., *Rude and Barbarous Kingdom. Russia in the Accounts of Sixteenth-Century English Travellers*. (Madison, Wis., 1968), pp. 315-317. Also Volume 13 of this series.

47. Although erdan is a variant of iordan, which refers to the ceremony at the hole in the ice through which the river water is blessed on January 6 in commemoration of the Epiphany (Theophany), it might pertain here, on August 1, to the Feast of the Procession of the Holy Cross.

48. His name is rendered elsewhere in the text and in the Index to the Soviet edition as Yevsevy.

49. In this case the elected elder was known as a gubnoi starosta, an elected elder with the duties of district criminal magistrate. When criminal activity increased in the mid-sixteenth century, local government agents were unable to cope. As a result, in 1539 the crown introduced in a number of districts the elected office of gubnoi starostsa, together with sworn assistants, and instructed the razboinyi prikaz (Chancellery for Criminal Affairs) to investigate criminal cases and punish offenders. In the seventeenth century the office of gubnoi starosta became a general institution in Muscovy. Peter I abolished it in 1702. Pushkarev, *Dictionary*, pp. 146-147.

50. See Note 40, above.

51. Metropolitan Job, a friend of the regent Boris Godunov, became the first Muscovite patriarch in 1589. Jeremiah II, patriarch of Constantinople, agreed to this elevation with considerable reluctance, although he recognized that he

was conferring *de jure* authority where it already existed *de facto*. Later the remaining Eastern patriarchs fell into line and gave their approval. The prestige of the Muscovite church was enhanced substantially by this elevation to the highest office in the Orthodox world. It led to both an improvement and an enlargement of the clerical hierarchy through the appointment of new metropolitans, archbishops and bishops at a critical time in Muscovite history. Job was deposed upon the triumph of the first False Dmitry in 1605 and died in 1607. See Riasanovsky, *History of Russia*, pp. 155-156; also the entry by Lupinin, MERSH, Volume 15, pp. 136-138.

52. Following the death of his first wife Anastasia, Ivan IV apparently lapsed into periods of madness and inaugurated a reign of terror, which almost destroyed the realm. Its instrument was the dreaded oprichnina, or crown estates. During his fits of rage, which alternated with hours of praying, Ivan brooked no opposition. When Metropolitan Philip dared to remonstrate with Ivan, he was imprisoned and killed by oprichnina members (1569). See entry by Graham, MERSH, Volume 11, pp. 131-133.

53. John Chrysostom (347-407), native of Antioch, was the greatest of the Greek Fathers of the church. He fell out of favor after insisting that the court forsake its sinful ways, and refused to condemn certain monks who were falsely accused of heresy. Empress Eudoxia, succeeded in having him charged falsely by an illegal synod in 403. Later he was exiled to Armenia, where he resided until his death. In 438 Eudoxia's son Theodosius II ceremoniously brought his remains to Constantinople, and did penance for his mother's offense against the saint.

54. Mark 3:24-25 "If a kingdom is divided against itself, that kingdom cannot stand. And if a house is divided against itself, that house will not be able to stand." Luke 11:17 "Every kingdom divided against itself is laid waste, and a divided household falls."

55. Entitled mnogoletie in Russian, it is a traditional song for special occasions expressing the wish for "many years" or a long life.

56. Luke 16:22 "The poor man died and was carried by the angels to Abraham's bosom."

57. The imagery of this passage is based upon the lyrical poems comprising the Songs of Solomon, or the Song of Songs, a book of the Old Testament which has been interpreted by the Christian, and particularly Byzantine, fathers as an allegory of Christ's love for His church, and the love of the church for its flock.

58. Vechere tvoei taine, literally "On the Evening of Your Mystery," a hymn commemorating the institution of the Holy Eucharist.

59. On Maunday Thursday it was the custom for the ruler to wash the feet of a selected number of beggars, in commemoration of Christ's washing of the disciples' feet. See John 13:5.

60. The tserkov' rizpolozheniia, church of the Deposition of the Robe, was constructed in the Moscow Kremlin between 1484 and 1448 by a team of Pskov architects. It was the private chapel of the metropolitans and patriarchs of

Moscow until the building of the Twelve Apostles church (1653-1656), also within the Moscow Kremlin.

61. Genesis 3:19 "In the sweat of your face shall you eat bread till you return to the ground, for out of it you were taken; you are dust, and to dust you shall return."

62. In those days everyone dreaded sudden death.

63. Soloviev refers to the *Domostroi*, a manual of rules for noble household management, daily religious observance and behavior, emphasizing the unquestioned authority of a father, the tsar-batiushka being a surrogate father to his people. It also contains a catalogue of homilies, rules and recipes. The work, mostly a compilation of homilies from sixteenth-century Muscovy, is attributed to an archpriest named Sylvester, who in the years 1547-1553 was a close adviser to Tsar Ivan IV. It has been edited and translated by Carolyn Johnston Pouncy as *The Domostroi. Rules for Russian Households in the Time of Ivan the Terrible* (Ithaca, N.Y., 1994).

64. Known as the bolshoi dvorets, it was a vast complex of buildings and land belonging to the tsar, whose large contingent of servants and peasants saw to the needs of the tsar's extensive household. The dvorets proper, out of which its chief operated, was the central office for management of buildings, lands and people. Pushkarev, *Dictionary*, pp. 15-16.

INDEX

THE EDITOR AND TRANSLATOR

Marian Jean Rubchak (Konopka) was born in Saskatoon, Saskatchewan, Canada. She began her higher education by pursuing a degree in Slavic Studies at the University of Manitoba. Subsequently when a family move took her to the U.S., she worked in Chicago as an advertising executive, and later in New York City was engaged as an editor-translator for *The Digest of the Soviet Press*. When the family relocated to New Jersey she resumed her studies, received a B.A. in history at Douglass College, and was elected to the Phi Beta Kappa national honor society. An M.A. in European history at Rutgers University followed. Back in Chicago she continued her studies and began a teaching career in various Chicago-area colleges and universities. Her Ph.D. in Russian and Soviet history was awarded by the University of Illinois, Chicago in 1988. Presently she is Professor of History at Valparaiso University, where she was named University Research Professor for 1997. In 1998 she was a Senior Fulbright Fellow. Rubchak is active at national and international conferences, and has contributed numerous articles and reviews to scholarly journals in the United States, Canada, England, Sweden, Holland, Belarus and Ukraine on Ukrainian national consciousness in early modern and contemporary periods, Ukrainian and Lithuanian diasporas, and feminism in Ukraine and Russia, as well as comparative manifestations of a national consciousness in Ukraine and its diaspora.

FROM ACADEMIC INTERNATIONAL PRESS*

*Request catalogs. Sample pages, tables of contents, more on line at www.ai-press.com